Communication
in Business and the
Professions

Speaking Up
Successfully

Communication
in Business and the
Professions

Speaking Up
Successfully

Artie Adams Thrash
Sam Houston State University

Annette N. Shelby
Georgetown University

Jerry L. Tarver
University of Richmond

Holt, Rinehart and Winston

New York   Chicago   San Francisco   Philadelphia
Montreal   Toronto   London   Sydney
Tokyo   Mexico City   Rio de Janeiro   Madrid

Acquisition Editor: THOMAS W. GORNICK
Project Editor: CARLA KAY
Production Manager: ROBIN B. BESOFSKY
Art Direction: GLORIA GENTILE
Book and Cover Design: ARTHUR RITTER

Library of Congress Cataloging in Publication Data

Thrash, Artie Adams
  Speaking up successfully.

  Includes bibliographies and index.
  1. Communication in management.   2. Communication in
organizations.   I. Shelby, Annette N.   II. Tarver,
Jerry, 1934–   .   III. Title.
HF57.18.T47   1984   658.4'5   83-8409

ISBN 0-03-061851-7

CBS COLLEGE PUBLISHING
Holt, Rinehart and Winston
The Dryden Press
Saunders College Publishing

Acknowledgments

William V. Haney, "The Story." Copyright © 1979 by William V. Haney. Adapted, by permission of the author, from *Communication and Organizational Behavior: Text and Cases,* 4th ed.

"Investments and Social Responsibility." Courtesy of the *Hoya,* Georgetown University, Washington, D.C. 20057.

The following were reprinted by permission of Sperry Corporation, New York, N.Y.: "It Pays to Listen," "Listening Can Improve Your Vision," "Listening Well Doesn't Mean Saying Yes," and the photographs on pages 1 and 97.

Seven diagrams of meeting room arrangements were reprinted from *Leaders Digest,* 1979, Audio Visual Division/3M Corporation: St. Paul, Minn.

"Propositions in Interview Behavior" was adapted by permission from *Public Communication in Business and the Professions* by Jerry W. Koehler and John I. Sisco. Copyright © 1981 by West Publishing Company. All rights reserved.

"Trial by Television" was reprinted by permission of Kaiser Aluminum.

"What Ever Happened to Fair Play?" and "Why Do Two Networks Refuse to Run This Commercial?" © 1982 by the Mobil Corporation. Reprinted by permission of Mobil Corporation.

The photograph on p. 137 was reprinted by permission of 3M Corporation.

Dedicated To Our Parents

Preface

Students in the 1980s—and their parents—have been greatly concerned about the usefulness of higher education in earning a living. Although this concern is legitimate, it needs to be kept in perspective. Only a few of the courses that any student takes will help directly in "qualifying" that student for a position upon graduation. Of course, a literature course fits directly into the plans of an English major who hopes to get a Ph.D. and teach in a college. And an accounting class obviously advances a student toward the goal of becoming a CPA in an accounting firm. But most students who take literature do not major in English, and not every member of an accounting class goes on to become a CPA.

This does not mean, however, that only those courses leading to a specific career are helpful in contributing to success in a job. A lawyer may benefit from knowing accounting and a salesperson may benefit from knowing literature. A student, then, should take the long-range view. *Some courses help a graduate get a job, while other courses help a graduate keep a job and advance in it.*

There was a time when an educated person was expected to know everything taught in a university. There were no majors in early colleges because all students took the same courses. This is no longer possible with the broad range of subjects available today. Students are forced to settle for specialization in one or two major academic areas while getting only a sample of the knowledge available from other departments.

The debate over what should be in that sample rages long and loud. Perhaps it never will be settled. Most colleges recognize that students must be allowed to decide the courses that fit their individual needs and interests.

This text is designed for a course focusing on the skills necessary for business and professional communication. Students will learn principles and strategies necessary for such professional and organizational types of communication as interviewing, group decision making, corporate advocacy, presentations, speech writing, and conducting a meeting. The supporting bases for these methods of communication include listening skills, interpersonal skills, nonverbal skills, leadership skills, and skills in delivery and the use of visual aids. Basic parliamentary procedure is included as an appendix.

The content moves from communication in dyads to communication within groups and to public types of communication. This approach allows students to gain confidence in interpersonal communication before attempting the less familiar, and perhaps more frightening, communication in public.

Students will have an opportunity in this course to enlarge their capacity to communicate successfully. The principles set forth in this book and the guidance of an instructor will enable students to understand a variety of communication situations and to participate in them with improved results.

Colleagues, friends, and students who have helped during the preparation of this manuscript by reading, typing, and advising, include Diana Douglas, Marianne McCahill, Nancy Gustafson, Greg Odjakjian, Hollis Thrash, Sheila Moreland, Lawrence Clayton, Michael Lewis, Elizabeth Chant, Thomas W. Gornick, and Carla Kay.

Table of Contents

Preface   ix

UNIT 1 OVERVIEW OF COMMUNICATION IN BUSINESS AND PROFESSIONAL ORGANIZATIONS

1. Communication in Business and Professional Organizations   **3**

The Importance of Communication in Business   4
     Communicating to Do Your Job Well   5
     Communicating to Serve Special Company Needs   7
     Communicating to Enhance Your Own Self-Worth   9
Learning Communication Requires a Lifetime Effort   10
     College Education   10
     On-the-Job Training   11
     On Your Own Time   11
A Speech on Speaking   12
Exercises   18
Suggested Readings   18

2. The Nature of Successful Human Communication   **21**

A Model of Communication   24
     Sender and Receiver   24
     Messages and Codes   26
     Communication Gaps   26
The Process of Communication   28
Summary   28
Exercises   29
Suggested Readings   30

3. Nonverbal Communication   **31**

The Significance of Nonverbal Communication   31
Definition   31
Strategies for Assessing and Using Nonverbal Elements of Communication   32
     1. Use Space for Successful Communication   32
     2. Use Time to Influence Communication   35
     3. Plan Your Physical Appearance to Affect Communication Successfully   36

4. Use Appropriate Gestures and Other Body
 Movements 36
5. Use Touch with Caution 37
6. Use Appropriate Voice and Paralanguage 38
7. Use Objects with Caution 38
8. Understand What Facial Expressions Reveal 39
Summary 39
Exercises 40
Suggested Readings 40

UNIT 2 INTERPERSONAL COMMUNICATION IN BUSINESS AND PROFESSIONAL ORGANIZATIONS

4. Successful Interpersonal Communication 45
A Definition 46
Personal Attributes Influencing Interpersonal
 Communication 47
 Trust 47
 Open-Mindedness 48
 Authoritarianism 49
 Dogmatism 49
Barriers to Interpersonal Communication 50
 Attitudes toward the Other Person 50
 Self-Behaviors 51
Strategies for Improving Interpersonal Communication 52
 Creating a Supportive Atmosphere 52
 Improving Message Effectiveness 54
Summary 55
Exercises 55
Suggested Readings 56

5. Listening 57
Active Listening 60
 Active versus Passive Listening 60
 Listening and Responding to Feeling Messages 60
Listening Steps and Skills 61
 Listening Step 1: Hear the Message 62
 Listening Step 2: Interpret/Understand the
  Message 64
 Listening Step 3: Test Understanding 67
 Listening Step 4: Revise Interpretation 68
 Listening Step 5: Evaluate the Message 68
 Listening Step 6: Remember the Message 70
Listening Models 70
 Self-centered Listening 71
 Responsive Listening 71
 Critical Listening 71
Improving Communication through Listening 72
Summary 72
Exercises 73
Suggested Readings 74

6. Interviewing   **75**

Functions of Interviews   76
    Getting Information   76
    Giving Information   77
    Problem Solving   78
    Persuasion   78
Kinds of Interviews   78
    Selection Interviews   79
    Counseling Interviews   83
    Appraisal Interviews   86
    Grievance Interviews   88
    Exit Interviews   89
Interview Strategies   90
    Information-Giving Strategies   91
    Information-Seeking Strategies   91
    Problem-Solving Strategies   92
    Persuasive Strategies   93
Summary   93
Exercises   94
Suggested Readings   95

UNIT 3 COMMUNICATION IN GROUPS AND MEETINGS OF BUSINESS AND PROFESSIONAL ORGANIZATIONS

7. Group Work through Meetings   **99**

To Have or Not to Have a Meeting   99
    Hold a Meeting . . .   100
    Do Not Hold a Meeting . . .   101
Types of Meetings   102
    Staff or Team Meetings   102
    Committee Meetings   103
    Conferences   103
    Conventions or Extended Conferences   103
Functions of Meetings   104
    Meetings to Share Information   104
    Meetings to Solve Problems   106
Interaction in Meetings   111
    Size of Group   111
    Group Cohesiveness   111
    Norms   112
    Roles   112
    Personal Agendas   113
    Status   114
Summary   114
Exercises   115
Suggested Readings   115

8. Leadership and Participation in Meetings   **117**

The Nature of Leadership   117
    Leadership as Influence   118
    Formal and Informal Leadership   118

Personal Characteristics	118
Intelligence	119
Achievement	119
Dependability	119
Participation	120
Leadership Styles	121
Authoritarian Style	121
Bureaucratic Style	121
Democratic Style	122
Nondirective Style	122
Situational Leadership	123
Leader Functions and Responsibilities	125
Responsibilities for Planning	125
Responsibilities for Conducting Meetings	129
The Role of the Participant	133
Summary	134
Exercises	135
Suggested Readings	136

UNIT 4 CORPORATE SPEECHES AND PRESENTATIONS

9. Public Relations and Corporate Advocacy — **139**

The Corporate Image	139
The Corporation's Audiences	141
Customers	141
Stockholders	141
Employees	143
Mass Media	143
Unions	144
Special-Interest Groups	144
General Public	146
Media for Corporate Messages	146
Internal Media	146
External Media	148
Communication Strategies for Public Relations	153
Providing Facts about the Industry or Product	153
Filling Consumer Need	153
Identifying with Something the Public Considers Positive	154
Communication Strategies for Advocacy	154
Withdrawal from Confrontation	154
Sleight of Hand	155
Challenging Opposing Facts and Arguments	155
Redefining the Issues	155
Presenting the Company Position	156
Adopt a Proactive Approach	156
Summary	157
Exercises	158
Suggested Readings	158

10. Successful Speeches for Corporate Advocacy   **161**

Audiences	162
Occasions	162
Strategies for Organizing the Speech	162
Determine the Purposes and Goals	163
Organize the Introduction	164
Organize the Content of the Speech	168
Organize the Conclusion of the Speech	171
Use Transitional Devices	172
Strategies for Winning Approval	172
Use Examples	172
Use Analogies	173
Use Quotations	174
Use Definitions	175
Use Statistical Data	175
Summary	176
Exercises	176
Suggested Readings	177

11. Making a Presentation   **179**

Examples of Presentations	180
Common Features of Presentations and the Public Speech	180
Delivery	180
Research and Evidence	180
Language	181
Organization	181
Special Features of a Presentation	181
Audience	181
Length	182
Visual Aids	182
Team Presentations	183
Handling Questions	183
Preparation for a Presentation	184
Establishing Objectives	184
Audience Analysis	185
Visual Aids for a Presentation	186
Models and Objects	186
Projecting Images	187
Handouts	187
Delivery of the Presentation	188
Organizing the Ideas in a Presentation	188
The Opening	189
The Background	189
The Criteria	189
The Proposal	189
The Justification	190
The Action	190
Special Considerations for a Team Presentation	191
Coordination and Rehearsal	191
Presentation Review and Critique	192

Summary 193
Exercises 193
Suggested Readings 194

12. Visual Aids 195

When Should You Use a Visual Aid? 195
The Degree of Audience Focus on Visual Aids 197
    Full Focus 197
    Primary Focus 198
    Variable Focus 202
Guidelines for Using Visual Aids 206
Working with the Audiovisual Department 208
Summary 209
Exercises 210
Suggested Readings 210

13. Delivering a Message 211

Modes of Delivery 211
    Reading a Speech 211
    Memorization 212
    Off-the-Cuff Delivery 212
    Speaking from Notes 212
Conversational Delivery 213
    Eye Contact 213
    Posture 214
    Gestures 215
    Voice 216
Appearance 217
Approaching and Leaving the Speaker's Stand 217
Handling the Question-and-Answer Session 217
    Types of Questions 218
Using the Microphone 219
Stage Fright 220
Practicing a Speech 220
Summary 221
Exercises 221
Suggested Readings 222

14. Speech Writing 223

The History and Status of Professional Speech
    Writers 224
Speech Writing in Business and the Professions 224
The Relationship between Speaker and Writer 225
    Conferences 225
    The Approval Process 225
The Language of the Speech 226
    Oral Style 226
    Clarity 228
    Forceful Language 228
    Stylistic Devices 229
    Inoffensive Language 230

Humor in the Speech	232
Relevance	232
Taste	232
Freshness	232
The Speaker's Manuscript	233
The Manuscript as a Guide to Speaking	234
Summary	234
Exercises	235
Suggested Readings	235

Appendix: Parliamentary Procedure   237

Index   241

Communication
in Business and the
Professions

Speaking Up
Successfully

OVERVIEW OF COMMUNICATION IN BUSINESS AND PROFESSIONAL ORGANIZATIONS

1

Communication in Business and Professional Organizations

1

A complex set of skills helps each of us successfully send and receive the varied spoken messages we must handle every day. Some of these skills, such as efficient listening and effective non-verbal communication, are so subtle we hardly realize we are using them. Others, such as making a good speech or running a meeting smoothly, sometimes seem so difficult that we might be tempted to assume they are to be left to "gifted" speakers or "natural" leaders.

Many centuries of study of human communication make it clear, however, that the skills involved in speaking can be learned. A careful examination of people who communicate effectively will show that they have acquired this ability by hard study and many hours of practical application. As you make your plans to enter a business or a profession, you need to assess frankly the demand for communication skills in your future career. You will take your first job at a time when the recognition of the need for people in business and the professions to communicate effectively has grown as rapidly as any of the other more obvious advances in science and technology.

At the beginning of the twentieth century there was, for all practical purposes, no such thing as business communication. In the ten volumes of collected speeches called *Modern Eloquence,* published in 1900, not one single speech by a business executive was presented. But by the second edition in 1923, two full volumes were devoted exclusively to "leaders of the industrial world." As the editors noted, representatives of business had moved "into the forum of public discussion."[1] A glance at any recent issue of *Vital Speeches of the Day* will show that leading corporate officers compare favorably with leaders in government and education in speaking out on public issues.

The growth of communication in business has not been limited to formal public speaking. In the 1980s American business executives have been startled to see countries such as Japan leap ahead of the United States in productivity of workers. As a result, U.S. companies have begun to employ the Japanese approach of

---

1. Ashley H. Thorndike, ed., *Modern Eloquence* (New York: Modern Eloquence Corporation, 1928), vol. 1., p. xix. The preface of the 1923 edition is cited in the 1928 edition.

increased communication from workers to management through "quality circles." In the regular quality circle meetings, workers communicate to share their suggestions for improved productivity and pass these suggestions on to a receptive management. The increased amount of communication flowing up the line in business has placed a premium on listening skills and on the ability to run a successful meeting.

The amount of communication flowing down from management to employees has also increased. Plant managers are facing ever greater demands to make oral presentations directly to their workers. Forms of business communication, almost unheard of a few decades ago, are flourishing. For example, companies and firms now publish regular newsletters and magazines to keep employees informed. The number of copies of such publications distributed in the United States exceeds by far the number of newspapers printed throughout the country.

The Importance of Communication in Business

When you enter a business or a profession, you should be aware of the number of professional communicators who are employed exclusively to get the "company message" over to employees and to the public. Even though communication may not be your profession, you will need to know something of the scope of modern professional and business communications.

The company magazines mentioned above are edited by professionals who belong to such organizations as the Public Relations Society of America or the International Association of Business Communicators. In the ranks of this group are communicators trained in the use of television and other audiovisual aids. Their knowledge of communication technology is used within organizations to prepare presentations, displays, and even sophisticated electronic bulletin boards to keep employees informed.

Professional communicators are also at work in transmitting information to the public. If you examine a bill from a utility company, you are likely to find more than just information on the amount of money owed for services. Frequently an insert will be added to convey a company message. Advertising on radio, TV, and billboards, in newspapers and magazines, and in a variety of other media represents a substantial outlay of energy and money in most companies. Public speaking remains a vital means of contact with the public. In addition to the speeches made by top corporate officers, there is a demand for middle managers and even hourly wage earners to represent their companies in speeches before a wide variety of audiences.

In short, any organization you work for does far more than supply a product or service for its clients or customers, and it does more than provide work and wages for its employees. A modern organization must communicate to survive. Employees and the public must be informed, and at times persuaded, if a business hopes to be successful in producing and marketing its wares. The skills of oral communication that you will study in this course will help you speak up successfully as you advance in your career.

COMMUNICATING TO DO YOUR JOB WELL

Even though you will probably be hired because of some business or professional ability you have acquired, this ability will not in and of itself be enough for you to accomplish your job. In 1973 Iowa State University's industrial administration department surveyed alumni to determine the importance of courses they had taken in relation to success in their occupations. Twenty courses were rated. English and Speech—written and oral communication—led all the rest in importance. They came out ahead of such courses as Economics, Computer Science, and Industrial Engineering. A number of other studies have consistently placed communication at the top of the academic skills needed to succeed on the job.[2] These findings should not be surprising when you consider the number of different categories of people with whom you must communicate to accomplish your work.

Communicating with people you manage. A few years ago a young lieutenant was shocked to discover on his first week on the job that he was called on to referee a bitter disagreement between two sergeants whose combined length of service amounted to more than thirty years. In order for the unit to function smoothly, the dispute had to be settled and the young officer had to accept the responsibility. Fortunately, he decided not to make an arbitrary judgment and instead called the two men in for a conference. He let them talk out their problem in the neutral territory of his office, and the problem was settled to everyone's satisfaction. But nowhere in the young officer's military training had there been any warning that communication skills in such situations were essential to his job.

Career advancement and salary increases are often tied rather closely to the number of persons who report to you. As your responsibility for the supervision of the work of others grows, so does your standing in your company or firm. To do well as a manager, you must know how to listen to others and how to interpret as well as send important nonverbal messages. You will require skills in running a meeting, and those skills must cover every situation from a hurried consultation at the water cooler to a formal conference for all your employees. The way you say good morning, the manner in which you give instructions to a secretary, and the style with which you make the speech explaining new purchasing procedures in your department are all instances of communication

2. Judy C. Pearson, Paul E. Nelson, and Ritch L. Sorenson, "How Students and Alumni Perceive the Basic Course," *Communication Education* 30 (July 1981): 301-2.

that will help determine whether you can make the grade as a manager.

Communicating with your peers. As women have been entering the work force in increasing numbers during the last few years, they have felt the need to establish lines of communication with other working women. Frequently they discovered that men had already established "networks" that were working successfully. Pointing out that "networking" is not a new concept and that it exists off the job as well as on, Marilyn Loden of New York Telephone urged women to form networks "to relieve job stress." "By networking," she said, "I mean an expanding web of relationships with other women for the purpose of building support, solving common problems and enhancing individual growth."[3]

It is sometimes suggested that the experience men have had in team sports makes it easier for them to join or establish networks; but the ability to communicate with peers is crucial to both sexes. The team sport analogy gives a fairly accurate picture of the process. Members of a team, or a company, must work together if they are to achieve their joint goals. But at the same time there is competition among the players. Who will be recognized and rewarded? Who will be the captain of the team? The answer will depend in part, of course, on the raw talent and ability any "player" brings to the corporate team. But it also depends on the ability to communicate with others.

When two engineers are working on a presentation to be given to higher management, they will fail if they do not work together. If one makes a "grandstand" play, their effort will probably fall short of what they could have done. But the engineer who both does a fair share of the work and is willing to let the other person take part of the credit will be the one who is best rewarded in the end.

Networks are not built overnight. Getting along with your colleagues must be worked at constantly. Successful interpersonal relationships depend on your ability to communicate with others.

Communicating with your superiors. Your capacity to communicate will be under constant scrutiny by your supervisors. The way you handle yourself in your job interview starts the process, and it continues as your progress is observed every time an executive sees you at work.

Your first formal report in front of your boss can be a harrowing experience. You know that you are being judged not only for the substance of what you say but also for the logic of your organization, the clarity of your language, and the force of your delivery. A weak presentation will leave a negative impression that may affect the evaluation of the rest of your work. A crisp, smooth report can mark you as someone on the way up.

3. *Vital Speeches,* August 1, 1981, p. 614.

You will want to present your report in a positive, confident manner. Your aim will be to display what you know about the topic in the most effective way possible. You can succeed if you realize that a good formal presentation does not come about by chance. You will apply the principles of effective communication in presenting the report, just as you applied your professional skills in selecting the material to present.

Communicating with the public.   Unless you are buried in a back office somewhere, you will almost certainly come into contact with the public on your job. It must be stressed that when a customer or a client talks to you, at that moment you *are* the company to that person. How you conduct yourself will largely determine the impression that someone has of the total organization. In these days of increasing consumer concern, a positive result can be most helpful to your employer. A negative result could produce a complaint against your organization.

Many of your public contacts are likely to be by telephone. If you are not aware of the danger involved, you may be careless about your communication. If you are annoyed at being interrupted, an irritated tone may creep into your voice. If the caller has a problem that is not in your department, you may be too callous or too hasty in your reaction. Remember that a caller does not care that your company is divided into departments; the caller knows *you* have answered the phone, and *you* should be able to help. Good communication technique demands that you see the problem from the caller's point of view.

You communicate to the public by the way you dress on the job and by the way you drive the company car. You may even find you are trapped in a corner at a party by someone who wants to complain about your prices, or your product, or your service. You will learn that, unlike a taxi, you cannot display a sign saying you are not available. You are always communicating even when you wish you were not.

COMMUNICATING TO SERVE SPECIAL COMPANY NEEDS

Company speeches before the public.   In addition to the public encounters that are part of your daily routine, you may be asked to participate in a formal public speaking program for your organization. You may, for example, be asked to become a part of the company speakers bureau. Through such a bureau, the company sends out speakers who are prepared to deliver a company message to desired audiences. Corporate advocacy, then, will become part of your responsibility.

Unfortunately, many students regard speeches as an outmoded form of communication. This view may be explained, in part, by the fact that modern taste and style have little place for the "oratory" of an earlier age. It is true that the dramatic platform behavior of such orators as William Jennings Bryan is no longer in vogue. And the language of the more famous speeches of Abraham Lincoln would strike the ear of a modern audience as strange. In fact, though, more speeches are being given today than in the "Golden Age of Oratory." The twenty-minute talk has replaced the two-hour oration, but more people are hearing more speeches than was possible in an earlier day.

The formal public speech remains a viable medium of communication. In an age of electronic wizardry, the speech retains the powerful attraction of one live human being delivering a talk tailored to fit the needs and interests of one particular audience. The audiences for the business message range from the civic club to the environmental action group to the legislative panel. With its accompanying question-and-answer sessions, the speech personalizes a message and humanizes an organization in a way that no other form of communication can match.

The sooner you become involved in corporate advocacy in public speaking, the sooner you will begin to hone the speaking skills required to represent your company at a higher level of management. The higher up the ladder you go, the greater the demand placed on you to be a company spokesperson. Looking ahead to the type of leaders that corporations will be requiring, David Rockefeller delivered a speech entitled "The Chief Executive in the Year 2000," in which he said:

> Finally—and perhaps most importantly—the chief executive in the year 2000 will have a personal responsibility for advocacy, activism and outspokenness. Increasingly, the CEO will be expected to represent articulately and coherently his company and industry to their critics. This will mean departing from the serene seas of the boardroom and plunging into the rough and tumble waters of the hearing room and the press room. . . . It will be risky, controversial and often painful. But it will be imperative in the years ahead if business freedom is to be preserved.[4]

Internal communication for company interests. In some instances you will be asked to make speeches or presentations within your company on matters not relating to your immediate job but of importance to your employer. Many of these speeches involve the civic responsibility of a company. You may be called on, for example, to make an appeal for a united charity drive. Most companies take such matters seriously, and they want to see the best possible case made for employee participation. Space will generally be made available on company bulletin boards for posters, and part of a company newsletter may be devoted to the drive. But much of the communication will be direct. Speeches must be made to call for volunteer workers or to urge contributions.

In addition to encouraging monetary contributions, companies often support other kinds of community projects. You might

4. *Vital Speeches,* January 1, 1980, p. 164.

deliver appeals on topics such as blood donations or requests for a volunteer to coach a company-sponsored ball team. You could also be called upon to promote company programs such as safety. Again, talks and meetings may be necessary. Or you might find yourself with the responsibility of communicating to internal audiences on the subject of buying bonds or joining a credit union. Some employees are sent out to organize individual meetings with a very special kind of company audience—stockholders. In a wide variety of cases, then, you may need to communicate to company audiences for company purposes that have almost nothing to do with the business or professional skill that won you your job.

COMMUNICATING TO ENHANCE YOUR OWN SELF-WORTH

A psychologist once made the observation that he had never encountered anyone with a severe mental problem who did not also have difficulty in communicating. The psychologist did not mean to imply that improved communication would cure mental illness, but we can recognize the fact that for most of us, problems in communication may lead to some kind of unhappiness with ourselves or with others. This is certainly true on the job. The normal frustrations of work will be magnified if a person is unable to communicate.

Communicating to avoid frustration.　Much of our sense of self-worth grows out of our ability to express ourselves well. Few people can avoid the frustration and unhappiness that comes with not being able to get others to see the value of their ideas.

Some people get the mistaken idea that "facts speak for themselves." This is seldom if ever true. Facts must be explained, defended, made interesting, and applied to the needs of those who listen. Have you ever had a brilliant teacher who was boring? Who knew the facts but could not inspire students to care about them or even to learn them? Such teachers often blame the students for their failure, but the fault may well lie with the teacher, who has to suffer through an unhappy career because of poor skills in communication.

Communicating to reduce conflict.　Communicating clearly will not solve all your problems when you have an unpleasant experience with someone on the job. Clear communication may lead you to discover you have real differences of opinion that *cannot* be resolved. On the other hand, you may resolve a major conflict if you are willing to listen, to explore what the other person means, to seek out areas of agreement, and to be open to change.

Using your communication skills to resolve conflict means that you must think of communication as a process, a process you can affect. If you realize that, then you are not locked into a hopeless situation in which you can only defend or attack. You will have the freedom to search for a solution to the conflict that will permit all parties to work toward a consensus or accept a compromise.

What used to be called "adult education" now has the title "continuing education." The new title helps convey the proper idea much better. Education is a lifetime process. It is not something you acquire only in a block of twelve or sixteen or twenty years of formal school enrollment. It is truly a "continuing" process that begins with earning the traditional degrees from school and lasts for as long as a person needs to learn.

The ongoing nature of learning has a special relevance for communication skills. These skills are not acquired by memorizing a set of facts or even by understanding fundamental principles. Communication skills come from a blending of knowledge with practice. No two speeches or meetings or conversations are exactly alike. Each situation calls for a unique application of what you know about communicating.

COLLEGE EDUCATION

For over 2,500 years the study of communication skills has been part of the curriculum of "higher" education. Aristotle introduced the study of speaking into Plato's Academy. The lectures he gave to Greek students of public speaking are preserved in his book *The Rhetoric,* which offers principles still sound for today's student. Through the Middle Ages, when rhetoric was taught along with grammar and logic as the three subjects for advanced students, to today's departments of speech communication, the subject matter of communication has been regarded as appropriate for those who will enter the world of earning a living and communicating on social and political issues.

It is important, therefore, that you do not regard your college course in business and professional communication as merely satisfying requirements, collecting credits to graduate, or adding to your grade point average. You are at a crucial point in your move from school to work, and you should view your participation in this course as a practical effort to start you on your way.

One useful piece of advice to remember from the beginning is that you should take careful notes and save them for future reference. No one can remember all the important points in a class after months or even years have passed. But nothing refreshes the memory as effectively as the original notes that you used to prepare exercises in class. They can be most helpful to you when you are about to conduct an important conference, interview for a job, or prepare a presentation.

You should also save any evaluations you get in this class so you can later review your strong and weak points. Save your exam papers as well as any reports you give. This is a good time to start building a professional library. Your textbook can become the cornerstone of that library. It should be marked freely to emphasize points you think are important, and your own opinions and elaborations can be indicated in the margin. Copies of any outside reading you do for the course should be kept with the book for future review.

Above all, do not forget that this course should be viewed in the context of the use to which you plan to put the skills taught. Always think of how you expect to apply what you will learn.

ON-THE-JOB TRAINING

The *New York Times* has counted approximately 2,000 courses being offered for academic credit, not by colleges or universities, but by 138 corporations including AT&T, General Electric, General Motors, and Xerox.[5] Companies offer a much larger number of noncredit classes to improve employee skills. Some of the training is remedial, but a significant portion is at a much higher level. Along with the graduate-level work offered in some technical fields, there is also advanced work in communication.

It would be a great mistake to think that learning is a process that ends in college. Increasingly, education is moving past the college years and away from the college campus. McDonald's "Hamburger University" is but one example of a corporate effort to establish training suited to particular needs. In some instances, such as the Sun Company's Sunbrook training facility in Radnor, Pennsylvania, companies have even built their own dormitories.

A student who surveyed the communication offerings among companies located in Richmond, Virginia, found that Reynolds Metals Company gave its employees the opportunity to take company courses in written communications, business communications, interviewing, and information systems. The survey found that a branch of Du Pont stresses communication skills in a supervisory training program lasting for twelve weeks. In addition, the company offered specialized training in public speaking, interviewing, and motivation. Similar programs were found in banks, insurance companies, and government departments.[6]

The *Times* estimated that IBM spends $1,000 to $2,000 per employee on formal training. Like other corporations, IBM provides some of its own instruction and sends some of its employees to seminars sponsored by hundreds of colleges, consultants, and professional associations. The employee of a modern corporation or firm has all but unlimited opportunities to pursue the development of communication skills.

ON YOUR OWN TIME

You can supplement your college training and your on-the-job training by learning more about communication on your own initiative. Many speakers join Toastmasters to get further instruction

5. *New York Times,* March 30, 1981, p. 20ff.
6. Dorie Lee Griggs, "Business Communications Training in the City of Richmond: A Survey," paper completed in partial fulfillment of requirements for an independent study project, University of Richmond, April 1981.

and experience. This organization, devoted to improving public speaking skills, gives members a chance to speak at every meeting. Toastmasters publishes guidelines for effective speaking, and other members give speakers an evaluation of their performances at meetings. The official monthly publication, *The Toastmaster,* features useful articles on techniques of speaking.

Night classes are available in most cities covering a variety of communication topics. Some may be highly specialized, such as "Speech for Women" or "How to Negotiate," whereas others cover broader topics dealing with nonverbal communication, group interaction, interpersonal communication, or argumentation. Even if the cost for such courses is not paid by your employer, you may find the small expense involved to be a good investment. Because the quality of classes may vary, you should try to determine in advance whether a course is taught by a competent instructor. Ask for the names of business people who have taken the course so you can telephone some of them to get their opinions.

You can get valuable experience just by joining clubs where you will be asked to give reports and serve on committees. Similar activity in churches or civic associations will be helpful. Or offer your services to a political group in helping a candidate. The opportunities for experience are there if you are willing to look for them.

Like any skill, your ability in communication will decay if you do not use it. Remember that no two communication situations are alike. Every time you participate, you learn a slightly new application of your skills. For the rest of your life, you can continue to grow in your ability to communicate.

A Speech on Speaking

Following is the text of a speech given by one of the authors of this textbook.[7] The speech, delivered to the Chicago Chapter of the International Association of Business Communicators (IABC) on March 11, 1981, deals with the role of speaking and speech writing in the modern corporation. In reading the text, you should study the techniques of communication the speaker uses, such as making points stand out, telling stories to attract interest, and speaking in a conversational style. Also, you should read the speech to learn the speaker's position on the credibility of speech as a medium of communication.

Opening

I've been looking forward to the opportunity to be with you today ever since David Clevenger invited me to speak back in October and told me you were building your entire program for the year around communication issues rather than mechanics and techniques of communication.

I thought maybe Lou Williams might have had a hand in decid-

7. Jerry Tarver, "Communication and Credibility: Corporate Speech Making in an Incredulous Age," *Vital Speeches of the Day,* April 15, 1981, p. 412.

ing on that approach, because it is certainly consistent with IABC's constant emphasis on enhancing the professionalism of communicators.

In my conversation with Dave I agreed to consider this issue of speechmaking and corporate credibility.

All of us who earn our livings as professional communicators know how difficult it is to get a message over to a viewer or a listener. Our words often get an incredulous reception.

Our attempt to analyze our problem is made somewhat difficult by the fact that the human spirit seems to have a healthy measure of gullibility mixed in with its skepticism.

The classic manifestation of this mixture, I suppose, has been the carnival where the country bumpkin is skeptical regarding the existence of the bearded lady, but gullible enough to pay a dollar to take a look. Today, in what some people may consider a more sophisticated situation, the modern gullible skeptic sits in front of a TV set watching a monkey do the dishes on "That's Incredible."

The tension between gullibility and skepticism affects business in its effort to make its message credible not merely to customers but to employees and to the public at large. In that effort, I believe the typical corporation is caught in a double bind. Far from being able to manipulate public opinion easily as critics charge, business faces an embedded skepticism. A skepticism made ironically more tenacious by the gullibility which so often causes people to fall for the simplistic argument that a company with the goal of making a profit is innately callous, shortsighted, and downright evil.

Under these circumstances, the job of corporate communication is being done amazingly well. This is no small tribute to the professionalism of you in this room and your counterparts throughout IABC. You have made remarkable progress in insisting that communicators must have access to all the relevant facts and that the bad news must be told along with the good. You have brought to the corporate world technical skills in communication that are—if I may use the word—incredible.

In your remarkable effort to solve communications problems with modern technology and our new sense of the range of the visual arts and the printed word, I contend we should not forget plain old public speaking. I submit that corporate speechmaking is an indispensable weapon in the communications arsenal you must maintain to gain credibility in our incredulous age. *Thesis statement and preview*

Let me support my thesis by first exploring the special characteristics which make speech a credible medium, and then I'd like to examine briefly what I consider to be some of the hazards you want to avoid in a speaking program.

First, then, let's explore the special features of speech. *First main point*

Special feature number one—speech humanizes your message.

I think we would all agree it is easier to reject the argument of a faceless corporation than to dismiss out of hand the remarks of a demonstrably decent, live human being standing in front of us.

In spite of all the exaggerated nonsense being written these days about how to read a person like a book, we need only to look at our everyday experiences to realize that we often *do* in fact tend to judge credibility less on *what* is said than on *how* someone communicates nonverbally.

I was visiting a friend recently when his young daughter came out of their house carrying a blanket. He asked her if her mother had given her permission to play with the blanket outside. The little girl ducked her head, looked to one side, and softly said, "Yes."

The father said, "Go ask her *again*."

A few minutes later the little girl came back out proudly carrying a different blanket. She walked past with head held high and a spring in her step. She said, "This time she *really* said yes."

I would never question the ability of a good writer to give words on the page the stamp of earnestness. But the best of writers lack tone, gesture, and the ability to look the listener in the eye.

I may be taken in by the pitch of an occasional hustler or con artist, but I would rather judge veracity face to face. And I agree with Gerda Fogle of Indiana Bell who insists she doesn't need polished orators speaking for her company. She wants speakers who simply have a grasp of the fundamentals of public speaking combined with firsthand knowledge of the company and an honest conviction of the soundness of company policy. These speakers will *become* the company for skeptical listeners. They will add a dimension of credibility with voice and action that words alone could never have.

The humanizing aspect of speechmaking does not come just from physical delivery. Aristotle noted centuries ago that speakers could enhance their messages with direct statements demonstrating their personal knowledge, their genuine concern, and their integrity. A couple of weeks ago I heard a utility company speaker say, "Let me tell you how we are trying to cut costs in my department." She went on to show how she was personally involved in efforts to be more efficient. Her examples would hardly have been worth the space in a news story or a bill insert, but in the context of her speech they were compelling.

I urge you to read a handful of speeches by John Hanley of Monsanto. He uses himself as a means of humanizing a chemical company. He gains credibility by citing facts drawn from his own experience, he expressly states that he cares, and he puts his character on the line for his convictions.

Let's look at credibility feature number two—speech is readily adaptable to an audience's needs and interests.

We are all familiar with the decline of the general interest magazine and the rise of the special interest publication. As editor of a speech writers' newsletter, I am pleased to know I belong to a group big enough to attract newsletters for editors of newsletters.

Some day we will no doubt have newsletters for editors of newsletters for editors of newsletters.

But no medium exceeds speech in adaptability. For three years now I have trained the members of a speakers bureau for a company located in Washington, D.C. In that short time I have seen the messages shift in emphasis. As one theme is no longer needed, it is discarded and replaced by another. But more important, each speech offered by the bureau can be fine-tuned to meet special needs. One of the talks is on energy conservation. It is developed one way to meet the needs of apartment house owners and another way for home owners in the suburbs. The excellent booklets on conservation distributed by this company will never have the credibility of the speeches.

Tom Paine's fiery pamphlets inspired the colonists in their resistance to the British. But reading one of the essays would have had little effect in St. John's Church on March 23, 1775, when Patrick Henry moved to arm the Colony of Virginia. It took Henry's speech to make that objective credible—a speech taking into account the fears and the hopes of a particular group of King George's subjects assembled at a special time in the unfolding story of the Revolution.

Now, speech credibility feature number three—speech permits interaction.

Twentieth-century audiences are a rather tame lot (with exceptions noted for much of the decade of the sixties). But it is not in the nature of the human animal to sit passively during the act of communication. Go back and read the Lincoln-Douglas debates so often cited as models of reasoned political argument. You will discover the speakers were forced at times to respond to shouted questions and comments from the audience.

I think people in this country today are starved for the opportunity to participate in communication. I'm sorry to see Walter Cronkite leave the evening news. I always talked back to him, and occasionally he gave me the impression he heard me. But what I'd really like to do is hear Cronkite in person. To nod, smile, shake my head "No," or maybe even groan a little bit.

Speech permits that interaction and in so doing adds a measure of credibility. Even the person who reacts negatively tends to go away feeling less hostile. The question-and-answer portion of the speaking assignment has become all but mandatory. Great. Give people a chance not merely to clarify points they don't understand but to have their own say and even to zap the speaker on occasion.

A company can gather valuable information on what people are thinking and on what they need. Occasionally an annoying problem can be solved or a policy modified on the basis of audience feedback.

No nonspeech medium—not letters to the editor; not suggestion boxes; not bulletin boards—permits such a satisfying level of interaction.

My speech credibility feature number four may not seem plausible at first, but I believe speechmaking allows you to probe an issue in considerable depth. Most of us—perhaps necessarily—are exposed to a great deal of quick and shallow communication. Is it any wonder we are skeptical? The evening news boils the world's events down to twenty-two minutes. I used to turn off the sound when Eric Sevareid came on. I couldn't tolerate a 210-second explanation of international trade one night and crime in the streets the next. Thank goodness, when PBS decided to explain the cosmos to me they gave Carl Sagan thirteen hours to do it. Billions and billions of tiny microseconds! (Sevareid would have polished that story off in fifteen minutes at the outside!) By contrast, a corporate speaker in the fairly typical time limit of fifteen to twenty minutes has a decent opportunity to explain credibly the effect of federal regulation of a given industry or to discuss the impact of a new plant on a community's environment.

The days of the two-hour speech are gone forever except in such isolated outposts as Castro's Cuba. But even the reduced time left for today's speaker compares most favorably with the rather narrow message of, say, the thirty-second commercial. I would even argue that the twenty-minute speech—in spite of the expense it entails—is often a better bargain than a mass message delivered to sleeping dogs and the backsides of people waddling away toward the refrigerator or the bathroom.

The issues you need to defend can hardly be made credible in a small compass. I realize that speakers usually want to cover too much. You must fight to keep them in bounds (I admit I had to throw away my favorite point to make my speech fit the time limit today—for those who can stay after we adjourn I have ten more minutes on the history of public speaking from the Greeks to the present). As a general rule, I urge you to consider slashing most initial topics by as much as one-half or two-thirds in order credibly to develop a topic in the depth needed.

Transition

I doubt if I could convince you of the credibility of speechmaking if I did not deal with the widely held belief that the printed word is somehow more reliable than human speech. Obviously we have proficient liars speaking in our society. Indeed, the words *oratory* and *rhetoric* are generally pejorative, and *speech* is not far behind. But note this. We also have a lot of bad writing. Sloppy writing and sleazy writing. We do not conclude, however, that writing per se is evil. Almost no one since Plato has made a serious attack on writing as bad in and of itself. Why?

At the psychological level I suppose the blame must be placed on the transitory nature of speech. It doesn't leave behind the solid evidence of the printed word. Even the tape recorder and the video camera do not capture the totality of a speaking event and have done little to weaken our emotionally negative reaction to the temporariness of speech.

I suspect our attitudes in the future will change, however, as more and more people store and retrieve the spoken word on video disks, while at the same time more and more of what we read will be called up by computer and displayed on a screen in a form hardly more permanent than speech itself.

But I am inclined to believe that a major part of the attack on the trustworthiness of oral communication can be traced to an elitism among writers. A newspaper columnist recently asserted, "The spoken word coming through a television set does not engage the brain as vigorously as does the printed word." That vivid phrase tells us more about the depth of the writer's scorn than it does about any fundamental flaw in spoken communication.

And it does not reflect the general view of consumers of communication.

The typewriters and the printing presses are in the hands of the intellectuals. We have elaborate initiation rites through which the novice must pass before being allowed to use the printed word in a responsible medium. But any crackpot or shyster is free to make a speech. What good are our style books, our rules, our years of training, if old John Randolph of Roanoke was right when he said years ago, the most eloquent speaker he ever heard "was a slave, sir, and her rostrum was the auction block"?

But I think the elitist position is simply wrong. Much that is written fails to engage the brain vigorously—or at all. And you can lie as easily with ink as with sound.

I'll not accept the collected sermons of the late Reverend Jim Jones as representatives of truth in speaking unless you will accept the *National Enquirer* as a fair sample of truth in print.

So, then, I argue that speech is a credible medium.

Let me now briefly deal with some of the major problems I think we face in running a speaking program.

Second main point

One problem is wasted effort. Companies often give speeches that seem to have no purpose other than to fill the allotted time. A certain amount of preaching to the converted is necessary, but many companies need a more aggressive program of seeking out audiences who are not otherwise likely to get the company message.

A second problem is failure to measure results. The simplistic counting of the number of speakers, the number of topics, and the number of listeners doesn't tell us much about the impact of a speaking campaign. More sophisticated measurement techniques are available and should be used.

A third problem is poor speakers. Speakers who have not reached the minimum level of competence needed to get a message over. Speakers who destroy your best efforts. Speakers who insist on bad jokes, dull charts, unintelligible language, and perhaps worst of all, speakers who read the manuscript for the first time on the way to the airport.

A fourth problem—and perhaps this is the basic problem from which all the others grow—a communications office without the status and staff to do its job. I have already said there is such a thing as natural eloquence. But not everybody has it. It is true that anyone can write a speech in the same sense it is true that anyone can perform surgery. I am capable of removing the appendix of a volunteer from this audience. I assure you I would accomplish the job eventually. But I would leave a horrible scar on the corpse.

We have too many butchered speeches resulting from situations where either no professional help was available or where the status of the writer was too low to make sound advice stick.

I have, of course, described the worst cases. I know of corporations where not one of the problems I cite can be found.

Conclusion   I believe the future is bright. Corporations today are committed to communication programs. The business world was once willing to let the product be the message. Now business seems to agree with historian Carl Becker, who said, "Left to themselves . . . facts do not speak; left to themselves they do not exist, not really, since for all practical purposes there is no fact until someone affirms it."

I would add to that only the observation that in affirming facts, no more credible medium can be found than the ancient art of speechmaking.

EXERCISES

1. Prepare a report on the Toastmasters. Discover all the services the organization offers. Visit a local meeting.
2. Interview several company communications directors to discover all the types of communication training their companies make available to employees.
3. Gather the details on the operation of the speakers bureau of some corporation such as a power or telephone company in your community. Find out how many speeches are given and what topics are covered.
4. Survey six months of *Vital Speeches* and prepare a summary of the business topics published. Determine which corporations are represented. See if you can find any trends.
5. Read Marilyn Loden's speech on networking in *Vital Speeches,* August 1, 1981, and report on it to the class.

Suggested Readings

Goldhaber, Gerald M. *Organizational Communication,* 2nd ed. Dubuque, Iowa: Wm. C. Brown Publishers, 1979.
This text provides organizational theory for the advanced student.

Harris, Thomas E. "Empathy, Communication, and the 'People' Perspective." *Business Education Forum* 36 (1981): 22–24.

Ouchi, William G. *Theory Z: How American Business Can Meet the Japanese Challenge.*

Reading, Mass.: Addison-Wesley Publishing Co., 1981.

This popular book focuses on a management style taken from a Japanese theory designed to increase productivity and improve employee morale by giving employees a voice in decision making.

Reuss, Carol, and Donn Silvis (eds.). *Inside Organizational Communication*. New York: Longman, 1981.

Sponsored by the International Association of Business Communicators, this volume surveys the functions of communication in the modern organization.

Vital Speeches of the Day. Published by City News Publishing Company, Southold, N.Y. This twice-monthly publication seeks to present the speeches of "recognized leaders of public opinion" and includes many talks by business executives as well as speeches on the subject of communication.

The Nature of Successful Human Communication

2

The word *communication* means different things to different people in different contexts. You may have complained about your professor's failure to communicate; you may have suggested that a quarrel with a close friend would not have occurred if the two of you had been able to communicate. Frequently people assume that talking is communicating. This misconception creates its own problem: "I told you all about that!" Talking is not necessarily communicating, just as hearing is not necessarily listening. You may have been in situations in which you *heard* the sounds of a person talking without *understanding* the information the person was trying to communicate. If you have ever received directions in a strange town and arrived at the wrong place, you understand how difficult it is to share meaning. Or you may use *communication* to mean the mass media: newspapers, books, magazines, radio, television, and films. Technologists may use the concept to describe certain systems; transportation by railroads or trucks, for example, may be seen as systems of communication. Physicians even refer to *communicable* diseases: those transmitted from one person to another. The study of communication, therefore, requires a common meaning for the word.

The word communication *is defined here simply as the transmission of messages through interaction.* This definition is appropriate only if such an exchange or sharing actually takes place. Each profession has its own need for sharing information. A patient who can communicate to a doctor the symptoms of an illness or the location of a pain increases the accuracy of that doctor's diagnosis; the ability of the doctor to communicate the instructions for the prescribed medication increases the effectiveness of the patient's treatment. An attorney must be able to communicate with a client to improve the chances that their case will succeed. A manager must be able to give direction through communication with subordinates. To ensure effective public relations, a chief executive officer must be able to share a corporation's philosophy with others.

The concern, however, is: How does anyone know when a person has succeeded in communicating? Most people think they are successful communicators. They think that if they *say* the words, and if other people *hear* those words, then the message is automatically *understood*. Do not fall for this fallacy. This chapter focuses on the total communication process so that you may determine when communication occurs and when it falters.

First, look at what happens when a person has information that needs to be shared with another person. Suppose, as an example, that Sally, who is the firm's public relations officer, needs to explain to Ray, the advertising manager, her expectations for the next publicity campaign. They have agreed to meet at 10:00 A.M. in Ray's office for the discussion. The communication process already has begun. They have selected as a *channel* oral-aural sound waves; that is, they have agreed to *talk* and *listen* (they could have chosen to exchange memos).

At the meeting, Sally starts the conversation; at this time, she is the *sender* of the message. She puts her message into a *code:* she uses the English language as her verbal code; the place she sits and the way she dresses become a part of her nonverbal code. These codes are symbols for the meaning she sends. She selects specific words and actions because of her own past experiences and because of her knowledge of Ray. She uses examples that are common to both.

Ray hears the words and sees Sally's emphatic gestures. He acknowledges (maybe subconsciously) that Sally has appropriated his desk by sitting on one end. As the *receiver* of these messages, he interprets the code, or gives meaning to what he sees and hears, based on his own past experiences and knowledge. No one has ever taught him that "a person sitting on top of your own desk is trying to dominate you" but, based on his experience, he may have attached that meaning to the action. Sally's experience may never have led her to that meaning; she may have felt more comfortable by sitting on the desk. She is sending an unintentional message through her nonverbal code. She notices that Ray shifts his chair backward and a slight frown appears on his face. These responses are *feedback,* and they act as a message that Ray now sends to Sally (either intentionally or unintentionally). Sally then becomes the receiver of this new message; she attaches a meaning to the nonverbal code; she adapts her next message to this meaning by getting off the desk and sitting on a chair beside Ray while she continues talking to him. She also may have made a verbal adaptation to the feedback she received by saying "Do you mind if I sit here?"

Through the communication process, Sally transmits many messages to Ray. She has shared her plans for an advertising campaign. Sally and Ray have agreed on some aspects of the plan and disagreed on others. The communication has been *successful* in that both share the same understanding of what those plans are.

Figure 2.1

Sender: Speaker; stimulus; the person who transmits verbal and nonverbal messages.

Example: *Sally,* who is explaining her expectations for the next publicity campaign.

Receiver: Recipient of the message; the listener; the audience.

Example: *Ray,* who is listening intently to the explanation and following instructions.

Messages: • Primary message (M_1), or the intended message that the sender originates.

Example: The *explanation* of Sally's expectations for the campaign.

• Responses, or feedback, that constitute the transaction of a new message (M_2).

Example: Ray's *frown,* which causes Sally to get off the desk and sit on a chair.

• Environmental messages (M_3), or the influences from the setting or circumstances that create additional messages.

Example: *Telephones* are *ringing,* which "sends" the message that this work is always important.

Codes: Symbols; verbal (words or language) and nonverbal (gestures, posture, movements, vocal sounds such as quality, pitch, rate, and nonfluencies such as *uh*).

Example: Sally's choice of *words,* her emphatic *gestures.*

Channel: The medium used to transmit the message, such as sound waves, pencil and paper, or space.

Example: The sound waves between Sally's voice and Ray's hearing; the space between Sally's gestures and Ray's eyes seeing those gestures.

Feedback: Responses; the interaction between people (M_2).

Example: Ray's *changing expression* to reveal annoyance.

> *Noise:* Detractions from the communication pro-
> cess.
>
> > Example: The *hot room* making it difficult
> > to concentrate.
>
> *Communication Gap:* Any lack of shared experiences that hinders
> successful communication.
>
> > Example: Ray's *unfamiliarity with mass-
> > media deadlines.*

A Model of Communication

In order to increase the probability of successful communication, you need to understand each component of this process called human communication. Perhaps the easiest way is to look at a simple model.[1]

SENDER AND RECEIVER

The communication model described here is composed of two rather odd-looking configurations.

One configuration will be a character named *S*. This *S* represents the *sender,* the *source,* the *stimulus,* or the *speaker* of the message. *S* has an odd shape: an arc (*A*), two straight lines the same length (*B*), two short straight lines (*C*), and one long line (*D*). (See Fig. 2.2.)

The other configuration is designated by *R*. The *R* represents the *receiver* or *responder* to that message. *R* looks similar to *S* in that it is composed of an arc (*A*), two equal lines (*B*), and a longer line (*D*). *R*, however, is missing two lines (*C*). (See Fig. 2.3.)

Just as no two people are alike, *S* and *R* are not alike, although they do share many of the same characteristics. Assume that these two configurations are the two people, Sally and Ray. They share the same language and many of the same interests; they are both employees of the same organization; they are the same age; they both have lived in large metropolitan areas. On the other hand, they are not the same gender and they are from different ethnic and religious backgrounds. The shared experiences of the two configurations are indicated by the overlap of *S* and *R* in Figure 2.4. The shaded area created by the overlap indicates the needs, values, knowledge, and experiences that *S* and *R* share.

---

1. For other models of communication, see the following books: David Berlo, *The Process of Communication* (New York: Holt, Rinehart and Winston, 1960), p. 72; Samuel Becker's model in *The Prospect of Rhetoric,* ed. Lloyd F. Bitzer and Edwin Black (Englewood Cliffs, N.J.: Prentice-Hall, 1971), p. 34; Michael C. McGee's conception in *Exploration in Rhetoric,* ed. Ray E. McKerrow (Glenview, Ill.: Scott, Foresman and Co., 1982), pp. 26–27; Wilbur Schramm, *Men, Messages and Media* (New York: Harper & Row, 1973), pp. 42, 102–3, 297–301.

Figure 2.2 Speaker = Sender

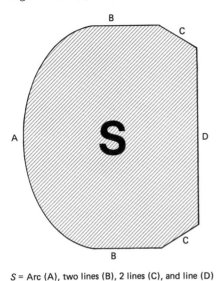

S = Arc (A), two lines (B), 2 lines (C), and line (D)

Figure 2.3 Receiver = Listener / Respondent

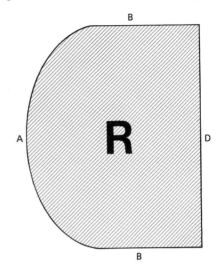

R= Arc (A), two lines (B), line (D)

Figure 2.4 Communication Model

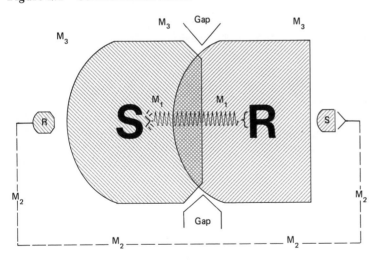

It is this *commonality* that allows them to communicate with each other. When Sally wants to communicate with Ray, she must draw upon her own past experiences and knowledge to choose the words, examples, and even the gestures with which to express herself. Ray can use only his own past experiences and knowledge to interpret what he sees, hears, and feels from Sally.

MESSAGES AND CODES

Sally wants Ray to understand the necessity for a new publicity campaign to begin in March. The significance of the deadline is her primary message (designated M_1 in Fig. 2.4). The primary message uses both verbal and nonverbal codes to communicate. Sally uses language (verbal code) that she assumes Ray will understand. She asks this question: "Do you think the graphic designer can complete the layout by March?" Ray receives the message and might interpret this question in one of several ways. Is she interested in what *he* thinks ("Do *you* think . . . ?"), or is she asking if the *designer* is *able* to finish (" . . . can the graphic designer *complete* the layout . . . ?")? Or Ray might respond by asking her to clarify what she means by the phrase "by March" (Does she mean *before* the month or during the month?).

Sally may add to her meaning with a nonverbal code: she might point to Ray (body gesture) as she says the word *you* to let him know it is *his* opinion she is asking for. She also might have emphasized a specific word by stressing that word: "Do *you* think . . . ?" This vocal emphasis (loudness) provides an additional nonverbal code (it is not a verbal code because its meaning comes from the sound of the voice rather than from the word itself).

Ray begins to respond to Sally's message immediately upon receiving it. He may smile, nod, and even mumble, "Uh-huh." These responses, or feedback, are new messages (designated M_2 in Fig. 2.4). On the other hand, he may look blankly at Sally; this also is a message. Sally must interpret the blank look and adapt her next message accordingly.

Other messages occur simultaneously with M_1 and M_2. These are messages in the environment (designated M_3). Ray is affected by environmental "messages" such as the temperature of the room, the ringing of the telephone, or maybe the clock dial; Ray is hearing and interpreting these messages at the same time he is receiving Sally's messages. Most M_3 types may be termed *noise* because they distract from the primary message. M_3's also may be either verbal (voice on radio) or nonverbal (passing of time) and they may be either audible or inaudible (the temperature).

COMMUNICATION GAPS

Notice the two "gaps" in the communication model (Fig. 2.4). These gaps represent a lack of shared experiences, knowledge, or understanding. Sometimes gaps occur in the codes of communication, as when two people do not speak the same language or do not have the same terminology for a technical field. Communication gaps may occur as a result of a difference in ages (and therefore experience): "We could have food rationing as we had in World War II." The differences in gender or in cultural and ethnic background create communication gaps. For example, nonverbal feedback may be misinterpreted: does the "nod" mean the listener agrees, or does it mean the listener merely understands? (Females nod their heads to indicate that they are paying attention more frequently than males.)

Communication gaps are present to various extents in all communication. These gaps may be bridged, however, even when the persons have not shared past experiences. For example, perhaps Ray has never experienced sexual discrimination, but Sally has. She may refer to other types of discrimination with which he is familiar to explain how it feels: maybe he was discriminated against in his family because of being the youngest child. Knowledge and understanding gained through education, literature, or films have bridged many communication gaps. It is necessary, therefore, to understand where the gaps are so that the sender can appeal to other experiences and knowledge to bridge them.

Use the guidelines in Figure 2.5 to discover the knowledge, experiences, needs, values, and attitudes of your listeners. Use this information to decide where communication gaps are likely to occur. Will your audience understand your reference to a "bullish stock market"? If not, how can you explain it based on what knowledge they *do* have? Would this audience understand the need for greater efficiency? Do they know what it is like to be "poor"? When you have gained an understanding of the listeners, you can either adapt your message to your shared characteristics or bridge the gaps by other means.

Figure 2.5 Audience Analysis Guide

General Characteristics

A. *Social and economic background*
   1. Description of audience's social and economic standing
   2. Description of special values or needs inherent in this environment which will relate to this presentation

B. *Training, education, and experience*
   1. Description of the expertise of the audience on this subject

C. *Special interests*
   1. Description of special interests held by this audience

D. *Background and physical attributes*
   1. Description of geographic and ethnic background
   2. Description of age, gender, or other physical attributes

Specific Characteristics

A. *Reasons for meeting*

B. *Attitudes toward the corporation and issues in this speech*
   1. Description of attitudes
   2. Possible causes of the attitudes

The Nature of Successful
Human Communication

In summary, the communication model in Figure 2.4 symbolizes two people talking together in an environment in which other verbal and nonverbal messages occur. It illustrates the necessity of using shared meaning (such as knowledge and experiences) if the communication is to be successful. Now that you see a symbolic representation of the communication process, look at concepts underlying this model.

The Process of Communication

A process is an ongoing movement that has a purpose; it always changes; it never is still, or static.[2] In the model, you saw that while Sally was talking, Ray was sending new messages, and that the environment was creating other messages. All of these interacted and influenced the message sent by Sally. The actual communication effort also was influenced by what happened before it was "frozen" into a model, and continued to have influence after it was "unfrozen" (maybe Ray reconsidered Sally's request after she left, and changed his mind).

Communication is a process: it is difficult to determine when it began and when it will end. Successful human communication would be much easier if you only had to consider the message transmitted at a specific moment. However, when you study people communicating, you need to be sensitive to what has happened to them prior to the event you are observing. You also need to understand what might result from this communication. Through developing such awareness, you will be more likely to use those reasons, examples, words, or actions that will aid your communication.

SUMMARY

People communicate almost constantly. The question is whether or not they are communicating what they *intend* to communicate. Sally knew what she wanted to communicate to Ray. She had a specific message she wanted him to understand. Everything she said and did should have contributed to his understanding. Her word choice, vocal tones, stance, and movements were all part of a message. If Ray misunderstood (misinterpreted) what he saw and heard, then Sally failed to accomplish her intended message, and Ray has now received a message he erroneously assumes to be accurate. His response will be based on a misunderstood message.

2. For a detailed explanation of communication as a process, see Berlo, *The Process of Communication*.

No one can guarantee total success in every communication effort. As you continue your study in this class, you will look at communication on an interpersonal level (between people); at communication in groups (a small number of people interacting in meetings); and at communication when speaking before audiences. You will focus on particular parts of the process as you study: the speaker, the listeners, the message (both verbal and nonverbal), and the environment (the setting and circumstances in which communication takes place). Such studies will enable you to increase the probability that you will communicate successfully.

EXERCISES

1. Select someone in the class to interview. Write a description of that person using Figure 2.5 as a guide. In which ways are you alike? In which ways are you different? Is it easy for you to communicate effectively with each other? Why?

2. Give the class a three-minute talk about the person you interviewed in Exercise 1. Include information that will help the listeners communicate effectively with that person. For example: "Bennett would understand examples related to music because he has played in the symphony for three years."

3. After everyone in the class has completed Exercise 2, write an analysis of the class as an audience. Include a section in which you give examples of how the information will be useful in communication.

4. Divide the class into pairs. One person in each pair will be the employee and the other will be the manager. The employee, with pencil and paper, will sit facing away from the chalkboard. The manager will face the chalkboard in order to see diagrams placed there and be able to give directions to the employee. The president (instructor) will draw three geometric figures on the chalkboard in any manner as long as they touch or overlap one of the other figures. The figures may be triangles, rectangles, squares, circles, or combinations. The manager will explain to the employee how to reproduce those figures on paper. The employee will listen carefully to the directions and see how accurately the drawings are reproduced. Were all the employees' final figures alike? Reverse the roles of managers and employees and try to reproduce a new drawing.

5. Attend a meeting of an organization. Write an analysis of one person's effectiveness in communicating. What was said that caused you to determine the extent of effectiveness? If you cannot attend a meeting, observe a salesperson and write the same type of analysis.

6. Divide the class into groups. Each group should draw a model to illustrate a segment of communication as a process.

Suggested Readings

Hamilton, Cheryl; Cordell Parker; and Doyle D. Smith. *Communicating for Results; A Guide for Business and the Professions.* Belmont, Calif.: Wadsworth Publishing Co., 1982, pp. 16–31.

This reference provides definitions of the traditionally accepted components of the communication process: stimulus, code, channel, feedback, environment, and noise.

McCroskey, James C. *An Introduction to Rhetorical Communication,* 4th ed. Englewood Cliffs, N.J.: Prentice-Hall, 1982.

Chapter 1, "The Nature of Rhetorical Communication," covers models and goals of communication. Chapter 3, "The Nature of the Receiver: Attitude Formation and Change," discusses characteristics of attitudes, how they are formed, and how they are changed. The theories are well documented.

Shannon, C. E., and W. Weaver. *The Mathematical Theory of Communication.* Urbana, Ill.: University of Illinois Press, 1949.

This source discusses one of the earliest models of communication, the Shannon-Weaver model, and should be used to study the development of models as a means of understanding communication.

Nonverbal Communication

3

If it is true that "actions speak louder than words," then you need to have a thorough understanding of what your actions may be saying to others, as well as what others are saying to you through their actions. This chapter will focus on how people assess and use nonverbal communication.

Most people have learned to interpret nonverbal communication more accurately than verbal communication. For example, if you give two contradictory messages simultaneously ("I believe you," said in a doubtful tone), which message does the listener accept as an accurate indication of your meaning? Most, if not all, listeners will accept the tone of voice. Your nonverbal communication may be at a subconscious level, with the result that you disclose feelings you never intended. In other words, you may want the person to believe your *words,* but you are revealing your true *feelings* through nonverbal means.

The Significance of Nonverbal Communication

Nonverbal communication is the transmission of messages through a method other than the literal interpretation of words. A listener assigns meaning not only by word choice and word combinations, but also by the way a speaker *says* words (the duration, tone, inflection, and quality of the voice); by the way the speaker *behaves* while saying those words (gestures, movements); by the use of *objects* (using a desk as a barrier); and by the use of *time* (keeping appointments) and *space* (keeping a certain distance from another).

Definition

A psychoanalyst has determined that ten minutes of conversation can reveal personality traits such as depression, impulsiveness, and dogmatism.[1] He analyzes speech according to such variables as the number of pauses, the number of nonpersonal references ("*One* should do that"), and the number of personal references ("*I* think . . ."). He concludes that a large number of *me*'s indicates a dependent person and a large number of such qualifiers as *it seems to be* indicates vagueness and indecision. Pauses and the rate of

1. Walter Weintraub, *Verbal Behavior: Adaptation in Psychopathology* (New York: Springer Publishing Company, 1981).

speaking may reveal certain psychotic disorders as well as other traits: "Silence serves an obvious self-protective function for those who distrust themselves"; it may also be used to discourage the company of unwanted individuals.[2] Be sensitive to what you may be disclosing nonverbally to others and what they are revealing to you.

If you are wondering how you became so perceptive and sensitive in interpreting nonverbal communication, think about how you learned your verbal communication. As a small child you misbehaved and someone shook a finger at you with a frown and a shake of the head. You learned that your behavior was unacceptable. Now, in an interview, you see the company president look at the clock, then down to some papers, and move slightly forward as if to rise. You determine that the interview is over. The president has "said" it is time to leave.

Strategies for Assessing and Using Nonverbal Elements of Communication

Assessing the meaning of another person's behavior is as risky as any other part of interpersonal communication. Many books and magazine articles have popularized the idea of "body language." Some authors imply that you can judge the encouragement being given you merely by watching the crossing and uncrossing of another person's arms and legs. This oversimplified view of nonverbal communication is misleading. It is impossible to say with certainty that any one gesture conveys only one meaning. This chapter does not imply that. Neither does it imply that you should manipulate people by nonverbal means. This chapter does say that people in our culture tend to consider the following nonverbal strategies important to communication effectiveness.

Any person in the professional and business world should know how to assess the use of nonverbal elements by others and should learn how to use these elements to communicate successfully. (See Fig. 3.1.)

1. USE SPACE FOR SUCCESSFUL COMMUNICATION

Most animals have a certain territory that "belongs" to them. When another animal encroaches on this area, the "owner" may consider it a violation. Humans also seem to exhibit territoriality. You can see the influence (real or imagined) of this concept when sports teams play on their "home ground."

Territoriality also exists in the business and professional world. The question of whose office to use for an interview is a good example. The person "owning" the office and seated behind the desk is perceived as having higher status. At certain times, the high-status person may want to emphasize the power associated with this territory; at other times, a high-status figure may prefer

2. Weintraub, p. 23.

> **Figure 3.1 Strategies for Effective Nonverbal Communication**
>
> 1. Use *space* for successful communication.
> 2. Use *time* to influence communication.
> 3. Plan your *physical appearance* to affect communication successfully.
> 4. Use appropriate *gestures* and other body *movements*.
> 5. Use *touch* with caution.
> 6. Use appropriate *voice* and *paralanguage*.
> 7. Use *objects* with caution.
> 8. Understand what *facial expressions* reveal.

to minimize status to encourage interpersonal communication, as discussed in the next chapter.

You may affect the perception of your status and power by the way you arrange office furniture, even if your desk and office space are assigned and thus beyond your control. You should determine how to use the existing conditions for maximum communication effectiveness.

Conference rooms. As a general rule, *the person seated in a position to have eye contact with the most people should be able to exert the most control or power.* The person sitting at the "head" of a table is generally perceived as the authority. Therefore, rectangular tables are best used in conference rooms when there will be a designated leader controlling the discussion. Round tables encourage equality of participants, but they become too large for groups of more than ten.

Office arrangement. The arrangement of furniture in the office itself, of course, depends on the size of the room. Ideally, an office should be large enough to allow several types of seating arrangements. Each type of arrangement is best suited for specific types of communication purposes.[3] Figure 3.2 illustrates an office arrangement for a large room that offers three seating arrangements. Each type is labeled. If you are unable to use all of them, you must be able to adapt, scale down, or decide which type will suit your needs best.

The *Type A* diagram illustrates the usual desk and chair arrangement. The visitor-subordinate may be seated in chair 2, close to the owner-executive (in chair 1) for informal business-oriented interviews. This position implies that both people recog-

---

3. For experimental and psychological studies of arrangements of professional settings to produce different interactions and climates, see Albert Mehrabian, *Silent Messages: Implicit Communication of Emotions and Attitudes,* 2nd ed. (Belmont, Calif.: Wadsworth Publishing Co., 1981), pp. 36–40; 117–21.

Figure 3.2

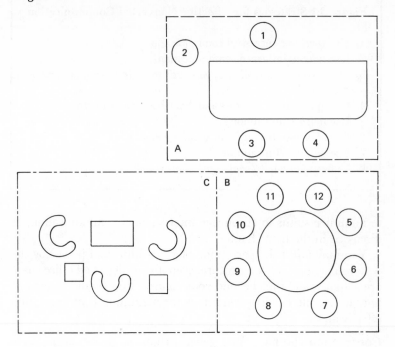

nize the inequality in roles but want to talk on a confidential or personal level about professional matters. Such an example would be a counseling interview (see Chapter 6). On the other hand, a person seated in chair 3 or 4 will consider the interview to be rather formal. This arrangement suggests the executive wants to maximize the status or power that his or her role carries. An attorney might use this arrangement while talking to a client.

The *Type B* diagram illustrates an arrangement that encourages participation by all members of a group. It implies equality. However, the executive who wants to minimize status should not choose either chair 11 or chair 12 because the power of the desk is seen behind those chairs. Remember, however, that if the meeting is held in this person's office (territory), this fact alone may be sufficient to endow the "owner" with status.

The *Type C* diagram is for informal, intimate, interpersonal communication. Its design, which resembles a social conversation grouping of living room furniture, promotes equality. A doctor visiting another doctor might choose this setting. If the president of the company comes into a subordinate's office, both would probably sit in this Type C grouping. If the high-status person took chair 2 in an office of Type A, the "owner" (low status) sitting in chair 1 probably would feel uneasy.

These three types of arrangements may be found in most company and professional offices. All three are not always found in one office. The chief executive officer, for example, may use a separate room for conferences. Sometimes Type C is found in the lobby, the reception area, or an outer office.

This discussion has so far focused on professional or executive use of the seating arrangement. If you are an interviewee, wait to be given a cue as to where you should sit. If in doubt, and if you wish to recognize the status of the other person, sit in chair 3 in a Type A setting.

2. USE TIME TO INFLUENCE COMMUNICATION

The use of *time* is particularly important in business and professional environments. Yet an appointment for 2:00 P.M. has different meanings for people of different cultures. Even within a given culture, a specific time may be interpreted differently according to occasion or purpose. As your own experience no doubt has shown, invitations to parties that give the time as 8:00 P.M. frequently are interpreted to mean that arrival time should be closer to 8:30 P.M. On the other hand, business appointments are scheduled with the intent that 2:00 P.M. *means* that the interview will start at 2:00. Therefore, some occasions present problems in clarity: what time does a business dinner begin if the time given is 8:00 P.M.? You may have to ask for help to find out what time your new boss expects you to arrive for such an event.

Some people are quite rigid about the use of time. These people arrive "on time" and expect everyone else to do the same. Sometimes they actually arrive early to be certain a meeting or an interview will begin promptly. They may perceive another person's failure to keep appointments promptly as a personal insult and an indication of irresponsibility.

Perhaps you have friends who rarely arrive at the appointed time. They may assume that such flexibility communicates a relaxed personality. They may feel that a late arrival focuses attention on them in much the same way a person arriving late at a party is able to "make an entrance." They may perceive the always-on-time person to be closed-minded and authoritarian. Perhaps it is the idea that the person being waited *for* has higher power: a patient waits for a doctor; a client waits for an attorney; a student waits for a professor. The problem, of course, occurs when two people with different attitudes toward time have business appointments. It is best, therefore, to keep appointments at the scheduled time and not risk alienating the other person.

Interruptions also are a part of the use of time. The protocol concerning outside interruptions during a meeting or interview usually is established between an executive and a secretary early in their working relationship. The secretary usually knows when to interrupt or keep other people out. The executive who asks the secretary to "hold all calls" gives a visitor or interviewee a feeling of importance. On the other hand, constant interruptions will convey the impression that the visitor has interrupted a busy day. The visitor may soon become irritated at not being given priority and assume the other person does not want to continue the meeting.

Of course, there are times when interruptions are necessary. The people involved in a meeting need to understand how to handle these occasions. The executive may make an explanation such as "I have a long-distance caller on the line who needs an immediate decision" and ask, "Do you mind if I leave for a few minutes to take the call in the other room?" The visitor then might respond, "Would you like me to wait in the reception room?" Neither person feels under pressure. If the call must be taken in the office and the visitor makes no motion to leave, the executive might instruct a receptionist, "Show Polly around the plant" or "Take Sam to the lounge for coffee while I handle this call."

3. PLAN YOUR PHYSICAL APPEARANCE TO AFFECT COMMUNICATION SUCCESSFULLY

A subject that is peculiar in its controversiality is that of a person's hair. Controversies focus on length, style, and color, and even on facial hair. Restrictions on length of hair have been the object of legal suits. Individual rights are pitted against safety regulations and uniformity. Whatever your individual preferences, many people will view your hair style as a statement. It may be a statement concerning your liberal philosophy, or your conservative philosophy. It may have religious significance. The color may be perceived as an indication of your personality or life-style. You may decide that, on principle, it is your right to wear your hair in any fashion you want. However, if you are trying to gain acceptance in a business meeting, you may want to analyze the other person's philosophy and adapt your hair style accordingly.

Generally speaking, it is best to avoid fashion extremes in a professional setting.[4] The best advice usually is to wear tailored or "nonfussy" clothes in subdued colors. Jewelry and other accessories should not distract from the message you intend to convey.

4. USE APPROPRIATE GESTURES AND OTHER BODY MOVEMENTS

Most of the time, a person will use gestures or body movements that reinforce the content of verbal communication. Rarely would anyone be so blatant as to *say*, "I'm delighted you have time to come in for this interview," and then stand and look out the window. The "welcoming" movements probably would be to rise out of the chair and indicate with a wave of the hand which chair the visitor should occupy.

People also make body movements that indicate meaning with-

4. William I. Gorden, Craig D. Tengler, and Dominic A. Infante, "Women's Clothing Predisposition as Predictors of Dress at Work, Job Satisfaction, and Career Advancement," *Southern Speech Communication Journal* 47 (Summer 1982): 422–34.

out using any words at all. For example, a person may shift in a chair and turn the body slightly away from another person when there is a disagreement. Neither may be consciously aware of the movement, but the one "receiving" the communicative feedback will *know* that the other person did not agree. The person who begins to tap a foot or swing a leg communicates an uneasiness with the conversation or the situation.

Other elements of movement that communicate include posture and the energy of an action. For example, a public speaker who slumps over the lectern may be seen as expressing lack of interest to the audience; one who shuffles slowly to the podium may appear to be communicating, "I really have nothing important to say." Someone genuinely interested in communicating with other people might be expected to demonstrate that interest by alert, energetic movements.

5. USE TOUCH WITH CAUTION

Touching another person may have a decidedly positive or negative impact in communication. There is a certain dichotomy when using touch in communication. Touch facilitates interaction; but it can also repel. Touch can increase communication; it catches the other person's attention; it may create a warmth between the two people; it encourages the other person to communicate.[5] It is difficult not to listen when someone is touching you. The Bell Telephone commercial capitalizes on the significance of touch by suggesting that you "reach out and touch someone" via telephone.

Tradition and culture determine where and when two people can touch. In the typical American business culture, men shake hands (but don't hold hands), slap each other on the back (but rarely hug), and are generally unsure whether or not these same principles apply to women in a business situation. (On the football field, where our culture permits patterns of behavior strikingly different from those in the office, men pat each other on the buttocks and hug frequently.) Women may or may not shake hands. Proper etiquette at one time dictated that women did not shake hands; later a man was told to shake a woman's hand *only* if the woman first offered her hand. Today, professionals generally make no distinction between males and females in shaking hands. It is a sign of recognition and acceptance.

From another standpoint, touching has sexual and coercive implications and should be used cautiously. A person who pats another on the shoulder or on top of the head may be suggesting a parent-child (authority-subordinate) relationship. The person may *intend* the touch to be conciliatory or to show approval; the one receiving the touch may perceive it to be patronizing or condescending.

Some people exert slight control by touching someone lightly on

5. Mehrabian, *Silent Messages,* pp. 23, 25.

Nonverbal
Communication

the arm while asking such questions as "Don't you think so?" Or they might put an arm around the shoulder of another person and give a slight, decisive pressure to indicate the same type of control. In both instances, the people have exerted *pressure* to have their ideas accepted.

Touch may be the single most important nonverbal element of communication. Used wisely, it can increase the listening, attention, and retention of interpersonal communication. Used unwisely, it can promote legal suits charging sexual harassment. Avoid any touch that may be perceived as coercive and an unfair use of status or power.

6. USE APPROPRIATE VOICE AND PARALANGUAGE

The term *paralanguage* refers not to the intellectual content of our words but to the way we use vocal inflection, vocal quality, and even the syntax of language. A simple example can be seen in the upward inflection at the end of a sentence that indicates a question rather than a statement. Without written marks of punctuation, the receivers of your message are dependent on your voice and manner to let them know you are emphasizing a point or that you have finished your message.

Certain vocal mechanisms reveal characteristics that may be detrimental to your credibility. For example, nonfluencies *(uh, um)* communicate a lack of self-confidence, hesitancy in committing oneself, or uncertainty over the issue being discussed. Nasal vocal tones may communicate a lack of intelligence (accurate or not, the perception is there). A speaker with a strident voice or harsh vocal tones may be showing irritation. A person who makes breathy, babyish sounds is not taken seriously. Substandard pronunciation and grammatical errors also hamper credibility.

Strive for the pleasant vocal quality that occurs when you relax your throat and say "ah." Use the pronunciation that most educated people use. Of course, you do not wish to become excessively self-conscious about your voice or words.

7. USE OBJECTS WITH CAUTION

Speakers frequently use objects as an extension of their gestures in making a forceful statement or in pointing to something. For example, a person may point with eyeglasses, a pencil, or a pipe, or may even slam a book on the desk to indicate a certain emotion.

Accessories in the office may communicate status, just as accessories on a person influence the perception of a listener. Unfortunately, some people use these same objects to reveal emotions such as nervousness, impatience, anxiety, and uncertainty. Not only does playing with jewelry, tapping a pencil on the desk, or straightening papers distract from the primary communication, but such behavior may communicate an unintended message. A sexist poster on a man's wall may eloquently express ideas he has no desire to transmit.

8. UNDERSTAND WHAT FACIAL EXPRESSIONS REVEAL

People's facial expressions (sometimes called *affect display*) probably reveal more than any other form of nonverbal communication. You can "read some people like an open book"; other people have "poker faces." But even the enigmatic person tells you something—perhaps that he or she believes "one should not reveal one's emotions." Many people also mirror another's expression. Watch the audience in a movie theater, and you will discover that in their expressions many people mimic what they see on the screen. Affect displays are a form of self-disclosure. When your face reacts, you reveal how you feel, what you are thinking, and whether you are listening. *Be careful to communicate your intended message through your facial expression.*

Facial expressions should reinforce the content of your message. If you are telling an employee that what you are discussing is "a serious and important matter," then your expression should reflect that seriousness. If you are sympathetic to what an employee is saying, allow your facial expression to reveal your sympathy.

The most important aspect of facial expression is eye contact with others. You probably have heard eyes described as "mirrors of the soul." If you do not want someone to know what you are thinking, then you probably will not look at that person. Because most people are perceptive, a person who *sees* your unwillingness to maintain eye contact may realize you have "something to hide."

The importance of eye contact is suggested by the word *contact*. When physical touch is too risky, or impossible because of distance, then eye contact becomes an excellent and acceptable substitute. If you do not consider eye contact comparable to touching, try establishing eye contact with someone in a place such as an elevator. People usually react as if you were guilty of touching them—a violation of cultural norms. Be cautious about the duration of the eye contact in a professional environment. A prolonged steady gaze may make another person feel uneasy, for it approaches the intimacy of touching.

SUMMARY

Nonverbal behavior is an important aspect of communication. It includes the voice, the body, and the environment. How you use these elements determines how effective you will be in communicating with others. In this chapter you learned the following principles.

1. Your listener is more likely to believe what you *do* than what you *say*.
2. Perceptions of nonverbal behavior usually are accurate.
3. Your perception of nonverbal communication is an outgrowth of your culture.

Nonverbal
Communication

4. Some influential elements of nonverbal communication include your use of space, time, physical appearance, gestures, movement, touch, voice, objects, facial expressions, and eye contact.
5. Eye contact may be used as an acceptable substitution for touch.

EXERCISES

1. List all of the expressions concerning *eyes* that you have heard.
2. Try making the following statements with no facial expression. Then make them with your "normal" expressions.
   a. That was a sour pickle.
   b. That was the funniest joke I ever heard.
   c. I saw a terrible accident on the way to work.
3. Read the following sentences aloud, stressing the word that is italicized:
   a. *I* believe you.
   b. I *believe* you.
   c. I believe *you.*
4. Prepare a three-minute pantomime of some office procedure or work-related behavior to be given in class.
5. Arrange to interview one of your professors. At the beginning of the interview ask if you may sit in the professor's chair during the interview. Be prepared to discuss your own feelings and your perception of the professor's feelings.

Suggested Readings

Benthall, Jonathan, and Ted Polhemus (eds.). *The Body as a Medium of Expression.* New York: E. P. Dutton & Co., 1975.
This source is a volume of essays written primarily about the use of the body in communication. They include such topics as "The Communicative Hand" and "Paralinguistics." Use the book for advanced study of nonverbal communication.

Burgoon, Judee, and Thomas Saine. *The Unspoken Dialogue: An Introduction to Nonverbal Communication.* Boston: Houghton Mifflin Co., 1978.
This text provides a comprehensive treatment of the use of nonverbal communication. The authors offer the theories surrounding the use of the body, space, time, artifacts and the cultural, sex, and personality differences in the use of nonverbal communication. They describe the functions of nonverbal communication in first impressions, attraction, affect displays, the regulation of interaction, the presentation of self, and the manipulation of others.

Fisher, Jeffrey D.; Marvin Rytting; and Richard Heslin. "Hands Touching Hands: Affective and Evaluative Effects of an Interpersonal Touch." *Sociometry* 39 (1976): 416–21.
Students who want to pursue a study of the influence of touching will find this article interesting.

Kendon, Adam; Richard M. Harris; and Mary Ritchie Key. *Organization of Behavior in*

Face-to-Face Interaction. The Hague: Mouton Publishers, 1975.

This volume of essays underlines nonverbal interaction from an anthropological viewpoint. Each essay is comprehensive and well documented.

Leathers, Dale G., and Ted H. Emigh. "Decoding Facial Expressions: A New Test with Decoding Norms." *Quarterly Journal of Speech Communication* 66 (1980): 418–36.

This article enables the reader to gain an understanding of interpretations assigned to facial expressions.

Obudho, Constance (comp.). *Human Nonverbal Behavior: An Annotated Bibliography.* Westport, Conn.: Greenwood Press, 1979.

This bibliography is useful for finding articles and books about human nonverbal behavior written during the period 1940–1978. The annotations provide descriptions that enable serious students to narrow their research to specific studies.

INTERPERSONAL COMMUNICATION IN BUSINESS AND PROFESSIONAL ORGANIZATIONS

2

Successful Interpersonal Communication

4

Many people assume that technical competence in a given field will ensure their success in the world of work. In some cases, that assumption may be correct. The medical researcher, the computer specialist who talks only to computers, or the lawyer who prepares only legal briefs may be able to excel without strong interpersonal skills. But for those who must work with other people to do their job effectively, an ability to communicate well is often the difference between success and failure.

To do their jobs well, corporate managers must communicate effectively with subordinates; doctors must communicate effectively with patients; teachers must communicate effectively with students; managing partners of accounting firms must communicate effectively with other partners and with auditors. In short, these people must interact with others on a one-to-one basis. The interpersonal skills that supplement their technical competence will give these professionals a competitive edge in the marketplace.

As Chapter 2 suggested, communication is a two-way process that involves speaking, listening, and sharing of meaning. Interpersonal communication is, most simply, interaction between people. How well people get along with each other (the level of support and trust between them) will affect how well they work together. As a manager, you can make the organizational climate better or worse through your interpersonal communication.

To improve the climate, take a look at the way you treat other people and how they respond to you. Do they believe and trust what you say? What kind of interpersonal climate do you create? Are you open to others' ideas or are you certain your own are always right? Would subordinates feel free to knock on your door and share with you their hopes and dreams as well as their project plans? What is your response when others are explaining themselves? Do you judge, evaluate, interrupt, ridicule, or otherwise minimize them? If so, you are not only undermining the climate, you are restricting the amount and accuracy of information you will receive from others; you are limiting the potential for cooperative problem solving; and you are minimizing the probability of others' commitment to you and the goals of your profession.

After you have assessed your interpersonal communication, look for ways to correct the negatives. To build trust, be consistent—with what you do and say; with your verbal and nonverbal messages; with the way you treat all your colleagues and subordinates. This chapter should increase your awareness of the personalities and strategies of the people involved in interpersonal communication.

A Definition

Interpersonal communication is the verbal and nonverbal interaction between people. The manager sending a message over the intercom is not participating in interpersonal communication. That person indeed may be sending a message to another person, but an important element is missing: feedback. There is no *interaction* between the people.

Interpersonal communication frequently is interaction between *two* people (called a *dyad*) in a face-to-face situation. You can still communicate, however, on an interpersonal basis when three or more people are talking. Look at the simple diagram (Fig. 4.1) illustrating such a conversation among *three* people (a *triad*).

Suppose, for example, that Mary, Bill, and John have entered the reception room and begun a conversation. You can study the interpersonal communication of each dyad within the triad. Mary and Bill form dyad M-B; Bill and John form dyad B-J; John and Mary form dyad J-M. One or more interpersonal communication transactions are occurring simultaneously during the conversation. That is, at the time verbal interpersonal communication occurs in dyad J-M, the *nonverbal* interpersonal communication in dyad M-B may be equally significant. For example, John and Mary may be discussing the need for increasing efficiency in production, and Mary may be using gestures indicating to Bill that he is not to leave the room because he needs to hear the discussion.

Even public speaking situations may be studied as complex interpersonal transactions with multiple dyads. Such a situation

Figure 4.1

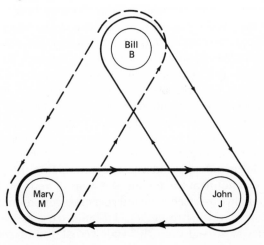

Figure 4.2

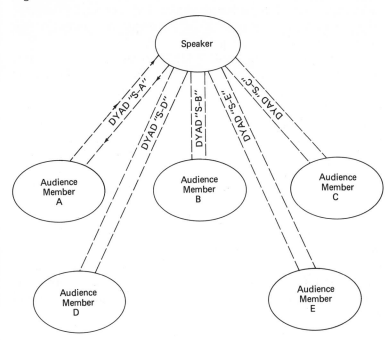

might look like that in Figure 4.2. Remember that each individual audience member is sending messages back (feedback) to the speaker. This interaction between the speaker and *each* listener is a dyad involved in interpersonal communication.

In the business and professional world, you frequently will be engaged in interpersonal communication. Sometimes this communication is a formal interview. Managers, for example, may schedule a session to talk with employees about organizational problems. Subordinates may ask supervisors for advice on writing a report. Professionals talk with colleagues during business luncheons. Any time people talk and listen to one another, they engage in interpersonal communication. Many factors will influence how you achieve success in this interaction. Some of these factors relate to the people involved. They include the personalities of the communicators and their willingness to risk self-disclosure in building trusting relationships.

TRUST

Trust is essential to successful interpersonal communication. Of course, the trust has to be mutual. Each person has to trust the sincerity of the other and be completely free to say whatever is appropriate. The trusting person neither threatens others nor fears reprisals from them. A trusting manager views the organization as a group of people working *together* to solve problems (increasing production, increasing sales, or building the corporate image).[1] The executives or managers and their employees are not adversaries within the corporation.

To develop a trusting relationship, one must be willing to risk self-disclosure. *Self-disclosure* is "verbally and nonverbally sharing with another some aspects of what makes you a person, aspects the other individual wouldn't be likely to recognize or understand without your help."[2] As a trusting subordinate, you may have to risk the displeasure of a supervisor; as a trusting manager, you may have to risk a loss of status with a subordinate. For example, if you ask for help, you risk the other person's assumption that you cannot cope with the problem. Before you decide to *trust*, in this case, you would weigh the possible loss of prestige against the possible gain of solving the problem. You might decide the possible loss outweighs the possible gain and therefore not admit your need for help. You may turn to a method of solving the problem that is not dependent on interpersonal communication, such as delegating the responsibility for the problem to someone else. Any organization must decide, through its executives, what information and which decisions should be shared with employees.

Trust is not established immediately. It takes time to determine to what extent certain information can be shared. The type of disclosure must be appropriate and the time and place must be appropriate. A new employee orientation session is not the time or place to reveal any misgivings about the financial stability of the organization. Building trust is a risky, time-consuming effort, but the long-range benefits far outweigh those risks.

OPEN-MINDEDNESS

The open-minded person is one who is receptive to a wide range of ideas, explanations, and knowledge. Such a person does not judge before considering a variety of opinions. Beginning a discussion with "I don't want to hear any silly ideas" will inhibit unique suggestions; most people would hesitate to express opinions that disagree with the supervisor. The open-minded person withholds critical evaluation until all the information is considered.

Judgments and critical evaluation should center on *what* is said, not *who* is offering those ideas. Thus, people are encouraged to speak without fear of being rejected. There is a difference between saying "It's difficult for me to understand how that suggestion would work" and offering a judgment about the person: "That suggestion just shows how stupid you are."

1. Fritz Steele, *The Open Organization: The Impact of Secrecy and Disclosure on People and Organizations* (Reading, Mass.: Addison-Wesley Publishing Co., 1975).
2. John Stewart, *Bridges Not Walls,* 3rd ed. (Reading, Mass.: Addison-Wesley Publishing Co., 1979), p. 112.

AUTHORITARIANISM

The authoritarian personality is based on the assumption that the person in authority "knows what's best." Subordinates of such figures believe that "the boss knows what I should do and will tell me." The boss may also use this approach toward subordinates: "I must tell my employees what to do or they won't do the correct thing." Words like *dictator, tyrant, paternalistic,* and *maternalistic* may describe the authoritarian manager. This personality type is institutionalized in the home, church, and school. The traditional family unit is based on authoritarianism. The parent "knows what's best" for the child. The church is headed by God (the ultimate authority) and godlike figures. Who can argue against someone who is speaking for an all-knowing God? The school has teachers and principals or deans. With such role models, it is no wonder the authoritarian personality is common in our culture.

The authoritarian finds interpersonal communication difficult with anyone other than a peer. Interpersonal communication implies reciprocal communication—two or more people who are equal in their desire to share their knowledge. If person A believes that person B is "always right," then A is reluctant to offer suggestions or information or in any way to initiate communication with B.

In organizations and in the professions, communication between two authoritarian personalities is based primarily on a status hierarchy; the manager speaks, for example, and the subordinate listens. If something is done incorrectly or if a problem arises, then the manager solves the problem and issues orders. Both are satisfied.

If only one of the two persons is strongly authoritarian, however, then interpersonal communication may result in dissatisfaction and a sense of frustration. The effective manager minimizes authoritarianism by minimizing status and power and by maximizing the open exchange of ideas.

DOGMATISM

The dogmatic personality is characterized by feelings of certainty on every issue. The person is opinionated, "always right," and closed-minded. A question of *probability* is rarely raised; there is no room for disagreement or discussion.

The dogmatic person does not use phrases such as "it seems to me" or "I think," which recognize that people's perceptions differ, but instead makes statements as if they were realities or truths ("You caused the problem when you . . ."). Do not be misled by the use of *we* by the dogmatic person, for this person frequently presumes to speak for everyone: "We will accomplish this in the following manner." Notice that the dogmatic person says *will,* not *may* or *might.*

When an authoritarian manager is dogmatic with an authoritarian subordinate, the subordinate accepts this because the person "in authority" is perceived as having "truth." Remember, however, that dogmatic statements discourage *communication* between people.

Barriers to Interpersonal Communication

People make decisions, communicate, and act according to their perceptions of both their environment and the people with whom they interact. These perceptions (how they interpret information) may sometimes be incomplete or even inaccurate. People tend to see and hear only what they want to see and hear or what they expect to see and hear (selective perception).

Barriers to effective interpersonal communication commonly arise from two sources: the attitudes a person holds toward another and the person's self-behavior.

ATTITUDES TOWARD THE OTHER PERSON

The following attitudes toward another person will distort your perception and thereby affect your communication with him or her.

Stereotyping. A significant barrier to interpersonal communication results from stereotyping a person. That is, the assumption that persons of the same "group" (gender, ethnic background, profession) all have the same traits will seriously hinder your ability to talk to a member of that group as a unique individual. For example, a problem in some offices is the inability to see female employees in ways other than such stereotypes as "Women are emotional" (therefore cannot reason logically) or "Women are helpless" (therefore cannot make the decisions to get the job done).

Labeling. Attaching a label to a person based on *current* or *past* behavior may keep you from communicating successfully with that person in *future* situations. Once labeled a "clown," a person has difficulty being taken seriously in decision-making situations. A person labeled as "accident prone" will be prone to accidents. When talking with others, do not be guilty of accepting yesterday's label as true of today's person.

Projecting. One of the most difficult things for people to see in themselves is that they project, or place, their own attitudes, beliefs, and values onto others. A person who values privacy may assume that a closed office door indicates a desire for privacy. But not everyone thinks that way. If you assume everyone would steal from the company if given the chance, you might be projecting your belief that *you* would do so.

Transference. This barrier to interpersonal communication is created when you transfer a trait held by one person to another person merely because the second person possesses certain characteristics. For example, if you always responded to your parents as authoritarian figures, you may transfer the same type of response to your boss, another authority figure. You have, in essence, transferred your parents' traits to your boss. Thus, you would have difficulty communicating with your boss if he or she acted other than as an authoritarian personality.

SELF-BEHAVIORS

Not only can your attitudes and perceptions about another person hinder the way you relate to each other, but your own behavior can provide a barrier to interpersonal communication.

Withdrawing. Withdrawing from interpersonal communication does not have to be the physical act of leaving a room. Some people do use this means of showing dissatisfaction with interpersonal communication, but usually they do so in personal relationships rather than professional ones. Rarely does a professional person become sufficiently upset to leave the room abruptly and slam the door in a working environment. But many people will emotionally and mentally withdraw from an interview or meeting when the communication is not satisfying. Perhaps they hear something threatening or boring, so they stop listening. They may still be hearing, as explained in Chapter 5, but they are no longer actively communicating in positive ways.

Frequently people indicate their withdrawal by nonverbal behavior. They shift backward and slide down in the chair, or may turn to one side as if using their bodies as barriers between them and another person. Such action discourages the other person from continuing in the conversation.

Ignoring the issues. Do not be guilty of talking all around the subject without getting to the issues. If an interview has been requested, it is for a purpose. If you ignore the issue, you only succeed in frustrating the other person. If an employee wants to discuss the company's evaluation procedure and you try to placate him or her with compliments, the employee will feel angry because you not only have ignored the issue, but have minimized or discounted the employee.

Pretending agreement. To pretend to agree only postpones the inevitable. For the moment, the other person may believe the interpersonal encounter has been successful; you both have communicated and reached agreement. Imagine the disappointment and resentment when that person discovers that you did not mean what you said.

Attaching blame. A problem arises, so you blame the other person. What does this accomplish? Does it solve the problem? The guilt (if the person is indeed guilty) just keeps the two of you from communicating effectively. The person may defend his or her actions. If you have used the person as a scapegoat (someone to take the blame for your own actions), then you probably have damaged the relationship so severely that positive interpersonal communication cannot occur. You must first reestablish a trusting relationship.

Rationalizing.   The opposite of accepting the responsibility for your behavior is to become defensive about what you have done. You perceive the other person's communication as threatening, so you react by rationalizing: you insist on giving "excuses." Suppose you fail to complete a report because it was more difficult than you expected. When the supervisor asks why the report is not ready, you rationalize by responding that it is the secretary's fault for not helping. This defensive behavior only antagonizes both the supervisor and the secretary.

Some rationalizing is psychologically necessary, however. A person must be able to "save face." If people assumed responsibility for *all* their mistakes, they might feel so guilty that they could no longer function. It is important to be sensitive to others' needs when they are rationalizing.

Strategies for Improving Interpersonal Communication

Strategies for improving specific *types* of interpersonal communication are given in the chapters on listening, interviewing, and meetings. Some strategies, however, are general to all communication situations. The foundation of these strategies is a sincere desire to be successful in that reciprocal interaction which constitutes interpersonal communication.

Two prime ingredients for successful interpersonal communication are *trust* and a genuine *feeling of equality* between the two people. This sense of equality, or worth, has nothing to do with ranks, roles, titles, or position. The equality must be in the attitude that each has something to share with the other.

Two kinds of strategies follow: first those that focus on providing a supportive atmosphere for trust and equality, and then those that improve message effectiveness.

CREATING A SUPPORTIVE ATMOSPHERE

A study by Jack R. Gibb differentiates between two climates for communication: the defensive and the supportive.[3] Some barriers to communication that exist in defensive climates have already been considered. A supportive atmosphere may be developed in the following ways. (See Fig. 4.3.)

1. Practice self-disclosure.   To self-disclose is to open yourself to another person. You reveal your thoughts, attitudes, values, and even past behavior—good and bad—to another person. Self-disclosure allows that person to "have a hold" over you. Perhaps you have revealed your feelings of insecurity or fear of rejection.

3. Jack R. Gibb, "Defensive Communication," *Journal of Communication* 11 (September 1961): 142–48.

This person *could* use that to control you. To self-disclose is risky. However, it is the best method for building trust and providing a feeling of equality.

2. Increase proximity. The further away you are from someone, the more difficulty you will have in communicating with that person. Studies of proximity reveal that friendship is developed between those who live or work in close proximity.[4] People who work in the same room frequently exchange confidences (self-disclose) and begin to socialize. Work groups thus create their own norms, roles, and support of each other.

Increase proximity for a supportive atmosphere by using the nonverbal strategies discussed in Chapter 3. Arrange the seating to be close; maintain eye contact; use touch.

3. Minimize status and power. Status and power can be minimized indirectly by avoiding titles and references to rank. People who are on a first-name basis are implying equality. (Caution: be certain both people are ready for this type of equality before you dispense with a title; the "superior" may be ready to *minimize* but not to eliminate status and power.)

Avoid symbols of status and power. Sitting behind an office desk maximizes rather than minimizes the status or power of an office. A desk in our culture has considerable power as a status symbol. Use seating arrangements suggested in Chapter 3 for specific types of interpersonal communication.

4. Stress common goals. Interpersonal communication in a professional setting usually has a serious purpose. More than likely, business or professional interviews are set up to solve problems or decide on policy. Both parties are interested in achieving the best solution or in determining the best policy. They may disagree about the best *method,* but would not be communicating if they did not have some of the same ultimate goals. They should not lose sight of these goals. By stressing the shared purpose for communicating, they promote equality. They both want only what is best—or what will work.

4. M. Argyle, M. Lalljee, and M. Cook, "The Effects of Visibility on Interaction in a Dyad," *Human Relations* 21 (1963): 3–17.

5. Stress similarities. We tend to trust people who are similar to us. You can develop a more trusting relationship, therefore, by reminding the other person of areas in which the two of you are equal and similar. A manager who was once in the subordinate's position might emphasize his or her understanding of the problems associated with that position.

IMPROVING MESSAGE EFFECTIVENESS

The following suggestions for wording messages can reduce defensive communication and can improve the interaction between the people involved. (See Fig. 4.4.)

Figure 4.4 Improving Message Effectiveness

1. Be accurate and concrete.
2. Criticize without blame.
3. Make assertions without aggression.
4. Paraphrase and summarize.

---

1. Be accurate and concrete. Avoid generalities, vague terms, and ambiguous language. If you ask for a report "anytime next week," you should be prepared for its not arriving until 5:00 P.M. on Friday. Otherwise, be specific: "Anytime before noon on Friday."

Give specific details if exactness is needed. Do not assume that the other person knows what you mean.

2. Criticize without blame. It is possible to evaluate proposals, causes of problems, or possible improvements without blaming others for past failures. An example of blaming is when a manager says, "Why did you implement X when you knew it would cause problem Y?" The successful communicator can talk in terms of "if we changed X, then problem Y might be reduced." This statement does not evaluate anyone's behavior.

3. Make assertions without aggression. *Assertions* are clear statements of feelings or attitudes. *Aggression* characterizes statements that encourage the other person to become defensive. Assertions are descriptive statements whereas aggressive statements may be disguised threats. Notice the difference between these statements:

> Assertion: I don't think I want to use my weekend to write the report.
> Aggression: I don't *have* to write that report over the weekend. (Implied threat: And you can't make me!)

Be open in expressing your thoughts, but avoid forcing the other person to take action or become defensive.

4. Paraphrase and summarize. One of the most effective methods for ensuring understanding during interpersonal communication is by paraphrasing or summarizing what another person says. These methods will aid clarification and prevent many misunderstandings. They also indicate an interest in the other person's ideas and promote trust in a relationship.

SUMMARY

This chapter focused on the interpersonal skills that help you relate to others in your profession. Interpersonal communication is based on the development of trust and equality in sharing information. One way to increase a feeling of trust is to understand how the personalities, roles, needs, values, behavior, and attitudes of those involved affect one another. Another skill is to learn the verbal and nonverbal strategies that provide a supportive atmosphere and minimize defensive behavior. Understanding both yourself and other people while using the verbal and nonverbal strategies will increase successful interpersonal communication.

EXERCISES

1. Go to the library or student center and observe instances of interpersonal communication. Write an analysis of the degree of trust and open-mindedness you observed.

2. Reveal something personal about yourself to a friend, and write down the reaction. Reveal the same thing to a classmate with whom you have only an acquaintance. Was the reaction different?

3. Sit down in the chair next to someone in the library. Observe the person's behavior.

4. Rank the following topics from 1 to 8, in the order of "difficult to discuss with one of my parents"; "with my closest friend"; "with someone sitting next to me on an airplane." Let 1 be "most difficult" and 8 be "easiest."
   a. My religious philosophy
   b. My views on premarital sex
   c. My financial status
   d. My self-image
   e. Food
   f. My health
   g. Entertainment
   h. Drug use

5. Compare your rankings with someone else's in the class. Write an analysis of what may have affected your responses.

Suggested Readings

Adler, Ronald B., and George Rodman. *Understanding Human Communication.* New York: Holt, Rinehart and Winston, 1982.

The authors provide theory and application to developing useful interpersonal relationships in chapters 6 and 7. The style is interesting.

Hulbert, Jack E. "Interpersonal Communication: Replacing Passive Behavior with Assertive Behavior." *Business Education Forum,* February 1982, pp. 25–29.

This article gives a brief description of a technique for "analyzing, discussing, and evaluating potential solutions to interpersonal conflicts."

Shuter, Robert. *Understanding Misunderstandings.* New York: Harper & Row, 1979.

The author achieves his goal of making this text clear and lively. Chapter 7, on conflict management, is interesting and readable.

Yankelovich, Daniel, and Bernard Lefkowitz. "Work and American Expectations." *National Forum* 62 (Spring 1982): 3–5.

This article illustrates the change in American values as they relate to job expectations.

Listening

5

On the average, people spend more time listening than they do in any other kind of communication—speaking, reading, or writing. Whatever business or profession you choose to enter, you will need to listen effectively and efficiently, for it is through listening that you receive messages from other people. A medical doctor learns about a patient's illness by the blood test *and* the patient's description of aches and pains. A lawyer prepares a defense based on law *and* the client's testimony. The teacher prepares a lecture based on the textbook *and* on questions raised about past lectures. A mother feeds a baby because the clock says it is feeding time *and* the baby is crying.

Listening is essential to effective communication, but most people have little formal training in how to improve the skill. This chapter provides basic information on listening as an active process. Further, it outlines listening steps, skills, and models.

The general lack of listening training reflects four false assumptions, listed as follows.

False Assumption 1: Communication Is Sending Messages to Other People.

As Chapter 2 suggested, communication is a transactional process that involves both speaker and listener. Some people, for example, believe that unless a message is received, no communication has occurred. If you do not listen to my instructions, I have wasted my time giving them.

False Assumption 2: Listening Is Simply a Matter of Hearing What Is Said.

As this chapter argues, listening is much more complicated than that. For one thing, hearing is a physiological process, while listening involves psychological phenomena. That is, listening includes "making sense" of the messages we hear and attaching meaning to them. How well people listen will affect how much of the message they ultimately remember.

False Assumption 3: People Are Naturally Good Listeners.

Research suggests, on the contrary, that most people listen very poorly. They only hear some of the messages aimed at them. They distort those they hear and make up (substitute) their own messages. Further, they remember very little of what they initially "hear."

IT PAYS TO LISTEN.
Columbus' ideas fell on deaf ears for years before Queen Isabella finally chose to listen. It's a lesson that wasn't lost on Sperry. Listening keeps us alert to ever-expanding

possibilities in computer science, aerospace, and defense.
What's more, it helps us expand them ourselves.
Real breakthroughs increasingly occur when seemingly unrelated advances get connected—and then, suddenly, explosively fuse. This takes an attentive, imaginative kind of listener who combines the unlikely in

unexpected ways.
It's why, at Sperry's Research Center, scientists from eighteen totally different disciplines regularly meet.
To listen to each other.
We at Sperry are convinced that listening well ignites new insights, guides us into

uncharted areas of thought, and ultimately uncovers whole new worlds.

◆ SPERRY

We understand how important it is to listen.
Sperry is Sperry Univac computers, Sperry New Holland farm equipment, Sperry Vickers fluid power systems, and defense and aerospace systems from Sperry division and Sperry Flight Systems.

For a booklet on listening, write to Sperry, Dept. F5, 1290 Avenue of the Americas, New York, N.Y. 10104.

Figure 5.1

False Assumption 4: Listening Cannot Be Taught.

Not only *can* listening be taught, it *is* taught. Thomas Gordon, for example, has developed comprehensive seminars that focus on listening skills for parents, teachers, and aspiring leaders.[1]

Sales training has traditionally stressed the importance of listening to the prospect. Organizations emphasize listening as an important management tool, and executive training programs typically include sessions on improving listening. Sperry Corporation, which has developed a comprehensive in-house training program, has also launched an advertising campaign that emphasizes listening.

Why are organizations such as Sperry investing time and money in listening training and promotion? Obviously, they believe that it is to their economic advantage to do so. As the copy for one Sperry ad reads, "It pays to listen."

To understand Sperry's rationale, let us review for a moment what organizations look like. *Organizations are composed of people who work together in highly structured superior-subordinate relationships to accomplish goals.* How well they perform their work will depend to a large degree on how well they communicate—how efficiently they manage information and how effec-

1. For an example of Gordon's approach, see Thomas Gordon, *Parent Effectiveness Training* (New York: Wyden, 1972).

tively they work together to solve problems and make decisions. The flow of information between people in the organization, and the group decision making that occurs there, both demand high levels of interaction. That means listening!

If you choose a business career, you probably will begin at an "entry-level" position. That is, you will be "low person on the totem pole" in the management hierarchy. Your job will require you to take orders, follow instructions, and read directives. In short, you will do a lot of listening. As you move up the managerial ladder, you will start to do more talking. In addition to taking orders from your superiors, you will begin giving orders to your subordinates. But you will need to listen to them, too.

If you are a manager, you will probably spend as much as one-third of your work day listening to other people.[2] Primarily you will listen to accomplish the organization's goals. In other words, you will use listening as a management tool to help you plan, organize, staff, direct, and control your resources toward accomplishing your goal. If you are a lawyer, a doctor, a teacher, or any other kind of professional, you will listen for the same reasons managers listen—to do your job well. By listening, you can build more effective work relationships as well as get information you need.

2. Richard C. Huseman, James M. Lahiff, and John D. Hatfield, *Business Communication: Strategies and Skills* (Hinsdale, Ill.: The Dryden Press, 1981), p. 261.

Figure 5.2

Active Listening

To listen well you need to listen "actively." To understand the full implications of what that means, look at two definitions of active listening. In its most basic sense, active listening is energetic listening with the message receiver a full partner in the communication process. In a more specialized sense, active listening is hearing and interpreting the *feeling* part of messages and responding in ways that are helpful to the message sender.

ACTIVE VERSUS PASSIVE LISTENING

The active listener acts; the passive listener is acted upon. Listeners who are actively involved in the communication process are psychologically and physiologically tuned in, attempting to understand the *sender's meaning*. Passive listeners, on the other hand, make less effort to participate in a sharing of meaning. They assume the messages they hear and understand *(receiver's meaning)* are what the sender "said." For the active listener, effective communication is the responsibility of both sender and receiver; for the passive listener, that responsibility is the sender's alone.

Since what message senders *mean* is not always what they *say,* active listeners listen for (1) verbal and nonverbal messages, (2) what was not said as well as what was said, and (3) the content and feeling dimensions of messages. The passive listener, on the other hand, hears what is interesting, beneficial, or attention-getting.

LISTENING AND RESPONDING TO FEELING MESSAGES

Most listeners, particularly those in organizations, listen for content only. In so doing, they often miss the real message. "I'm going to throw this typewriter into the Atlantic Ocean" is not a content message. It has nothing to do with the seashore and likely nothing to do with the typewriter. The true message—"I'm frustrated" or some version thereof—may result from unreasonable workload, status problems in the organization, or typing errors. To respond to the message on the basis of its content—"I'm planning a trip to Atlantic City this weekend; would you like a ride?"—sounds absurd, even insulting.

Even when managers realize that a message is not primarily a content one, they may nonetheless reply on a content level. Though the response may be true, well intentioned, and clearly presented, it is not likely to be helpful to the subordinate since it fails to respond to the feelings expressed. Typical but *nonhelpful* ways a manager might respond to the typewriter message include the following.

1. *Give advice.* "Go back and try typing the report again. Maybe you won't make so many errors next time."
2. *Evaluate/judge.* "Let's face it. Typing is not your strong suit."
3. *Minimize.* "It's just a report. I don't see why you're so upset."
4. *Universalize.* "Nobody else in the pool types well either."

5. *Sympathize.* "I'm so sorry you aren't a good typist."
6. *Warn.* "Don't let Sam know you aren't going to finish the report."
7. *Withdraw.* "It's not my problem. I have plenty of my own work to do."

Active listening suggests that message receivers should not only recognize feeling messages when they hear them, but should also respond to those messages *on a feeling level,* playing back to the sender what they "sensed" or "heard" or "felt" the message to be. Carl Rogers calls the playing back of feeling messages *reflecting.*[3] Appropriate reflecting responses in the typewriter example might be "You're frustrated," "Something's really gotten under your skin," or "Gee, but you're mad."

Many managers resist reflecting their subordinates' feeling messages, believing that feelings have no place in a work environment. Yet feelings are everywhere people are. Recognizing and responding to feelings help humanize the workplace, making it a more congenial place for people to function. Also, by acknowledging feelings, managers prevent them from festering and erupting in other, potentially destructive ways.

Most managers are not trained to deal with feeling messages. The following comment is typical: "I can't confront John on his alcoholism. I don't know how to help him, and I could make matters worse. Besides, he doesn't want me meddling in his business. He'd deny he has a drinking problem anyway." The manager is missing the point. If John's performance is suffering, some *confrontation must occur on that performance.* If a problem with alcoholism is uncovered in the process, the manager cannot ignore it. Reflecting will probably be more helpful and less threatening than giving advice or questioning. Ultimately, however, John may be referred to a professional counselor.

Another reason some people are uncomfortable with reflecting is that they are afraid they will sound foolish. "I can't say 'You're frustrated.' That sounds ridiculous." Reflecting does sound phony if the person is not genuine in trying to feed back the sender's message. But the point many people miss is this: if they reflect the message they "heard," the sender will appreciate that someone is trying to understand. If they reflect correctly, the message has been communicated.

Listening Steps and Skills

You can become a better listener if you work to listen more systematically. Good listening is orderly; it is also developmental, with one stage building on another. You cannot respond thoughtfully to a message until you have "heard" it. Yet some people try. They assume they know what a message will be, tune out the

3. Carl Rogers, *On Becoming a Person* (Boston: Houghton Mifflin, 1961).

sender's words and nonverbal signals, and ask questions, answer, or argue—without ever having heard the message.

This section describes six sequential *listening steps* that should help you listen more systematically.

1. Hear the message.
2. Interpret/understand the message.
3. Test understanding.
4. Revise interpretation.
5. Evaluate.
6. Remember.

You will not always need to follow all of these steps. As we will discuss later in this chapter, your purpose for listening should determine which are most appropriate. Never reorder the steps, however; and when you skip a stage, *know you are skipping it* and *have a reason for doing so*.

In the following discussion of listening steps, you will find specific *listening skills* that are useful at various stages of the process. Some of these skills are nonverbal (eye contact, maintaining appropriate distance, leaning forward, nods, and vocalizations); others are verbal (questioning, reflecting, restating, paraphrasing, and summarizing). Each skill will be described in detail.

LISTENING STEP 1: HEAR THE MESSAGE

When you "hear" a message, you do more than take sounds into your ears. You absorb other messages as well—the nervous twitch; the overpowering perfume; the speaker's nearness; the "you know" that punctuates every sentence. You also "hear" or perceive the buzzing fly, the sunlight's glare on the chalkboard, the music next door, your neighbor's doodling. For everything you "hear," however, you miss even more.

You miss much that is going on around you because you cannot physically take it all in. You have only five senses to receive messages, and you probably cannot use more than one of them at the same time. You switch from seeing to hearing and back again—very quickly, of course, but you switch nonetheless. Even when you are trying to pay attention, you tune in and out like a weak radio station. You are probably not aware how short your attention span is (maybe as short as three or four seconds) or how you keep switching from channel to channel. Neither, when you are in a movie theater, are you aware of the thousands of individual frames of film you see with gaps between each of them; or the lapses in your own attention. Both, however, affect what you "hear." To compensate for listening gaps, message senders need to restate their most important points. They can repeat, paraphrase, or summarize them, or they can use supplementary channels (speaking and visualizing) to get their messages "heard."

If listening is selective, if we cannot "hear" everything, what determines which messages "get through" and which do not? The following true story provides some clues.

A young man of rural background won a scholarship to a university in New York City. The first day in town, he and his roommate hopped a bus to see the city lights. When they reached the heart of the shopping area, they decided to walk for a while to "get the feel" of the place. Near one busy intersection, the farmboy stopped, cupped his hand to his ear, and cried out excitedly, "I hear a cricket." His roommate, who was from a nearby city, looked at him in astonishment. "A cricket? There are no crickets in New York City, and even if there were, you couldn't hear them in this traffic." "But I do," insisted the farmboy. "I do hear a cricket—just listen." He reached down into a small patch of weeds growing by the bus stop sign, picked up a cricket, and triumphantly presented it to his friend. "See, I know a cricket when I hear one." "How did you ever hear that?" his friend queried. "I can't even hear myself think with all this noise." The farmboy thought for a minute. Then he took some coins from his pocket, tossed them into the air, and watched them hit the crowded sidewalk. People stopped in their tracks. A mad scramble began. Hands were frantically combing every inch of space, searching for the money. "You see," said the farmboy, "it just depends on what you're listening for." In the midst of car horns, endless chatter of pedestrians, a policeman's whistle, feet walking, shuffling and scraping, one person heard a cricket, another some coins clink; others heard nothing. The farmboy was right: *people hear what they are listening for.*

What do most people listen for? What do they voluntarily give their attention to? What things get their attention without their willing it so? People listen voluntarily to messages that are meaningful to them; that is, *if they see some personal benefit* in the message or *if the message is what they expect it to be.* People listen involuntarily to strong messages, to the unexpected, and to messages that are free from distractions.

If communication is a transactional process, then you as a listener have a responsibility to develop skills to "hear" others better. Nonverbal behaviors are particularly useful in increasing listener sensitivity to others' messages. Since these behaviors can be learned and developed, they are referred to as skills. The following discussion identifies *eye contact, maintaining "appropriate" distance, leaning forward, nods, and vocalizations* as nonverbal listening skills.

Eye contact.　By looking at others when they are speaking to you, you increase your chances of "getting" their messages. For one thing, your attention cannot wander easily. Also, you are better able to "hear" the nonverbal messages being sent. For example, if a sender's hands are shaking, you are aware of the nonverbal cue, and you interpret the message: is it nervousness, anger, or a physical disability?

Maintaining "appropriate" distance. If you sit as far away from the message sender as possible, you are more likely to miss part of the message than if you sit under the speaker's nose. On the other hand, you should not get so close that you are both uncomfortable.

Leaning forward. You usually "hear" more of the message if you are intently leaning forward listening than if you are sprawled out or slouched in the chair. Leaning forward can help you "tune in" to the sender's message. It also acknowledges the speaker by saying, "I'm listening." By reinforcing the speaker ("You're worth listening to"), you are encouraging the communication to continue.

Nods. By slowly moving your head up and down, you tell a listener that you understand. Be careful, however, that your nod messages are not misleading; the message sender may think you are agreeing. If you sense confusion, make clear that you are following the speaker's line of thought, not necessarily agreeing or disagreeing with the point. Because nod messages are reinforcing to the speaker, they encourage open communication.

Vocalizations. Although vocalizations or nonfluencies such as *um, uh,* and *ah* by a speaker detract from the message, vocalizations by a hearer can be a useful listening tool. As with the nod, these sounds of communication can send feedback that you are listening. Since such messages reinforce the speaker, they will likely result in increased information flow.

LISTENING STEP 2: INTERPRET/UNDERSTAND THE MESSAGE

The messages you "hear" are symbols—verbal and nonverbal codes. To "make sense" of those messages, you must process them or take them out of code (essentially a psychological process). In short, you *interpret* the messages you hear—from your own perspective. You leave out some details, add others, and give emphasis according to what is important to you. In interpreting messages, you often are far afield of the message the sender intended. Instead, you have made up a message that is consistent with your own view of the world. A number of factors influence how hearers interpret messages. Some of the most important include the following:

Relevance of the material to the individual's pressures and priorities
Knowledge level and past experiences
Attitudes, values, and belief structures
Presence or absence of conflicting messages
Physical setting

Comfort and trust level
Status and roles
Self-concept

In "making sense" out of the messages you receive, you draw conclusions about what you "heard." Typically, you generalize from bits and pieces of information (inductive reasoning). Or you try to fit information into your own set of premises about the world (deductive reasoning). Sometimes your conclusions may be inadequate or inaccurate because you do not have enough information, or the information you have is biased or outdated. Often, your conclusions are not useful because you have not reached them logically. You may infer too quickly, jumping to unwarranted conclusions, assigning intentions, and making judgments before you have understood the *other person's message.*

One particularly troublesome problem that prevents our understanding others' messages is the common tendency to confuse or fail to distinguish between what we see and hear (observations) and the conclusions we draw (inferences). In a court of law, for example, conflicting testimony from "eyewitnesses" is not uncommon. The problem is partly perceptual; in attempting to "make sense" of our observations, we must select and interpret messages according to our own experience. The difficulty arises when we *fail to differentiate the perceived message* (what is understood) *from the intended message* (what was said or meant). The exercise in Figure 5.3 will give you an indication of the extent to which you blur the distinction between observations and inferences.

After you have finished the exercise, share your answers with another person. Do you agree on every answer? If you were courtroom witnesses, would your stories be the same? If your answers are similar to those of numerous others who have completed this exercise, you have probably made a lot of inferences and are convinced they are facts. You may even be prepared to argue about them. Most likely, you have made some mistakes.

Making inferences is essential to survival. The city provides our drinking water. Since we believe water supplies are carefully monitored, we infer the water is safe and drink it. The doctor gives us a shot. Since doctors are "medical experts," we infer the shot will make us better, not worse. We've installed a burglar alarm. Since we believe these devices prevent burglaries, we infer we can sleep safely. We are not always correct in these inferences. Some city drinking water has small amounts of life-threatening chemicals; some shots paralyze or even kill; burglar alarms do not always protect us from harm.

How can we minimize the risk of being wrong? First we have to be *aware* we are making an inference. Then we need to validate it. Has the water been tested recently? What is its fluoride content? What are the most recent statistics on results of the tetanus vaccine? Is the burglar alarm activated? When we are listening to

Figure 5.3 Inference and Observation

A businessman had just turned off the lights in the store when a man appeared and demanded money. The owner opened a cash register. The contents of the cash register were scooped up, and the man sped away. A member of the police force was notified promptly.

Are these statements true (T), false (F), or not certain (?). Put a check in the appropriate box to indicate your opinion.

T	F	?	
			1. A man appeared after the owner had turned off the store lights.
			2. The robber was a man.
			3. The man did not demand money.
			4. The man who opened the cash register was the owner.
			5. The store owner scooped up the contents of the cash register and ran away.
			6. Someone opened a cash register.
			7. After the man who demanded the money scooped up the contents of the cash register, he ran away.
			8. Although the cash register contained money, the story does not state how much.
			9. The robber demanded money of the owner.
			10. The story concerns a series of events in which only three persons are referred to: the owner of the store, a man who demanded money, and a member of the police force.

Adapted from William V. Haney, *Communication and Interpersonal Relations,* 4th ed. (Homewood, Ill.: Richard D. Irwin, 1979), pp. 250–51.

others, we need to be sensitive to the inferences we make about their messages and examine them critically.

If message senders and receivers are to *understand* each other, both must assume responsibility for communicating the message. As a sender, you can increase the chances your message will be understood by identifying perceptual barriers (both your own and your hearers') and planning your messages to minimize or bypass them. As a listener, you need to be aware of barriers that prevent you from understanding what message senders really want to communicate.

Listeners can also improve understanding by wisely using the mental time lag between messages. Since people can think faster than they can speak, you will have a lot of "play time" waiting for speaker messages. Use that time to focus on the message by repeating it in your mind; asking yourself questions about it; synthesizing important points; and noting points that need clarification. Make a mental note of questions you need to ask to help you understand the message better. In order to understand messages others send, you will need additional facts, opinions, or clarification. *Questioning is a verbal listening skill particularly appropriate for getting or clarifying information.*

Questioning. Though we commonly think of questioning as a "talking" skill, it is also an important listening tool since it helps us interpret and understand messages (step 2 in the listening process). You may ask questions either directly or indirectly. *Direct questions* end with a question mark: "Do you think we should go into the New York market this year?" *Indirect questions,* on the other hand, request information, but they do it more subtly: "You must have some ideas on our market expansion plans." Sometimes you wish general information or to get the respondent talking on an issue. Ask *open questions* such as "Tell me about promotion opportunities at Acme." *Closed questions,* on the other hand, which aim at more specific responses, are useful when you know what information you need. An example of a closed question is "How many managers were promoted at Acme during the last year?" You may also use *follow-up questions* to probe for details or more precise information.

A final word of advice on asking questions: ask questions for information or clarification and not for accusation. "Why" questions, for example, often sound accusatory. "Why did you leave out the percentage ratio?" is not so much a question for information as a message that you did something unacceptable.

LISTENING STEP 3: TEST UNDERSTANDING

The message you interpret or understand may not be the message the sender meant. The only way to find that out is to "test" it. Testing your understanding of a message implies a willingness to see something from another person's point of view and, if necessary, to alter your opinion. As suggested, one way to clarify or better understand messages is to ask questions. You can also test understanding by feeding messages back to the message sender. *Reflecting, restating, paraphrasing, and summarizing are verbal listening skills useful in testing understanding.*

Reflecting. If the message you "heard" was a feeling message, the most appropriate response you can make is a reflecting one. By reflecting, you are saying to the individual, "I understand." You also clarify whether or not you interpreted the message correctly. In other words, if you reflect a message ("You've really had about all you can take this week") and are accurate, the sender will sigh in relief. On the other hand, if you have misread the message, the sender will correct you ("No, it's just that I have two reports to finish today").

Restating. Sometimes you may play back a content message *using the speaker's own words:* "We should not reassign staff until the guidelines are written." *Restatement,* or, to use Carl Rogers's term, "mirroring," *makes no judgment* about the other's message, but it does clarify for you and the speaker precisely what was said. Since you do not wish to imply that the speaker was unclear, word your response carefully. The following phrases are nonthreatening ways to begin: "Let's see if I've understood you"; "As I understand it"; "Why don't I go back over that so I'll be sure I understand." Be careful not to overdo restating, however. The message sender does not need an echo, only reinforcement.

Paraphrasing. Paraphrasing is another way to check your understanding of the message. In paraphrasing you play back the message, but *in your own words.* For example, "You think the guidelines will affect staff reassignment." You may wish to begin your paraphrase with language similar to that suggested for restating: "Let me see if I understand"; "Why don't I put that in my own words to see if I've got the idea."

Summarizing. Whereas reflecting, restating, and paraphrasing respond to a single message, a summary synthesizes. Summarizing does not go beyond the message you "heard." Neither does it include your own opinion. It simply tries to draw together material from a discussion. A typical summary statement would be: "So you really have three objections to the proposal—cost, time constraints, and reallocation of personnel."

LISTENING STEP 4: REVISE INTERPRETATION

After you have tested your understanding of the other person's message, you should revise your earlier interpretation of what you "heard." Essentially, you are making the leap from your own understanding to the sender's. In so doing, you have reached for a common "meaning," and that is what communication is all about.

LISTENING STEP 5: EVALUATE THE MESSAGE

Evaluation is the *critical* part of listening, the part where you deliberate about the message. Here you make judgments, accept or reject ideas, opinions, or reasoning, and place "value" on messages. Decision makers arrive at defensible choices through testing ideas, data, and alternative solutions. When listening critically, you need to apply some general standards to the propositions, arguments, and data you hear. These standards should include relevancy; accuracy; adequacy (completeness or representativeness); objectivity; expertise; reliability; and coherence.

Though evaluation is an important part of problem solving and decision making in organizations and other professional settings, it can also be a barrier to communication. Evaluation may limit the information and ideas that subordinates are willing to share with superiors and prevent others from openly discussing problems that negatively affect their work. Evaluation can be punishing, threatening, or demeaning—even to the most self-confident person.

How can you solve the dilemma of the need to evaluate versus the human and information costs of doing so? The following suggestions may help:

Evaluate in the appropriate situation. Sometimes the listener's job is to make judgments and give opinions. Such situations as problem solving, decision making, appraisal, and performance counseling call for evaluation. These face-to-face meetings allow feedback for all concerned and give others an opportunity to ask or answer questions and raise objections to the view expressed.

At other times, evaluation is inappropriate and potentially damaging. For example, evaluation can be obstructive during the sending or receiving of information. If you are explaining steps a person will need to take to implement a new policy, you do not want the discussion to disintegrate into an argument over whether the policy is good or bad. You just need it carried out correctly.

Evaluate at the appropriate time. Evaluate *after* you have understood the message. Some listeners evaluate before they hear a message; some hear only a part and judge; others hear the speaker out before offering an opinion; still others test their understanding and then respond. The last alternative is the most useful.

Evaluate the ideas, not the person. People become attached to their own ideas and find it hard to be objective about them. When their ideas are attacked, they may feel they have been attacked personally. You need to be sensitive to the difficulty of separating people from their ideas. When evaluating, you should make every attempt to support the individual while at the same time critically evaluating the suggestion. Positive, impersonal (avoid the pronoun *you*) language will help. Note the difference in "tone" in these two examples: (1) "*Your* marketing plan is *inappropriate* for a service industry." (2) "The marketing plan before us seems more appropriate for manufacturing than for a service industry."

LISTENING STEP 6: REMEMBER THE MESSAGE

How well you listen to messages and what you listen to will influence how much you remember. The *message sender* can increase the probability of listeners remembering the message by

- showing how the message benefits or affects the listener
- previewing the main points for the listener at the beginning of the presentation
- using signposts (*one, two,* and *three*) and transitions to emphasize the major points
- summarizing main points at the end of the presentation
- asking listeners questions
- requiring listeners to apply the materials (cases, etc.)

Listeners can improve their chances of remembering the messages they hear by

- using "thinking" or lag time to review and internalize main points
- taking notes
- making connections between what is being said and what the listener already knows

Listening Models

In the preceding sections, we have described six sequential steps in listening. Not all listeners follow all the steps, however. Some may skip steps because they do not know better or they do not *want* to listen effectively. Others skip steps for more legitimate reasons. Which steps listeners follow may depend on their reason for listening, their knowledge of the listening process, and their skill in responding to others.

People use at least three different approaches or strategies when they listen. These are *self-centered listening, responsive listening,* and *critical listening.* The following models show which of the listening steps each strategy includes.

Self-Centered Listening (ego-oriented)	Responsive Listening (people-oriented)	Critical Listening (task-oriented)
1. Hear or assume message.	1. Hear message.	1. Hear message.
2. Interpret/Understand.	2. Interpret/Understand.	2. Interpret/Understand.
3. ———	3. Test understanding.	3. Test understanding.
4. ———	4. Revise interpretation.	4. Revise interpretation.
5. Evaluate.	5. ———	5. Evaluate.
6. Remember.	6. Remember.	6. Remember.

SELF-CENTERED LISTENING

The self-centered strategy is probably the most commonly used, particularly among people with little or no listening training. The strategy is ego-centered: self-centered listeners listen to gain something for themselves. Some do not listen at all. Others pretend. Still others "listen" by monopolizing the conversation. A few listen to understand the speaker's message. They sometimes pay close attention to what the speaker says and often ask questions for information, but *self-centered listeners rarely test their understanding of the messages they receive*. Rather, they assume that others' perspectives do not differ significantly from their own or that theirs is the only valid approach.

RESPONSIVE LISTENING

Professionally trained counselors often use the responsive approach to listening.[4] Responsive listeners are more concerned with people than with a task. Their goal is twofold: to understand the *real* message, and to value or reinforce the message sender. Responsive listeners use reflecting, restating, summarizing, and paraphrasing skills extensively and are less likely to use probing questions, particularly in the early stages of the interview. *Responsive listeners rarely judge, and never judge prematurely* (before they have adequately reinforced the message sender and received the information they need to understand the problem). As early as 1952, Carl Rogers, who was instrumental in developing the strategy, argued that "the major barrier to mutual interpersonal communication is our very natural tendency to judge, to evaluate, to approve (or disapprove) the statement of the other person or group." For Rogers, "Real communication occurs, and this evaluative tendency is avoided, when we listen with understanding."[5]

CRITICAL LISTENING

Critical listening is not limited to evaluation. Rather, it balances the need to accomplish the task with the need to understand a message *before* judging it. Critical listeners use a range of listening skills—from those that support message senders (nonverbal acknowledging, reflecting) to those that expand, clarify, and test content (restating, summarizing, paraphrasing, questioning).

4. Carkhuff and Berenson distinguish two phases of counseling, the responsive and action phases, and suggest that most traditional therapies use *only* the first. R. R. Carkhuff and B. G. Berenson, *Beyond Counseling and Therapy* (New York: Holt, Rinehart and Winston, 1967), chap. 9. For more directive approaches that include evaluation, see F. S. Perls, R. E. Hefferline, and P. Goodman, *Gestalt Therapy: Excitement and Growth in Human Personality* (New York: Dell, 1965), first published in 1951. See also Albert Ellis, *Reason and Emotion in Psychotherapy* (New York: Lyle Stuart, 1962).

5. Carl R. Rogers and F. J. Roethlisberger, "Barriers and Gateways to Communication," *Harvard Business Review* 30 (July–August 1952): 47.

Regardless of the strategy you follow when listening to others, you will find some general suggestions helpful in improving your effectiveness as a listener. Further, as a message sender, you will need to get others to listen to you. The checklist in Figure 5.4 summarizes principles you may find helpful.

Figure 5.4 Listening Checklist

Suggestions for Improving Listening

1. Determine the value *to you* of what is being said.
2. Be aware of your biases and how they affect your listening.
3. Be prepared to listen (have necessary information; know the other person's position, etc.).
4. Use the time lag to review the major points.
5. Listen to understand, not to contradict.
6. Evaluate only *after* you have heard the other person out.
7. Listen both to what is being said and what is not being said.
8. Listen to feeling messages as well as the facts.
9. Listen for nonverbal messages.
10. Listen for the main idea. Do not get bogged down on details.
11. Ask questions, restate, paraphrase, and summarize to clarify messages.
12. Use nonverbal listening skills (eye contact, appropriate physical distance, leaning forward, and acknowledging).

Suggestions for Getting Other People to Listen

1. Tell listeners what benefits they can get from listening.
2. Use redundancy and multiple channels (visuals, etc.).
3. Have listeners "replay" what you have said.
4. Use feedback to determine whether others are listening.
5. Control distractions.

SUMMARY

Successful professionals need to be good listeners. They also need to plan their messages so others will hear, understand, and act on them. In short, listening is a tool that serves several important functions. It gives speakers feedback on their messages, provides information from others, enables people to "talk through" and solve problems, and improves morale.

Whether you listen, how you listen, or why you listen is a message to others. Listening nonevaluatively and "actively" is a message that says you are trying to understand. That message will strengthen communication between people and help build interpersonal trust.

Listening is a process. It is sequential, with the specific steps determined by the listener's purpose. It moves from (1) hearing to (2) interpreting to (3) testing to (4) reformulating to (5) evaluating to (6) remembering the sender's message. Not all listeners follow all the steps.

Listening is a skill. This chapter focused on nonverbal skills including eye contact, distance, body position, and acknowledging cues such as nods, vocalizations or nonfluencies. It also included questioning, reflecting, summarizing, clarifying, paraphrasing, and restating as verbal skills that help you listen better. Finally, it gave specific things both speaker and listener can do to increase the probability that a message will be understood.

Listening is also a strategy. How a person listens is determined by training, attitude, reason for listening, and assumptions about communication. This chapter described three strategies: self-centered, responsive, and critical listening.

EXERCISES

1. Have three class members observe listening behaviors during a teacher's lecture and report at the end of the class on what they observed. What were listeners doing or saying that told you they were listening? What were the nonlisteners doing or saying that told you they were not listening?

2. Divide the class into groups of three. Let one person explain an upsetting situation to a second person who restates the problem *to the satisfaction of the message sender*. The third person observes and reports to the class on listening skills used and not used.

3. Write reflecting responses to the following statements:
   a. If I have one more test this week, I'm going to jump out the window.
   b. John is a raving idiot.
   c. Nothing is ever good enough for my parents. They expect perfection.

4. Divide the class into pairs. One person explains a real problem to the other. The listener *uses only nonverbal responses*. After five minutes, break into small groups to discuss the difficulty listeners have in *not talking*. Was the situation awkward for the speaker? For the listener? Did the situation make the speaker feel more or less free to discuss the problem?

5. For one day keep a log on your listening to others. How much time did you spend? What strategy did you most often use (self-centered, responsive, critical)? Was your use of strategy appropriate for the situation? Explain. What listening skills were you most comfortable

using? Which did you find hard to use? Which did you fail to use? Write a two-page analysis based on the log.

6. Discuss in small groups (or write a short paper on) why questions are not appropriate for dealing with feeling messages.

7. Bring to class cartoons or news articles that demonstrate communication breakdowns. What role did listening play? What listening strategies would have prevented or minimized the breakdown?

8. Compare your class notes for one week with those of another person in the class. How are they similar? How are they different? How do you account for similarities and differences?

Suggested Readings

Barker, Larry L. *Listening Behavior*. Englewood Cliffs, N.J.: Prentice-Hall, 1971.
A practical, easy-to-read book that explains listening behavior and the listening process. The author provides the reader help in identifying listening problems and gives specific suggestions for improving listening. The listening quiz is an attention getter and a motivator for students.

Nichols, Ralph G., and Leonard A. Stevens. *Are You Listening?* New York: McGraw-Hill, 1957.
The standard reference work on listening. Though other works have updated Nichols and Stevens's approach, this book is the starting point for the student interested in pursuing this area.

Weaver, Carl H. *Human Listening*. Indianapolis, Ind.: Bobbs-Merrill Co., 1972.
The book focuses on the processes of listening behavior. Its major thrust is to improve the understanding of listening rather than to provide a "how-to" approach. Chapter exercises are excellent, and an appendix on teaching and testing listening is particularly useful.

Wolff, Florence I., Nadine C. Marsnik, William S. Tacey, and Ralph G. Nichols. *Perceptive Listening*. New York: Holt, Rinehart and Winston, 1983.
A basic, comprehensive textbook on listening, including chapters on the kinds of listening we do, productive listening techniques, and listening in business.

Wolvin, Andrew D., and Carolyn Gwynn Coakley. *Listening Instruction*. Urbana, Ill.: ERIC Clearinghouse on Reading and Communications Skills, 1979.
A short section on theory precedes thirty-eight classroom exercises for teaching listening skills. A good bibliography on listening is also included.

Interviewing

6

The interview is a common form of communication in organizations and other professional settings. This chapter gives guidelines for distinguishing interviews from other types of communication, describes functions and kinds of interviews, and sets out some things you can do to improve your skills both as an interviewer and as the person being interviewed. You need to remember, however, that providing a supportive climate for the interview is critical. The physical setting and the interpersonal relationship between interviewer and interviewee influence what is accomplished.

Interviewing is a special form of interpersonal communication used widely in business and the professions as a means of accomplishing organizational goals. Typically, interviews in an organizational setting share a number of common characteristics. These characteristics include the following:

1. *Interviews are person-to-person communication.* Usually they involve a dyad, but sometimes they may include more than two people. Board or group interviews, however, such as several candidates being interviewed at the same time for a job, are relatively rare in organizations.

2. *Interview participants have clearly defined roles.* The interviewer is usually the initiator, the questioner, the rulemaker, and the evaluator. The interviewee is the respondent. The interviewer sets the agenda and directs the course of the interview. Sometimes, if the interviewee assumes control of the discussion, it may force the interviewer on the defensive.

3. *Interviews are usually face to face.* Both interviewer and interviewee are usually in the same room at the same time in close proximity to each other. An exception is the telephone interview, though not all telephone conversations are interviews.

4. *Interviews involve interaction.* The interview is two-way communication with both people talking and both listening. The *level* of interaction will affect the success of the interview, that is, whether the individuals involved simply respond to each other's messages or really try to see each other's viewpoint. If people do not feel free to share ideas, they will likely interact at a low level; if the climate allows them to be open and honest, their communication will be more meaningful and more useful.

5. *Interviews have a purpose.* Interviews are more than conversations. They have a predetermined and serious purpose that *relates to the*

organization's goals. Sometimes interviews have a stated purpose that is at odds with the actual purpose. For example, a subordinate may request an interview to discuss a project deadline. The real reason for seeing the boss is to ask for a raise, show how much time and effort are going into the project, or get feedback on work already done. Superiors also request subordinates to "drop in" to discuss a project when the real reason for the interview is to reprimand, assign additional work, or get a "feel" for reactions to a new policy or procedure. False expectations about the interview purpose can negatively affect interaction.

6. *Interviews usually involve status.* In organizations, where interviews tend to follow formal channels, the superior usually interviews a subordinate. In the professions, doctors interview patients, and lawyers and accountants interview clients. Status is less important, however, in journalistic settings, as when a reporter interviews a politician.

7. *Interviews occur in both formal and informal settings.* An interview can take place in a wide variety of surroundings. A job (or selection) interview is usually highly structured and will usually be conducted in a relatively formal setting. On the other hand, a "coaching" interview, in which you ask your boss for help on a project, can take place in a much more informal setting.

Functions of Interviews

Interviews help managers and other professionals do their jobs. They are a major means by which people relate to each other, to get and give information and to solve problems. Further, interviews are sometimes used to persuade others to "buy" ideas, products, or services. The following discussion explores these four interview functions: getting information, giving information, problem solving, and persuasion.

GETTING INFORMATION

If you are a manager, you will not always have all the information you need to do your job well. Sometimes you will ask for specific information: sales figures for the last month; or comparisons with major competitors. Often, however, you need information you do not even know exists. To increase your chances of getting that information, you need to work to build relationships that will allow and encourage others to volunteer information.

Sometimes you must get information from superiors; at other times, subordinates can provide useful data. You will ask your superiors for job specifications, organizational plans and procedures, and feedback on how you are measuring up to expectations. You will also need to know how well your subordinates are doing on their jobs, what significant findings they have uncovered, and how co-workers relate to each other. You will find some of the data you need in memorandums, reports, surveys, and company publications, but you may also use face-to-face communication with both superiors and subordinates to get up-to-date, precise, accurate, and adequate information.

Each of the various professions has its unique requirements for information, and that information is obtained in a variety of ways. Lawyers use accident reports; accountants work from canceled checks and receipts; doctors use blood tests and X rays, and require patients to fill out detailed forms on past medical history. Rarely, however, are reports, documented records, or questionnaires sufficient. Lawyers, accountants, and doctors also meet with their clients and patients in interview situations to probe for additional information. The lawyer's skill in getting the "facts" from the client and the doctor's ability to get a precise description of the patient's aches and pains may directly reflect their success in defending the client in court or treating the patient's illness.

The problem for managers and other professionals is *how* to get the information they need from the interviews. The first way may be to ask questions. Most people think if they ask the right questions, they will get the necessary information. As the chapter on listening suggests, the kinds of questions you ask will affect the information you receive. Asking a question, however, does not mean that people will automatically tell you what they know. Rather, they will likely filter information through their own ideas about what you want to hear, whether you will like what they have to say, and whether you will "punish" them (either directly or indirectly) for giving information you are unprepared to hear. For example, Jim, who is vice-president for public relations and your boss, asks your opinion on a speech he has prepared for the company president. You *really* think the piece is a cover-up that distorts the facts. Your recognition that Jim wrote the speech, that he is your boss, that he will not like negative feedback, and that he can fire you if he wishes will likely affect your response to him. How you respond will also raise some ethical questions. Will you be truthful, vague, or outright dishonest? How can you present negative news in as positive a light as possible?

GIVING INFORMATION

Not only do managers and other professionals need to get information from others, they also may have to provide data to superiors (progress reports) and subordinates (work schedules). This giving of information is accomplished through memorandums and reports, and also in person-to-person interactions. Whether you use written or oral formats to communicate will depend in part on the nature of the material discussed, organizational norms, managerial style, the size of the organization, and time constraints.

Managers give information to subordinates; doctors give information to patients; accountants give information to clients; and lawyers instruct witnesses in face-to-face oral communication situations. Managers may assign work, give instructions, or explain procedures. Doctors explain to patients the nature of their illnesses and describe the prescribed treatment.

PROBLEM SOLVING

Interviews provide a forum for solving problems in organizations and other professional settings. Some problems are technological; some are financial; some arise from poor planning or implementation; others are people-related. Not all organizational problems can be solved in interviews. If the cutting machine is broken, call a mechanic. If you cannot reconcile the ledger, start over with your calculator. Some organizational problems, however, should be addressed in interview situations. Sam has not met production quotas. Request an interview with him to find out the problem and work out a way to solve it. Sales are off by one-third. Request an interview with the sales manager to find the cause and formulate a solution. Pete cannot get along with his co-workers, and his work is suffering. Request an interview with Pete to try to get his performance up to an acceptable level.

PERSUASION

Interviews may be used to persuade others to accept a point of view or to sell a product or idea. Persuasive interviews may be conducted inside or outside the organization or profession. Internally, managers try to influence *each other* (to lend a valued assistant for a special job); *their superiors* (to provide a larger share of the operating budget); and *their subordinates* (to work on a report over the weekend). Subordinates also try to exert influence at various levels in the organization. They initiate new plans and present new ideas to their superiors. They persuade their co-workers to swap work schedules, do extra work, or change personal habits ("I'm allergic to cigarette smoke"). They also try to modify the behavior of those below them in the organizational hierarchy.

Organizations also attempt to influence the external environment through persuasive interviews. In addition to sales personnel and advertisers promoting the organization's products or ideas through sales presentations, corporate advocates use interviews to present the company's case to its many publics. Chief executive officers, for example, hold press conferences; company representatives lobby members of Congress for favorable legislation; spokespersons appear on network talk shows. Chapter 9 sets out strategies these corporate advocates may use to influence public opinion.

Kinds of Interviews

Every organization and profession has its unique requirements for getting and giving information, solving problems, and persuading others. Each, therefore, has developed specialized kinds of interview formats to meet its particular needs. As an individual entering business or the professions, you should be prepared for a variety of interview situations (both as interviewer and interviewee).

This discussion focuses on five kinds of interviews commonly used in organizations: selection, counseling, appraisal, grievance, and exit interviews. Most of these interviews are also used in the professions depending on the size and structure of the staff. The following discussion describes the purpose, special characteristics, and participant responsibilities in each type of interview. It also includes a sample *interview plan* for each.

SELECTION INTERVIEWS

In the selection interview, a representative from an organization talks with an applicant about a job. Organizations may schedule one or more selection interviews with a job applicant. In large organizations, someone from the personnel department may do initial screening interviews, and line managers (those people whom the applicants would work for) conduct second, more comprehensive interviews.

The main purpose of selection interviewing is to hire the best possible employees. Specifically, the interviewer wants to find out as much relevant information as possible about applicants and match their qualifications with those of the job. Further, if the qualifications look promising, the interviewer may wish to "sell" the applicant on the organization, answering questions, providing information, suggesting benefits. Applicants, on the other hand, want a job offer. Most also want some specific information about the organization. Each party should be aware of the other's expectations.

As an interviewer, you will want to develop an interview plan that will generate the best information possible in the time allotted. In its "bare bones" form, your plan may resemble the one in Figure 6.1.

In putting applicants at ease, you may engage in some small talk—just enough to get the applicant talking. Then preview what will take place in the interview. After briefly describing the job and the organization, you are ready to get to the "meat" of the

---

Figure 6.1 Selection Interview Plan

1. Put applicant at ease.
2. Orient applicant to interview.
3. Give information about the job and the organization.
4. Get needed information.
5. Answer questions.
6. Sell applicant on the job (optional step).
7. Clarify next step in selection process.

interview: information about the applicant's qualifications for the job.

Develop your interview questions from the job requirements and the applicant's résumé. Steer clear, however, of personal questions that are potentially discriminatory. Federal Equal Employment Opportunity guidelines specify that questions about personal characteristics such as age, sex, marital status, and race *must be directly related to the job.* For example, a question about how much an applicant weighs is legal only if a weight constraint affects doing the job satisfactorily (for example, if the applicant is a football linebacker, a trapeze artist, or a model). Further, any job-related personal question should be asked of *all* applicants. Otherwise, you are open to charges of discrimination.

After you have the essential information you need and have provided an opportunity for the applicant to question you, you may decide to give a short sales pitch. Be careful, however, not to mislead applicants when you have no hiring authority or when the candidate is marginally qualified for the job. Finally, you will need to close the interview by describing the next step in the selection process. Will you call or write the applicant? When? What should the applicant do next?

As an applicant, you want to make a good impression. You can improve your chances of getting a second interview or a job offer by preparing for the interview and conducting yourself professionally. Preparation includes researching the organization and the job to find out what the interviewer will be looking for and the questions you need to ask. Preparation also means doing some serious thinking about your own qualifications. What does your résumé mean *to this organization?* What skills do you have to offer? (See Figs. 6.2 and 6.3.) What technical expertise do you have? What adaptive skills (integrity, dependability, resourcefulness) and functional skills (planning, communicating, organizing) can you offer? How do those skills relate to the job you are applying for? Be prepared to answer such typical interview questions as "What is your greatest weakness?" "Tell me about yourself." "Why should we hire you?"

Preparation will not be enough. You need to present a professional image in the interview. Dress neatly and appropriately, and adapt to the dress norms of the organization. A banking recruiter at an eastern university complained recently to the school's career planning and placement officer that men applicants were not making a good impression; they were wearing sports jackets to their interviews. Similarly, a multinational technical firm considers women applicants for managerial positions only if they wear tailored suits to their interviews.

Conduct yourself professionally in the interview. Try to control nervous mannerisms such as aimless manipulation of a pen or pencil. Lean forward in your chair—do not sprawl. Look at the

Figure 6.2 Sample of Chronological Résumé

SAMUEL E. SMARTS
1348 Kalorama Circle, N.E.
Washington, D.C. 20004
(203) 922-1222

OBJECTIVE
Human Resources Management position where knowledge of governmental regulations can be used in design of personnel policies.

EDUCATION
1980-84
University of Washington, Bachelor of Arts
Major: Speech Communication
Minor: Business Administration
GPA: 3.4 (scale 4.0)

1976-80
Central High School, St. Louis, Mo.
Honors curriculum

EXPERIENCE
1980-84
Office of Admissions and Records, University of Washington
File Clerk—Responsible for collating files on incoming students. Promoted to supervisor of work study students.

Summer 1983
Smith and Bros., Inc., Omaha, Nebr.
Secretary—Performed general secretarial duties including typing, answering phone, filing.

Summer 1982
Jones, Jones, and Jones, Attorneys, Omaha, Nebr.
Messenger—Responsible for delivering and picking up legal papers and other relevant materials.

Summers
1978-81
Self-Employed, St. Louis, Mo., and Omaha, Nebr.
Lawn service—Contracted with homeowners and apartment complexes to tend lawns and clip shrubbery.

ACTIVITIES
and HONORS
College: Pi Kappa Phi, scholastic honor society; Dean's List five semesters; Debate Club; Marketing Club (Vice-President); Rho Pi Rho, social fraternity.

High School: National Honor Society; Debate Club; Maskers Drama Club; Basketball; Baseball.

REFERENCES
Provided on request.

Figure 6.3 Sample of Functional Résumé

MARY KATHERINE NEWTON

Permanent Address:
813 North Cherry St.
Tyler, Texas 32200
(402) 988-2211

School Address:
1632 Surrey Lane, Apt. #4
Dalton, Arizona 13441
(922) 811-3236

OBJECTIVE

Position in public relations where training and summer work experience can contribute to the development of a comprehensive public relations effort.

SKILLS

Technical Skills
- Proficient in layout and design
- Created public relations campaign for wholesale company during summer internship
- Photography

Communication Skills
- Edited copy for school newspaper
- Composed copy for wholesale campaign
- Good interpersonal skills

Research Skills
- Marketing research tools
- Conducting sampling for wholesale campaign
- Designed questionnaire for class project

EXPERIENCE

Media Assistant, Arizona College Department of Educational Television, September 1982–May 1984.

Intern, National Wholesale Council, Washington, D.C., Summer 1983.

Student Assistant, Professor John James, September 1981– May 1982.

Messenger, Morgan and Company, insurance brokers, Tyler, Texas, Summers 1980–82.

EDUCATION

Arizona College, Dalton, Arizona. Expected date of graduation, May 1984. Major: English; Minor: Speech Communication. Courses included Introduction to Media; Communication Theory; Layout and Design; Photography.

ACTIVITIES AND INTERESTS

Copy editor of The Rag, school newspaper; jogging; photography; spectator sports; vintage films.

interviewer, but do not stare. Ask meaningful questions about the job and the organization. Answer the interviewer's questions seriously, not flippantly, and let your own personality shine through in the interview. So often job applicants come across as "wooden." The interviewer wants some sense of you as a *person*.

Keep your cool! Some interviewers use what is called a stress strategy. They deliberately try to throw you off guard with openers such as "You've got five minutes to convince me you're the person for the job" or "I'm really too tired for this interview, but go ahead and tell me about yourself anyway" or "Your résumé doesn't show me much." When faced with a stress strategy, clarify what the real question or real problem is. Ask a question such as "Are you particularly interested in my work experience or course work?" or "If you are tired, would you prefer to reschedule the interview?" or "What specific things about the résumé are you referring to?" Another thing to remember is *always respond on the content level*. Do not allow yourself to get frustrated or angry; answer as a professional.

COUNSELING INTERVIEWS

A second kind of interview commonly found in organizations is the counseling interview. This interview, which is based on the premise that a person in authority has a responsibility to help subordinates, usually occurs in response to a problem. In most organizational settings counseling tends to be directive. That is, the manager describes the problem and suggests a way of handling it; the subordinate listens and answers a few questions. In therapeutic situations, on the other hand, the counseling is often more nondirective: "I'm here to listen. If you talk long enough, you should come to a better understanding of the problem, which will allow you to solve it on your own."[1] In most business and professional situations, a useful approach is to combine a task orientation with a sensitivity to the human dimension. The interviewer using this approach can recognize and respond to *personal concerns* that are operating but also ensure that the *problem* will be addressed.

Counseling responsibilities in organizations relate primarily to performance. In discussing performance, however, personal problems sometimes surface. Occasionally, someone may want to discuss a personal problem with you. Though you may not have the professional training to handle personal problem solving, you can act as a sounding board. ("I'm afraid I won't be able to tell you what to do, but I'll be happy to listen.") You can allow a person to talk through and perhaps come to a greater understanding of the problem. Your reinforcing behavior also tells the person that you are concerned. That is a powerful managerial message. Ulti-

---

1. Carl Rogers, *Client-Centered Therapy: Its Current Practice, Implications, and Theory* (Boston: Houghton Mifflin, 1951). For examples of more directive approaches, see footnote 4, Chapter 5.

mately, you may need to suggest professional counseling in personal problem situations such as drug abuse or obvious psychological problems. To refer an employee to someone else at the beginning of the interview is rarely wise, however, since it can signify lack of interest and thereby cut off future communication.

When in-house career counseling centers are not available, you may be responsible for career counseling. Though you may not be professionally trained to direct others' careers, you can offer your experience and observations. You can also help subordinates identify training needs.

As an interviewer, you will need to formulate an interview plan *before* the counseling interview begins. At minimum, that plan should include the four steps outlined in Figure 6.4.

Figure 6.4 Counseling Interview Plan

1. Create a supportive climate.
2. Give feedback.
3. Request information.
4. Formulate action plans.

A responsibility you will have as an interviewer will be to counsel subordinates in a way that will minimize any tension that is normally associated with counseling. Create as supportive a climate as you can. Your willingness to listen and your genuine respect for the subordinate will help. The chapters on interpersonal communication and listening (Chapters 4 and 5) will help you develop skills that will enable you to accomplish these goals.

Whether the counseling interview relates to performance, personal problem solving, or career development, you have three major responsibilities in addition to building a supportive climate: to give feedback, get information, and help formulate action plans.

Giving feedback. Subordinates need feedback on their performance. Counseling implies that a problem "belongs" either to the manager or to the subordinate. Sometimes subordinates come to you for help. At other times, you must confront (and sometimes reprimand) them about behavior that is causing problems for the organization, such as poor work or erratic behavior.

How, when, and for what purpose managers confront subordinates will affect the success or failure of performance counseling. The confrontation should be as close in time to the behavior as possible. Its purpose should be to *solve the problem,* not to attach blame or attack the subordinate. Further, the feedback should include *positive* points as well as negative ones ("Your analysis of the salary structure was excellent"). Some managers give only negative feedback, however. They assume that unless they tell an employee otherwise, the person will know that his or her work is acceptable. Such a manager passes up an opportunity to reinforce good work and ensure that it will continue.

Getting information.   Another major responsibility in counseling subordinates is to get information from them that will help in understanding the problem. For example, you may need precise information about what caused a report to be late, what to do to get the report finished, and how to make certain future reports will be on time. Your subordinate may not want to give you that information; you may get excuses or rationalizations instead.

The true reasons for the late report may be personal and painful—alcoholism, a pending divorce, or financial problems. Sometimes the cause of the problem relates to the organization. The individual has not been promoted, was denied a raise, has uninteresting work to do. At other times, the problem may be you. You give confusing, contradictory directions or fail to give help when subordinates need it. Before you can effectively counsel an employee on job performance, you need a clear indication of what the *true* problem is.

Your listening skills will be invaluable in getting information from subordinates. (See Chapter 5.) By your nonverbal signals, reflecting statements, paraphrases, summaries, and restatements, you will encourage the other person to talk. You can also get information from questions, particularly if you ask them in a logical order. But you may close up communication if your questions seem threatening.

Formulating action plans.   Another responsibility in counseling is to encourage and facilitate the formulation of precise action plans to solve the problems identified. These action plans should (1) specify what is to be done (the report will be completed), (2) provide clear deadlines (by Friday, October 13), and (3) set out resources available from an executive or the organization ("We'll provide editing help").

In general, subordinates need to initiate their own action plans, but managers may have to give help. In most organizations, action planning is a cooperative effort between manager and subordinate. It involves clarifying goals and choosing a plan that is both acceptable to the manager's needs and consistent with the subordinate's willingness and ability to carry it out. If you can encourage the subordinate to initiate a solution to a problem, that person will be more committed to the plan than if you had suggested the idea.

As an interviewee (the person being counseled), recognize that all is not lost. You are not being fired; you are not receiving a formal appraisal that will wreck your career; your manager needs your help to do the job. Fight the tendency to be defensive, to justify your behavior. Anger, withdrawal, and rationalization are luxuries you cannot afford. Your energy must go toward ensuring that the report is finished.

Try to see the interview from the manager's perspective. The job must get done. You may not have done your part so far. Use the feedback to get yourself on track. Listen, too, for what is positive. Remember, you will never develop your career until someone tells you honestly the things you are doing well and the things you are not. Only then can you improve your performance.

APPRAISAL INTERVIEWS

Most large organizations and many small ones have comprehensive systems for appraising subordinates. Though specific methods differ, most appraisal systems have at least three steps, and each of these steps includes an interview. The steps are goal setting, interim performance counseling, and final appraisal.

Goal setting. Appraisal should start with a common understanding between manager and subordinate about precise job expectations ("You are responsible for the Smithson legal brief") and about the criteria for performance evaluation ("The brief must contain the three procedural and six legal issues we wish to raise; it must be clearly written using standard legal format; it must cite all relevant legal cases"). Sometimes a manager or other professional sets out expectations and criteria for evaluation in a memorandum to the subordinate. More often, those goals are clarified in an interview.

Because job expectations form the basis for appraisal, both manager and subordinate should insist on *clear, precise, easily measurable performance standards.* "You should write well" is probably an insufficient criterion for evaluation; what does "well" mean? You might anticipate an argument at final appraisal time over such a vague standard.

Not only should the manager and subordinate agree initially on performance goals, but they should also make provisions for modifying the standards during the appraisal period. The nature of the work may change, new goals may be set, and new standards may be applied.

Interim performance counseling. Whereas the goal-setting period allows for prior agreement about evaluation standards, the interim counseling provides feedback on performance before the final rating. Such counseling has the positive benefit of allowing subordinates to change unsatisfactory performance before the final rating occurs.

Final appraisal. If the goal-setting and interim performance counseling sessions have accomplished their purposes, the final appraisal interview should contain no surprises for the subordinate. The appraisal interview, then, becomes a review of adjusted performance in light of the goals.

If the subordinate's performance has been perfect, the appraisal interview will go smoothly. But if the manager's rating is not a "perfect 10," the subordinate will probably be hurt, upset, or angry. Appraisal can create great stress between the manager and subordinate when it is tied to a job assignment, salary, or promotion decisions.

As an interviewer, you will have different responsibilities in each of the three appraisal-related situations. In the goal-setting interview, you may tell the subordinate what the job expectations are or you may set performance goals together. In the interim performance counseling appraisal, you will need to follow an interview plan described in Figure 6.4. For the final appraisal interview, you should develop a plan similar to that in Figure 6.5.

Figure 6.5 Appraisal Interview Plan

1. Give (or come to an agreement on) appraisal rating.
2. Invite response from subordinate.
3. Answer questions.
4. Shift focus of discussion to counseling or problem solving. (See Fig. 6.4.)

As interviewer, your main responsibility in discussing the final appraisal is to present and explain your evaluation to the subordinate. In describing your evaluation, you may use the organization's appraisal rating form as a guide and discuss the ratings on each category, point by point. You may choose, on the other hand, to begin with positive ratings, move to any negative evaluations, and end with positive ratings, especially with subordinates who feel threatened by the appraisal process. Another approach is to work cooperatively with the subordinate to reach agreement on the ratings to be assigned. This approach is perhaps the most humane, though admittedly the most time-consuming.

If you choose to prepare an evaluation and present it to the subordinate (the manager's most common option), you will need to set out your ratings in a clear, objective, nonthreatening manner. To justify your evaluations, you will need specific evidence of performance. That means you should keep good records throughout the appraisal period. Some managers find a daily or weekly diary of incidents helpful at appraisal time. Be sure, however, to record and present a balanced picture of performance—the positive as well as the negative examples of employee behavior.

Allow subordinates to respond to your ratings and answer any specific questions or offer any explanations that are appropriate. Do not trap yourself, however, into trying to convince the subordinate that your position is the right one. You will not always get agreement that a poor appraisal is either correct or justified. At some point, you may have to say: "I understand that you do not agree with my evaluation. You are free to add your comments to the file."

Whenever negative appraisal occurs, try to move the evaluation toward a problem-solving session. How can the subordinate's performance be improved in the *future?* What implications does the appraisal have for career development? What resources (such as training) can you offer? What are the next specific, positive steps the subordinate should take toward improving performance? What are the immediate and long-term effects of such behavioral change?

As an interviewee, approach appraisal as an important tool of career development. Carefully note your positive ratings. These are areas where you need to continue doing the things you are doing well. Do not let the negative evaluations overshadow them. Control your emotional response to negative ratings. Realize that a defensive response is normal and natural, but it is not productive. An emotional outburst will not change your rating and may antagonize the manager. Avoid tantrums, the silent treatment, or argument. If you have questions, ask them. If you have a good case for a stronger appraisal rating, make it. But present it professionally—clearly, concisely, and logically.

Use the appraisal as an opportunity to grow professionally. Tap your manager's experience to help you improve your performance. Ask for help in making changes. Is training available? Will the manager "coach" you in your weak areas? Which of your superior's suggestions can you realistically use? Turn the appraisal to your advantage and use it to develop your career.

GRIEVANCE INTERVIEWS

Some organizations, particularly those with union contracts, have detailed formal grievance procedures that precede legal actions. If you are interested in those procedures, a labor arbitration text should give you detailed information. The discussion here relates to more informal grievance or complaint interviews.

Some employees come to managers to express general discontent with the organization. Others have specific complaints: they did not get a raise; the work load has increased; another employee is causing morale problems. Whether the grievance is general or specific, there is a *problem* (whether real or imagined) *that the employee feels strongly about.* The problem is so important, in fact, that the employee is willing to risk a negative reaction from the manager or censure from co-workers. To request an interview to discuss a complaint, the subordinate has risked upward communication.

As an interviewer, you need to plan how to communicate as effectively as possible with a disgruntled, if not hostile, subordi-

> **Figure 6.6 Grievance Interview Plan**
> 1. Create a supportive atmosphere.
> 2. Invite the person to state the grievance.
> 3. Ask questions for information.
> 4. Provide any explanation that is *necessary*.
> 5. Formulate action plans.

nate. The interview plan in Figure 6.6 should give you some ideas about what you need to do.

A supportive atmosphere is particularly important in the grievance interview since tension will probably be present. One way to relieve that tension is to let the other person do most of the talking, particularly at the beginning of the interview.

Use your listening skills to explore the problem area, to expand your understanding of the problem. Ask questions to get information; reflect feeling messages to "test" your own understanding; restate, paraphrase, and summarize to gain insight into the complaint. Then provide any *necessary* information to the discussion. Work cooperatively with the subordinate to come up with solutions to the problem. Are the solutions reasonable? Realistic? Will they satisfy the employee? After the plan has been implemented, get feedback about how it is working.

As an interviewee, center on the issue, not on a person. Approach the problem rationally, avoiding emotional language, tears, or threats. Explain the problem in such a way that the manager will see its significance to the organization. Work with the manager to come up with a mutually satisfactory plan to correct the problem. After the plan has been implemented, give the manager feedback about how it is working.

EXIT INTERVIEWS

Most organizations have high employee turnover, which results in great costs, both in dollars and morale. On the average, people hold about five or six different jobs in a lifetime. Sometimes people leave an organization because they are fired or laid off; often they leave voluntarily. When employees resign, the organization may request an exit interview.

Organizations have exit interviews for three main reasons. The first is public relations. Unhappy people can severely damage an organization's image, so the company wants employees to leave on a pleasant note. Further, exit interviews allow organizations to get feedback. Managers or staff can gain insight from those who are leaving about what needs to be changed in the organization. Finally, exit interviews provide information to the employee about

Interviewing

severance pay, compensation for vacation time, transfer of insurance, career development, and the kind of recommendation to be expected.

As an interviewer, you need a systematic plan to accomplish your goals. The suggested outline in Figure 6.7 will help you get information while minimizing potential conflict in the interview.

Figure 6.7 Exit Interview Plan

1. Create a supportive climate.
2. Ask for information (avoid providing data unless asked).
3. Listen nonevaluatively.
4. End on a pleasant, positive note.

As a first step you need to create a nonthreatening climate to allow the employee to be open and honest with you. This will help build a positive interviewer-interviewee relationship and result in your getting more and accurate information. Use the interview as a problem-solving session. Ask the employee's advice on how to deal with difficulties in the organization. Express your genuine interest in the person's career development.

If the employee is angry, "process" the anger; that is, listen. Do not allow yourself to be defensive. Neither should you spend a lot of time explaining. Your good arguments probably will fall on deaf ears. Try to support the individual as much as possible by being respectful and giving the person a hearing.

As an interviewee, control your emotions. Do not use the session to vent your personal frustrations. Give the interviewer information that can help to improve the organization. But give that information only if the interviewer is willing to listen. A defensive interviewer will not hear your good ideas. Respond pleasantly, and work to build good human relationships. You may need a recommendation from this interviewer, or you may wish to come back to the organization at a later time. Do not assume that you know all the policies and procedures related to your leaving. Ask questions to get the information you need. Ask questions about recommendations. Ask the interviewer's advice about your career. You may get some good suggestions.

Interview Strategies

At the beginning of this chapter, we suggested that interviews serve four functions in organizations and the professions. They help the interviewer to get and give information, solve problems, and persuade. Each of the interview *plans* described in the preceding section includes one or more of these *functions*. Figure 6.8 provides a summary.

Figure 6.8 Kinds and Functions of Interviews

Kind	Function
Selection interview	Get information, give information, persuade
Counseling interview	Get information, give information, solve problems
Appraisal interview	Give information, solve problems
Grievance interview	Get information, give information, solve problems
Exit interview	Get information

Whereas the interview plans suggest *what you need to do* in the various kinds of interviews, strategies for carrying out the four interview functions can give you direction about *how to do it.* Following are some strategies to help you accomplish your interview goals. Perhaps you can add to the list.

INFORMATION-GIVING STRATEGIES

1. *Demonstrate how the information affects the listener.* People listen more carefully when they understand how the information relates to them. Do not wait for your listeners to determine how they can use the material. Tell them at the beginning of the interview.
2. *Explain the information precisely and concisely.* Set out your information point by point, using specific language. Do not overexplain; just give the listeners the information they need and are willing to hear.
3. *Clarify information through examples.* Choose examples that will fit into the listeners' experience.
4. *Summarize the information or ask your hearers to restate what they heard.* By planned redundancy, you increase the probability your hearers will "hear" the message. By clarifying the main points through a summary and/or restatement, you will help them remember your *ideas* instead of an example or anecdote.
5. *Test understanding through application.* Ask about realistic "cases" or critical incidents that allow hearers to apply the information.

INFORMATION-SEEKING STRATEGIES

1. *Concentrate on building the trust level.* Avoid passing immediate judgment on everything someone says. Minimize your status.
2. *Listen.* How much have you ever learned by talking? Probably not much. But if you let other people talk long enough you will get a surprising amount of information from them.
3. *Choose your questions to get the kind of information you need.* If you want the person to talk generally without any direction on your

part, ask the most *open questions* you can think of ("Tell me about Acme Company"). On the other hand, if you need precise information, use a more *closed question* ("What products will Acme market this year?"; "Do you agree with the policy?"). To pursue something the other person has said, ask a *follow-up* or *probe* ("You mentioned a new plastics process. Can you be more specific?"; "Aren't you really saying that management is inefficient?").

4. *Order your questions to make your interview go somewhere.* Decide before the interview where you want to go, what you want to accomplish, what information you really need. Then plan a strategy to get there. When you already have a lot of information and need specific details to fill in the gaps, use a cone model to order your questions. Begin with specific questions and build toward more general ones.

Specific questions --→   --→   --→   General questions

Cone Model

The cone model is commonly used in selection interviews where the interviewer has a résumé. The reverse cone model is more helpful in counseling or appraisal where you need to get the interviewer talking—either to get information or to process emotional tension. In this model, you move from general to specific questions.

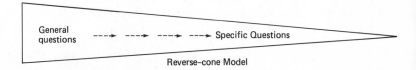

General questions   --→   --→   --→   --→ Specific Questions

Reverse–cone Model

PROBLEM-SOLVING STRATEGIES

1. *Gain an understanding of the problem.* Do not assume you know what the problem is. The problem you sense or the problem the subordinate admits to may be only a symptom of the real problem. You can increase your chances of getting at the real problem by listening and asking questions.

2. *Define the problem within the interviewee's sphere of influence.* It is not productive to spend a lot of time talking about a problem the subordinate has no chance of solving. You have to be more specific than "Sam is a nuisance." What can you do with "nuisanceness"? You are likely to find a solution if you define the problem more precisely: "Sam interrupts co-workers when they are on the phone." That is solvable.

3. *Establish problem ownership.* Whose problem is it anyway? The person who "owns" the problem must solve it. If your subordinate's car pool is late every day, the employee must take action to get to work on time. You are not responsible for arranging transportation.

4. *Develop specific action plans.* Spell out in detail who does what and when. Build in a system to monitor implementation.
5. *Gain commitment to action plans.* Subordinates will have greater commitment to plans they have suggested. You can increase commitment by emphasizing rewards for carrying through on the plans and negative consequences for ignoring them.

PERSUASIVE STRATEGIES

1. *Get hearer's attention and interest.* Stress the benefits to the listener. Show how the hearer may be affected.
2. *Explain proposal or product.* Give hearers as much information as they need to understand what is being "sold." Show how specific features of the product/proposal affect them: "This plan would move your office four miles, which would mean you'd be closer to your suppliers."
3. *Offer proof.* Back up your arguments or claims with good evidence and sound reasoning. Specific proof materials you can use include facts, statistics, expert opinions, tests, guarantees, and examples.
4. *Ask for action.* Do not hint around about what you want your hearers to do. Ask them clearly and plainly for the action. Then make it easy for them to respond. "I'd like to offer a motion on my recommendation." "Just sign on the dotted line."

SUMMARY

This chapter examines a special form of interpersonal communication, the interview. Typically, interviews share the following common characteristics: (1) They are person-to-person communication; (2) their participants have clearly defined roles of interviewer and interviewee; (3) they are usually face to face; (4) they involve interaction; (5) they have a specific purpose that relates to organizational goals; (6) they typically involve status; (7) they can occur either in formal or informal settings.

Interviews serve four important functions. They provide means of getting information, giving information, solving problems, and persuading others to accept ideas, services, and products.

The kinds of interviews used in organizations differ, but the following formats are the most typical: selection, counseling, appraisal, grievance, and exit interviews. Selection interviews are to secure employees for organizations. The interviewer is looking for the best possible employee, and the interviewee wants a job offer. These differing goals influence the interaction in the interview. Performance counseling is important as a means of providing employees feedback, getting information from subordinates, and developing action plans to improve employee performance. The appraisal process, which includes goal setting and interim performance counseling, culminates in the final appraisal interview. Potentially an emotionally charged interaction, the appraisal interview should go beyond evaluation to focus on employee development.

Both grievance and exit interviews provide opportunities for honest feedback from employees. Whereas grievance interviews are initiated by the subordinate, exit interviews are usually requested by the employer. Both can result in the organization's getting valuable information from its employees.

This chapter has included specific suggestions for both the interviewer and the interviewee in each of the interview situations. They should establish and implement an interview plan consistent with accomplishing their goals. They may choose from among four interview strategies: information giving, information seeking, problem solving, and persuasion.

EXERCISES

1. Interview someone who has been recently interviewed for a job. Compile a list of questions asked, and report on strategies the interviewer or interviewee used.

2. Tape-record an interview with your roommate in which you appraise his or her "performance" as a good roommate. Turn in the tape along with a written evaluation of how well the interview went.

3. Work with your roommate to develop an action plan to solve a specific problem you have (such as keeping the room neat, coordinating study hours, paying bills). Specify who does what, when. Include a provision for following up on the plan to ensure that it will be implemented.

4. Conduct an exit interview with a graduating senior. Record the interview and turn in the tape with a written summary of (1) information gathered that might be useful to you and to your school and (2) an *evaluation* of the interview process (include comments on the techniques you used that you found to be successful, and also include suggestions on how the interview might have been better conducted).

5. Develop an interview grading sheet for both leader and participants. What should the evaluator look for? How much weight (points) should be assigned to each criterion?

6. Conduct an interview in class (clear the subject and kind of interview with your teacher). Class members should grade the interview.

7. Divide the class into groups. Each group will invite a "visitor" from the business or professional world to class to be interviewed. Provide the interviewee with some closed and open questions that will be asked during the interview. This procedure conducted prior to the interview will give the interviewee some confidence and reassurance of your intent. Members of the group should conduct the interview in front of the class with the purpose of gaining information about the interviewee's business or profession.

Suggested Readings

Benjamin, Alfred. *The Helping Interview,* 2nd ed. Boston: Houghton Mifflin, 1974.

This book focuses on the interview in which the interviewer tries to *help* the interviewee, which implies problem solving. Professionals such as doctors, nurses, and counselors will find this book useful. Managers will find its material applicable to counseling situations.

Downs, Cal W.; G. Paul Smeyak; and Ernest Martin. *Professional Interviewing.* New York: Harper and Row, 1980.

Major sections of the book treat the basic processes of interviewing, the interview as a management tool, interviews used in the mass media, and the interview as a research tool. Based on theory, the book focuses primarily on skills development: planning interviews, managing interviews, and interpreting data.

Einhorn, Lois J.; Patricia Hayes Bradley; and John E. Baird, Jr. *Effective Employment Interviewing: Unlocking Human Potential.* Glenview, Ill.: Scott, Foresman and Co., 1982.

This text gives an in-depth treatment of many interviewing skills.

Mahler, Walter. *How Effective Executives Interview.* Homewood, Ill.: Dow Jones–Irwin, 1976.

A practical approach to interviewing as practiced by managers. Based on observations of successful executives.

Richetto, Gary, and Joseph P. Zima. "Fundamentals of Interviewing" in *Modules in Speech Communication,* ed. Ronald L. Applbaum and Roderick P. Hart. Chicago: Science Research Association, 1976.

A clear description of the nature of interviewing and interviewing barriers and biases. The book includes excellent discussion questions and practical sections on interview preparation and strategies.

Stewart, Charles J., and William B. Cash, Jr. *Interviewing: Principles and Practices,* 2nd ed. Dubuque, Iowa: Wm. C. Brown, 1978.

An excellent survey of general principles and techniques of interviewing, with an indepth discussion of six specialized kinds of interviews (survey, journalistic, employment, performance, counseling, and persuasive). An appendix on sample interviews provides excellent models for students.

COMMUNICATION IN GROUPS AND MEETINGS OF BUSINESS AND PROFESSIONAL ORGANIZATIONS

3

Group Work through Meetings

7

Most business and professional people spend a lot of time communicating on a one-to-one basis. They give instructions and advice, ask for information, and discuss problems with others. Communication also takes place with groups of people in a more formal setting. As managers and other professionals move up the organizational ladder, they spend more time communicating with individuals in formal meetings. Outside the work environment, they participate in other kinds of meetings such as service clubs, church groups, or conventions.

Meetings can be helpful in accomplishing an organization's goals, but sometimes they are frustrating and a waste of time. No matter how significant the information may be, a meeting may fail to accomplish anything worthwhile if the designated leader or an influential group member does not understand *when to have a meeting, how to organize it,* and *how to manage the people* who attend the meeting.

If you are going to be involved in meetings in your profession (sales conference, bar association meeting) or in your personal life (United Way drive, neighborhood beautification council), you will want them to be as productive as possible. By understanding how meetings operate and what their goals are, you should gain insight into how to increase their effectiveness. This chapter gives you some guidelines about when meetings are appropriate for accomplishing organizational goals. It explores types and functions of meetings; these will influence how you organize group work. Finally, it examines interaction in meetings and identifies those factors affecting group work that you can manage. Chapter 8 contains additional advice about planning and conducting meetings.

To Have or Not to Have a Meeting

Individuals may communicate with one another in writing, in individual face-to-face discussion, over the telephone, or in a group. Often, in organizations, the manager or another high-status professional must decide which option to choose. The guidelines listed in Figure 7.1 will help in determining whether a meeting is the best way to get your work done.

HOLD A MEETING . . .

If you need several people to receive the same information at the same time. Timing is the critical point here, particularly in high-tension situations. By explaining a new procedure or policy to all of your subordinates simultaneously, you will likely cut down on "grapevine" activity or gossip, and you will make your subordinates feel equally important. You should not call meetings, however, to disseminate routine information.

If information is potentially difficult to understand or subject to distortion. By allowing discussion, you can judge whether your hearers understand the information you presented. A meeting puts you in a better position to respond to questions and concerns and to clarify distortions you discover.

If coordination of tasks and staff is critical to accomplishing your goals. Sometimes one work group does not know what others in the organization are doing. Lack of communication can result in duplication of effort, failure to meet organizational deadlines, and misunderstanding over who is responsible for what part of the project. Examples of such coordination failures are numerous: a bridge for an interstate highway in Kansas is completed four years before the highway itself is constructed; subway lines in Washington, D.C., are finished three years before subway cars are available; an inventory buildup occurs when manufacturing is not coordinated with sales. By using meetings as a forum for discussion, you can coordinate projects for which you are responsible.

If you are open to creative ideas from your subordinates. Leaders often fail to realize that a group can generate more and better ideas than one individual can. The principle of synergy states that the result of a group working together is often greater than the sum of the individual contributions. Put simply, no matter how much information you have, no matter how smart you are, no matter how much experience you have, you can usually benefit from the ideas and suggestions of others.

If you need commitment from your group to implement new plans and procedures. Group leaders must never lose sight of the fact that those who help formulate a solution have a greater investment in seeing it work than those who are excluded from the decision-making process. If you tell others to implement your plan, they may "stand back" and see if it works. On the other hand, if they have been consulted in the decision making, they are more committed to making sure that the plan works.

If you need to build cohesiveness in your work group. The preceding reasons for holding meetings essentially relate to accomplishing a task. To do their work effectively, group members need to work well together, cooperate with each other, and function as a cohesive unit. Meetings can help increase group cohesiveness. Small talk, jokes, and other seemingly irrelevant discussions can aid in bonding the group into a unified whole. This cohesiveness helps in accomplishing the assigned task.

DO NOT HOLD A MEETING . . .

If you do not have a clear, legitimate goal for the meeting. As the preceding discussion suggests, meetings serve valuable functions in organizations. Meetings are not useful, however, if they are held out of habit ("We always have a meeting on Friday") or if they substitute for positive action ("We *are* doing something; we're having a meeting").

If a meeting is not the best way to reach your goal. A meeting may not be the most appropriate way to reach your goal. Guard against using meetings indiscriminately by asking: "What do I wish to accomplish? Is a meeting the best way to do it?"

If the time spent meeting cannot be justified. As a professional, you will never have as much time as you need to get your work done. Meetings, moreover, can take a lot of time. Sometimes, the time invested in a meeting is well worth it; at other times, the time could have been used more productively elsewhere.

If you need a quick decision. Occasions occur when you simply will not have time to call a meeting. If you receive a call at 5:00 P.M. on Monday from the chief executive officer, who wants a procedures report at 9:00 A.M. on Tuesday, you will need to make the necessary decisions on your own. In such a situation, time constraints simply do not allow you to consult your subordinates.

Avoid using time pressures, however, as an *excuse* to exclude others from decision making.

If you do not want feedback from your subordinates. Some managers, doctors, lawyers, or other professionals prefer that all communication in their organization be "downward"—that is, they do the talking, and their subordinates, patients, or clients do the listening. Just because you tell others something, however, does not necessarily mean they understand your message. Without providing opportunities for feedback and being open to the feedback you receive, you may never know whether or not you have been clear.

If you want to retain total control over decisions for which you are responsible. By allowing others to participate in decision making, you lose a degree of control over the decision. If you are responsible for carrying out a given task, you may be uncomfortable with a partial loss of control. If you plan to retain all the decision-making responsibility, be careful not to mislead your group into thinking it will have some control. Honesty is the best policy. If you have not yet made a decision and want ideas from your group, hold a meeting, but plainly state: "I would appreciate your ideas and suggestions, but ultimately, I must make the decision." If you have already made a decision, hold a meeting only to explain the policy.

Types of Meetings

When organizing your meetings, it is helpful to know what kinds of formats are available to you. Organizations typically use staff meetings, committees, conferences, and conventions or extended conferences. The purpose of your meeting, the people to be involved, and the size of the group will give direction as to which of these options to use.

STAFF OR TEAM MEETINGS

As a manager or other professional responsible for subordinates, you call staff and team meetings for task-related reasons—to solve problems, to coordinate work, or to get or give information. Positions on the organizational chart determine who will participate in a staff meeting. The hospital administrator meets with doctors, nurses, technicians, or managerial staff; the lawyer meets with paralegal aides; the manager meets with subordinates; the company president meets with the vice-presidents; the plant superintendent meets with the foremen; the administrative assistant meets with the keypunch operators. These are all examples of staff meetings. The key factor here is that since there is no doubt about who is leader or "boss," status is likely to be an important concern.

Staffs are relatively stable work units. Teams, on the other hand, are formed to accomplish a specific task and then disband after the task is accomplished. Members of a staff attend a meeting by virtue of the positions they hold; teams are put together on the basis of expertise, availability, and ability to work well with others. For example, in a steel fabricating subsidiary of a major U.S. corporation, the team leader for a specialized project was the plant foreman. The team members were three company engineers, a home office computer programmer, and a quality control specialist from the plant. As this example shows, a team usually has members from throughout the organization, not from just one hierarchical level or operating division.

COMMITTEE MEETINGS

Another way you may accomplish a task or coordinate work is to form a *committee*. Committees may meet over an extended period of time, or they may have a limited life and function. "Permanent" committees are called *standing committees*. Those you form to accomplish a specific goal and then disband are *ad hoc*.

CONFERENCES

Sometimes you need to build a communication channel that allows consultation between two work groups. When that is the case, you might schedule a conference. The consultation may be face to face, or it may use the telephone or satellite video equipment. In tracking a national drug ring, for example, Federal Drug Enforcement agents may be working in Houston, Miami, New York, and Chicago. To compare notes and coordinate their efforts, these agents may need to arrange a conference. They may fly to a central location to meet, or they may place a "conference call" on the telephone. If they are very sophisticated, they may install satellite "disks" on the roofs of their offices and communicate by video—using a scrambler, of course.

Large corporations with plants and offices scattered through the United States and the world are increasingly dependent on teleconferencing for communication between offices. The Bell System has facilities available for video meetings between major U.S. cities.

CONVENTIONS OR EXTENDED CONFERENCES

When you need to bring people together to meet for several days, you may schedule an extended conference or a convention. You have a lot of choices about the way to handle this meeting, since convention or extended conference formats differ widely. When planning a convention or extended conference, you may choose from the following formats, either individually or in combination: forum, symposium, lecture, panel discussion, and breakout or buzz session.

Forum. The forum is an open discussion related to a specific topic. Any member of the audience may participate. The forum has a designated moderator who opens and closes the discussion, defines its boundaries, and channels questions to the appropriate person.

Symposium. A symposium includes a series of prepared talks on a specified topic by selected participants, each of whom speaks for a designated period of time. Usually, participants in a symposium have expertise in the discussion area. They may take different positions on an issue, or they may explore different parts of a single topic. Questions or a forum may follow a symposium.

Lecture. Sometimes, the primary format for an extended conference is a lecture by an "expert" in a particular topic area. Questions often follow lectures.

Panel discussion. Unlike the forum, a panel discussion has a limited number of participants (usually four or five). They discuss a given issue in front of an audience. Panelists usually have expertise in particular subject areas of the topic. Questions or a forum may follow the discussion.

Breakout or buzz sessions. Sharing ideas is important even in extremely large groups. Not only does the group need the ideas of all its members, but having the opportunity to contribute builds individual self-esteem and increases group cohesiveness. A problem with large conventions or conferences is the difficulty of providing opportunities for widespread participation by group members. One way to increase participation is to subdivide a large group into smaller groups for short discussion. These small groups meet in breakout or buzz sessions. After a designated period of time, members of each small group report back to the larger group the ideas, suggestions, or comments of their breakout group members.

Functions of Meetings

Regardless of the kind of meeting you hold, it should serve one or more organizational functions: information sharing, problem solving or decision making, work coordination, or team building. The following discussion examines the *information-sharing* and *problem-solving* functions and provides models for each. Work coordination combines both these functions, while team building results from the positive interaction that occurs in groups. Factors that affect this interaction are explored later in the chapter.

MEETINGS TO SHARE INFORMATION

You can increase the effectiveness of meetings if you plan them in such a way as to adapt new information to your hearers. The following model describes a systematic method for giving new information to groups.

Information-Sharing Model

1. Create interest in the information.
2. Preview what you are going to talk about.
3. Set out the information.

4. Test the hearer's understanding of the information.

5. Reemphasize the benefits of the information to the hearer.

Create interest. The first step in effectively sharing information is to create interest in the information. You might start by telling group members what the information *means* to them and how it affects them. You may also want to clarify for them what they are supposed to *do* with the information. Finally, you may wish to show members of your group how the information can *help* them. If, for example, you wish to disseminate information about a new performance appraisal system, you might begin as follows: "As you know, Acme Corporation is committed to beginning a new performance appraisal system July 1 [*what information means*]. In that system you will be expected to fill out a form about each of your subordinates [*what to do with information*]. The purpose of the meeting today is to provide information that will simplify your task [*hearer benefit*]."

Preview material. You probably have heard the often-repeated advice: "Tell the audience what you're going to tell them. Tell them. Then tell them what you've told them." The first part may be called *preview*. A preview gives your listeners a road map of what you are going to talk about. Preview makes your presentation easier to follow and therefore easier to understand. An appropriate preview statement for the meeting discussing performance appraisal might be: "I'll explain the new performance appraisal process we'll be using, give you an opportunity to ask questions, and then provide a test case, which we'll use for practice."

Set out the information. A third step in the information-sharing agenda is to set out the information as clearly and concisely as possible. You may also use the following suggestions as a practical checklist.

- Use words your hearers will understand. Technical or specialized language that may be meaningful to you may not be meaningful to them. Don't assume they have the same knowledge and experience you have.
- Build in verbal "signposts." Use words that let your hearers know where you are in the presentation—words like *first, second, another,* and *finally*.
- Visualize information. Use diagrams, charts, graphs, or lists of key ideas to clarify complicated material. (See Chapter 12, "Visual Aids.")
- Use examples and simple analogies.

Test understanding. A fourth step in the information-sharing agenda is to test your hearers' understanding of the material you have presented. You may ask questions, give participants an opportunity to ask questions, and/or use sample "cases." Feedback enables you to find out how well your hearers understand the information you have given them and to clear up any misconceptions.

The questions you ask your hearers should be more specific than "Do you understand?" "Let's discuss any questions you may have about the coding system" will probably be more useful. Sample cases not only provide feedback on whether hearers understand the material, but also give your group members an opportunity to apply the information: "Patricia, you have a subordinate who is often late to work and has informed you that in the future, he'll need to leave on Fridays at noon to catch his carpool. Using the appraisal scale we've been discussing, how would you rate this employee on the category 'Meets Time Expectations'?" Patricia's response will give valuable feedback about how she will use the information you gave her.

Reemphasize hearer benefits. A final step in the information-sharing agenda is to reemphasize for group members the benefits they will receive by understanding and implementing the material you presented. The benefits hearers might receive from implementing a new appraisal system could be a more objective system of assessment, a time-saving device, or an instrument that will meet legal criteria and therefore minimize an individual's liability. In any event, whether your hearers like the appraisal system or not, they will be expected to fill out the new rating forms required. Therefore, it is to their benefit to understand how to do it.

MEETINGS TO SOLVE PROBLEMS

Groups typically solve problems in one of several ways. Some adopt the solution proposed by one member—usually that of the group leader or another status figure. Some groups choose sides and "fight," and the stronger (either the side with higher status or the majority) wins. Others follow a cooperative problem-solving approach.

Problem solving through group process implies that the group (not the leader) solves a problem through an orderly, progressive, goal-directed approach. In addition to a positive climate that allows for open and honest interaction, you need a process structure that prescribes rules for interaction. You can find a number of problem-solving and decision-making models in textbooks on group process.[1] This chapter outlines two widely used approaches that are easy to understand and apply. The first is the standard problem-solving model called *reflective thinking;* the other is a highly structured approach called the *nominal group method.*

---

1. For alternative problem-solving models, see C. Kepner and B. Tregoe, *The Rational Manager: A Systematic Approach to Problem Solving and Decisionmaking* (New York: McGraw-Hill, 1965); Carl E. Larson, "Forms of Analysis and Small Group Problem-solving," *Speech Monographs* 36 (1969): 452–55; B. Aubrey Fisher, *Small Group Decision Making,* 2nd ed. (New York: McGraw-Hill, 1980).

Reflective Thinking Model

Since John Dewey developed the reflective thinking process as a method for solving social problems, his model has been highly tested, widely used, and adapted to a variety of problem-solving situations.[2] The model provides structure for problem solving but does not contradict the notion of group process. Rather, as Applbaum and his colleagues observed, the steps of the model "interact with each other in a very systematic manner."[3]

The following six-step outline is a modified version of Dewey's problem-solving model.

Problem-Solving Model
1. Define the problem.
2. Analyze the problem.
3. Determine criteria.
4. List solutions.
5. Select "best" solution.
6. Implement solution.

1. Define the problem. Your group first must reach consensus on what the problem is. By insisting early in the discussion on a clear, one-sentence statement of what the group agrees the problem to be, you accomplish two important things. First, you determine what will and will not be relevant. This gives the discussion more focus and more direction, and it saves time in the meeting. Second, by getting early agreement on problem definition, you increase the probability of group agreement on a solution. Often, when groups argue over different solutions to a problem, they are really providing answers for *different segments of a problem area.*

The unwillingness or failure to focus on a precise problem undermines the work of many problem-solving groups. If, for example, a hospital board is meeting to discuss the need to provide quality health care for patients, the board is attacking a general problem area. Because the topic is too broad, the results of any general discussion are not likely to be fruitful in generating specific action plans. If, on the other hand, the board focuses on one segment of the problem area—for example, determining what pieces of equipment to purchase for the intensive care unit—the group is more likely to come up with precise recommendations.

2. Analyze the problem. In analyzing the problem, the group should examine such things as the background of the problem; factual information and authoritative opinions about the problem; existing policies and procedures; how the problem fits into the organizational scheme of things; and how the problem affects all

2. John Dewey, *How We Think* (Boston: D. C. Heath and Co., 1910).
3. Ronald L. Applbaum, Edward M. Bodaken, Kenneth K. Sereno, and Karl W. E. Anatol, *The Process of Group Communication* (Chicago: Science Research Associates, 1977), p. 102.

segments of the organization and its publics (labor, management, stockholders, consumers, and competitors). Analysis is more than collecting data, however. In analysis, you try to determine what data *means* in relation to the problem. What conclusions can you draw? What generalizations? What cause-effect relationships? What, for example, does the fact that a piece of equipment is ten years old tell you? What else do you need to know before that fact becomes meaningful? How does the fact that twelve heart attack victims were admitted to the intensive care unit last month affect your decision of what equipment to purchase? Why?

3. Determine criteria. The group should agree on the *standards or criteria that any solution to the problem must meet.* In other words, what are the yardsticks by which you will measure various solutions? The standards you set will come from the nature of the problem itself, from organizational constraints, and from predispositions of group members. Criteria that evolve from considering the importance of the equipment to saving lives, how much use the equipment will likely get, and how out-of-date or worn current equipment is, grow out of the particular problem—equipment needs. On the other hand, physical space requirements, costs, and personnel allocation are constraints imposed by the organization. Finally, the attitudes and priorities of the board members will influence criteria. The president of the board, who has a heart condition, may argue that the lifesaving need is a more important criterion than the cost of the equipment. The accountant's standard for judging, on the other hand, may be influenced by the costs of various pieces of equipment.

Since all the standards set out in our example are legitimate, the group may find it useful to set priorities—number them in order of importance. By ranking criteria *before* discussing solutions, groups will increase the likelihood of reaching more objective and thus better solutions.

4. List solutions. The group may want to write all possible solutions in a numbered list, preferably in the order that they are suggested. Listing is an occasion for brainstorming. One rule must hold absolutely: *no discussion of solutions can take place until all possible solutions have been generated.* By preventing early discussion of solutions, you are likely to increase the number of ideas. Also, people are less hesitant to make suggestions if their ideas are not immediately "shot down." Premature evaluation can be a major barrier to getting the best solutions in group problem solving.

5. Select "best" solution. If your group followed the preceding steps *in order,* selecting among solutions becomes relatively easy. Ideally, the solution picked is the one that "best" meets the essential criteria generated in step 3 of the process. Frequently, groups combine three or four solutions in order to meet criteria they have established. At other times, they negotiate a compromise between or among solutions.

6. Implement solution. Selecting a solution is sometimes not enough. The group must determine the steps necessary to put the solution into practice—that is, the group must set out a clear course of action to be followed. Sometimes this step is the prerogative of the group. At other times, it is delegated to others.

Nominal Group Method

The second approach useful for problem solving that is discussed in this chapter is the nominal group, which is a highly structured model for accomplishing a group task. As its name suggests, and its procedure confirms, the nominal group is a group in name only. That is, individuals are assembled to reach a goal, but they *do not interact with each other.* Thus, the first rule in using the model is that all communications should be channeled through the group leader.[4] (See Fig. 7.2.) A second rule for the nominal group is that group members should not openly evaluate the ideas or opinions of others. Third, the steps of the model, described below, are to be followed in order.

Since the nominal group method differs radically from the style of meetings group members normally attend, the leader must offer strong guidance, clarifying procedure and shepherding the group

4. See Richard C. Huseman, "The Role of the Nominal Group in Small Group Communication," in *Readings in Interpersonal and Organizational Communication,* 3rd ed., ed. Richard C. Huseman, Cal M. Logue, and Dwight L. Freshley (Boston: Holbrook Press, 1977), pp. 493–501.

Figure 7.2 Model of Interaction in Nominal Group

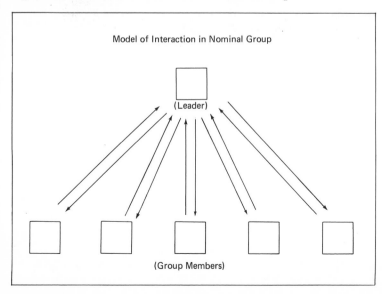

Model of Interaction in Nominal Group

(Leader)

(Group Members)

through the sequential steps of the model. At the beginning of the session, the leader will probably need to explain the reasons for using the model (it's an efficient way of getting a wide range of opinion; it gives all group members an equal opportunity to contribute). The leader should also define the nature of the work to be done (investigate causes of or provide a solution for weak sales in the plastics division; identify major employee problems arising out of the company's recent merger). During the meeting, the leader enforces the rules and records data and observations. Finally, the leader may tally meeting results or delegate the task to one or more group members.

A five-step outline describes the *procedure* for using the nominal group method. The model prescribes that the steps be followed in order.

Nominal Group Method

1. *List ideas independently.* Participants make separate lists of information or ideas that need to be generated (advantages or disadvantages of a problem, causes, effects, implications, standards, or possible solutions). They should have sufficient time to put as many things on their lists as they wish. Perhaps fifteen to twenty minutes should be devoted to this step.

2. *Compile group list.* Each group member is asked to name one item from his or her list. The group leader records those items on a board or a flip chart. The procedure of calling on each group member for an item to add to the group list is repeated until participants have no more items to add.

3. *Revise group list.* After a "complete" list of items has been generated, group members may reword or combine items, or they may remove duplications. All this discussion goes through the leader.

4. *Rank-order master list independently.* Individually, group members rank-order the total list. The meeting leader may save time by asking members to rank-order only their top three or five choices.

5. *Collate results.* Individual results are tallied, and the results are reported to the group.

When deciding whether or not to use the nominal group approach, you need to weigh carefully its disadvantages and its advantages. There are at least three important disadvantages of the method. First, it does little to facilitate group cohesiveness. Rather, the model restricts group dynamics by channeling all communication through the leader. Second, by precluding evaluation, the process may drive disagreement underground, which may result in a potentially explosive situation. Third, a lack of open discussion may prevent a full and thoughtful consideration of the merits of an idea or the advantages or disadvantages of a particular solution. Advantages of the approach are that it (1) allows for openness in sharing ideas; (2) ensures that every member's ideas get a fair hearing; (3) provides a way to control the dominant person(s) in the group; and (4) adapts easily to a variety of group tasks.[5]

One of the most difficult jobs any work group leader has is to *manage* group process—the dynamic, ongoing, ever-changing interaction in the group. How your group members relate to one another will influence, if not determine, the success or failure of the group's work. The following section describes six important factors that influence interaction in groups: group size, cohesiveness, norms, roles, personal agendas, and status.

SIZE OF GROUP

The size of the group will necessarily influence the amount and nature of interaction that occurs. Usually, the smaller the group, the more opportunity for each member to express ideas. As meetings become larger, the chance for individual group members to contribute diminishes. If feedback is important and if you want ideas from all participants, you should restrict your meeting to between six and twelve participants.

The number of members in a group will directly affect the physical room arrangement and, indirectly, the interaction of the group. As Chapter 3 suggests, seating participants around a table increases their opportunities to talk to each other. Using a classroom setup, however—as you must do with large groups—limits interaction. Sometimes you will have difficulty controlling group size, as with large conferences and conventions.

GROUP COHESIVENESS

You want and need your group members to work well together. On the other hand, they should not be so closely knit that they are unwilling to disagree with one another, to test ideas in debate, or to offer courses of action that differ from your own. Groups united by friendship, ideology, or loyalty may ignore or minimize the usefulness or validity of an idea under consideration and seek agreement for the sake of group cohesiveness. Ultimately, such conformity undermines the group's work.

If you have a cohesiveness problem in your group—either too much or too little—one thing you may look at is the self-concepts of group members. Persons with a positive though realistic evaluation of themselves tend to work well in groups. Those with low self-esteem tend either to withdraw from groups or to overcom-

5. For an excellent synthesis of the nominal group process, see Thad B. Green and Paul H. Pietri, "Using Nominal Grouping to Improve Upward Communication," in *Intercom: Readings in Organizational Communication,* ed. Stewart Ferguson and Sherry D. Ferguson (Rochelle Park, N.J.: Hayden Book Co., 1980), pp. 356–65.

pensate for their negative feelings by attempting to dominate the group. High self-esteem contributes to group cohesiveness; low self-esteem weakens it.

Another thing you may examine is whether or not group members like one another and whether they like you. People tend to work best with those they like. You may not be able to change radically the likes or dislikes of group members, but you can, in many cases, form groups from people who like one another.

Commitment to common goals also influences cohesiveness. Define clearly the group's goals, or help the group define its own goals. When individuals are guided by group goals and not by their personal objectives, the group will function more efficiently and more effectively.

A final factor affecting cohesiveness is the motivations of group members. To build cohesiveness in your group, you will want to emphasize rewards that the group can offer to each member—including *belonging or being accepted by the group, having influence on group outcomes,* and *being liked and valued.*

NORMS

New groups immediately begin to define what is and is not acceptable behavior. Since such rules—or *norms*—serve as criteria for "punishments" and "rewards" for group members, they have an important impact on the amount and kind of interaction that occur. If you are to begin work with a group that is already established, you should recognize that the group will already have its unwritten rules of behavior for its members.

Sometimes group norms are supportive of group work. Insisting on prompt attendance at meetings, being prepared, and completing assigned tasks are positive norms. Negative norms include such things as carrying on side conversations in meetings, squelching disagreement, and excluding or ridiculing certain group members or their ideas. Your task as manager is to influence group norms in positive directions. Your leadership style, your expectations of the group, and the sanctions and/or reinforcements you provide can help establish positive group norms.

ROLES

If you observe groups carefully, you will find that members work out with the group the *place* they will occupy in the group or the role they will perform.[6] Some group members are looked to for expertise, some for humor, others for procedural knowledge. Leadership is also a role, sometimes played by the designated leader, sometimes by a group member.

Roles can be extremely rigid in groups. "I am the appropriate

6. For a discussion of role emergence, see Ernest G. Bormann and Nancy C. Bormann, *Effective Small Group Communication,* 3rd ed. (Minneapolis, Minn.: Burgess Publishing Co., 1980), pp. 80–83.

person to present the budget data." "Only the designated leader has the authority to begin a meeting." If group members do not perform the roles *expected* of them, uncertainty and conflict can result. Group leaders need to be sensitive to the roles that members of their group play and to their own task and social leadership roles.

The *task role* focuses on getting the work done—meeting the assigned goal. This role is not the exclusive prerogative of the designated leader, but is sometimes shared or assumed entirely by group members. For example, if another member perceives you as uncertain about leading the group toward accomplishing the goal, that member may take over responsibility for the task—depending, of course, on status differences and reward structures in the organization. Or you may deliberately seek help from group members who are highly task-oriented. The point is that unless someone—either you or a member of your group—makes completing the task a priority, your group is not likely to get its work done.

Another leadership role is the *social role,* which focuses on the interpersonal relationships among group members. This role is important in building and maintaining cohesiveness. The "people dimension" may be effectively managed in groups by the leader, or it may be turned over to members of the group. Sometimes group members preempt the designated leader and *assume* the role (if, of course, the group agrees).

PERSONAL AGENDAS

Some group members have personal agendas so compelling that the work of the group becomes secondary, if not irrelevant. These agendas may reflect attitudes, past experiences, job satisfaction, personal likes and dislikes, territoriality, status, or feelings of exclusion from the group. When you chair a meeting, you will have to keep these agendas from undermining your task.

Sometimes personal agendas result from a single incident—for example, the boss assigns Mary's personal secretary to John and tells Mary to take her work to the secretarial pool. By threatening Mary's status and "territory"—what "belongs" to her—the boss's action will likely affect her priorities and performance in the organization, including the meetings she attends. Though such isolated incidents are not an uncommon cause of group member dissatisfaction, more often it is a series of episodes, either personal or work-related, that results in an overriding personal agenda.

Unsatisfied personal agendas can lead to behavior that will destroy a meeting. Both the individual who dominates a meeting with irrelevant or hostile comments and the introvert who "tunes out" the meeting disrupt the task. Dominators not only add little to a meeting, but also prevent others from doing so. Introverts, on the other hand, seldom preclude others from contributing, but by failing to participate fully, they rob the group of potentially valuable ideas.

As a meeting leader, you will sometimes have to cope with disruptions during the meeting. A more useful, long-term approach, however, is to try to find the underlying cause and work to minimize if not remove it. If exclusion is the problem, make a conscious effort to involve the person in group discussion. If personal likes are at issue, look for ways to resolve the tension. If territoriality is the point, offer reassurance or some substitute domain. If the problem is status, assign the individual a responsible job.

STATUS

Your status as a leader of the group may be a potential barrier to group interaction. In work groups where the manager or another professional is "boss," subordinates are often reluctant to offer contrary opinions. After all, the boss promotes, fires, assigns work, and gives positive and negative reinforcement—in short, the boss has power. One thing you can do to minimize this effect of your status is to listen to the ideas of your subordinates in meetings without agreeing or disagreeing.

Some members of your group may have status simply because other group members like them, trust them, or believe they have expertise.[7] The prestige that "experts" have is particularly noteworthy, since it can be misleading. Sometimes the label *expert* is sufficient to guarantee influence even in areas where the "expert" has no experience.

Status is clearly tied to the human needs to be recognized, to be included, and to control.[8] On the other hand, someone with "too much" status—such as the chairman of the board sitting in on a production meeting—can undermine open, honest communication. You should work to minimize status—whether your own or that of specific group members—when it interferes with or distorts communication within the group.

SUMMARY

In organizations—whether they are corporations, government agencies, or volunteer associations—formal group communication usually takes one of four forms: staff or team meetings, committee meetings, conferences, or conventions. This chapter has focused primarily on meetings that are small enough to allow for group interaction.

Meetings have a legitimate role in organizations, but they are also

7. French and Raven investigated expertise as a type of social power. See John R. P. French, Jr., and Bertram Raven, "The Bases of Social Power," in *Studies in Social Power,* ed. Darwin Cartwright (Ann Arbor, Mich.: Institute for Social Research, 1959), pp. 150–67.
8. See W. Schutz, *FIRO: A Three-Dimensional Theory of Interpersonal Behavior* (New York: Holt, Rinehart and Winston, 1958).

widely abused. Specifically, meetings can serve as a forum for sharing information, coordinating work, problem solving or decision making, and team building. Whether or not to hold a meeting should be a managerial choice made after a thorough examination of options.

Meetings should be *planned* to accomplish their goals. The agenda should facilitate group process. This chapter has outlined three alternatives: an information-sharing model, the reflective thinking or problem-solving model, and the nominal group method.

Central to an understanding of groups is an understanding of *process*, which suggests that the amount, kind, and quality of interaction between and among group members will affect whether the group goal will be accomplished. The leader must be sensitive to and exert influence on those factors that affect interaction among group members.

EXERCISES

1. Ask permission to observe a committee meeting at your university. Based on the principles discussed in this chapter, prepare a written analysis of the meeting.
2. Take notes of your observations during an information-sharing meeting at which you are a group member. Build a model of what you observed. How does your model differ from the information-sharing model in this chapter?
3. Do you exhibit primarily a task or a social role in meetings? What are the advantages and disadvantages of your style?
4. Observe a disruptive, self-centered role operating in a group. Describe the person's action. How did other group members react? What was the effect on the group? What was the leader's response?
5. Hold a meeting in class (plan a class party or project, prepare an exam on this chapter, or agree on a time to reschedule class). Follow the nominal group procedure. Evaluate the meeting.
6. Make a list of the legitimate meetings you attend (those held for good, defensible reasons). Then list those meetings you attend that should never have been called. What kinds of differences do you see between them?

Suggested Readings

Applbaum, Ronald L.; Edward M. Bodaken; Kenneth K. Sereno; and Karl W. E. Anatol. *The Process of Group Communication.* Chicago: Science Research Associates, 1974.

An excellent discussion of the group communication process. Integrates theory and application of general systems principles.

Bormann, Ernest G. *Discussion and Group Methods: Theory and Practice.* New York: Harper and Row, 1969.

A good explanation of techniques of group discussion and group methods. The discussion of roles is particularly helpful in understanding the functioning of groups. Chapter

15, "The Ethical Implications of Small-Group Discussion," explores the ethical problems associated with group work and sets out a code for the practitioner.

Fisher, B. Aubrey. *Small Group Decision Making*, 2nd ed. New York: McGraw-Hill, 1980.
Fisher's work focuses on decision-making groups as groups with a specific task orientation. The aim of the work is to generate an understanding of communication and the group process. There is less emphasis on practical application of general principles.

Gouran, Dennis S. *Making Decisions in Groups: Choices and Consequences*. Glenview, Ill.: Scott, Foresman and Co., 1982.
Grounded in theory and research, the book provides practical suggestions for preparation, participation, and evaluation of group work. Of particular interest is the distinction between "single-motive context" (where group members pursue the same goal) and "mixed-motive interaction" (such as that occurring in bargaining). Chapter 8 examines crisis decision making.

Mabry, Edward A., and Richard E. Barnes. *The Dynamics of Small Group Communication*. Englewood Cliffs, N.J.: Prentice-Hall, 1980.
This text is a systems approach to small-group communication. The authors examine group inputs (including personality, attitudinal orientations, and the environment); integrative processes (interaction, networks, and leadership); and outputs (interpersonal relationships, patterns of group development, and achievement). Of particular interest to students of business and professional communication are the numerous examples drawn from industry and other organizations.

Scheidel, Thomas M., and Laura Crowell. *Discussing and Deciding: A Desk Book for Group Leaders and Members*. New York: Macmillan Publishing Co., 1979.
This book contains a number of alternative procedures that leaders and group members may use in small group discussions. A very practical approach to group work, it is recommended as a handy reference for the professional who manages or participates in small-group work.

Zelko, Harold P., and Frank E. X. Dance. *Business and Professional Speech Communication*, 2nd ed. New York: Holt, Rinehart and Winston, 1978.
Chapter 8, "The Business Conference," includes good discussions of purposes and types of conferences. The description of conference process is clear and practical.

Leadership and Participation in Meetings

8

In the preceding chapter, you learned about the different types and functions of meetings common to most organizations. You recall from that discussion that managers and other group leaders call staff, team, and committee meetings and hold conferences and conventions to share information and solve problems. This chapter explores the nature of the leadership that occurs in those meetings and describes the personal characteristics most leaders share, leadership styles, situational leadership, and leadership functions and responsibilities. Further, it identifies specific responsibilities of the participants.

The Nature of Leadership

Do leaders have common characteristics, or is personality irrelevant to their leadership? Does leadership come from charisma, or is it a function of the group? Do we attribute good or bad leadership to people independent of what they actually accomplish? That is, does leadership exist "only as a perception"? Perhaps leadership is the "art of counteractive influence," adaptive responses to situations that group *members* can and should make.[1] What other specific factors affect leadership and how do they relate to each other? These are questions social science researchers have studied for over fifty years; yet they have reached no general agreement or precise answers.[2]

The difficulty of describing the nature of leadership is analogous to the Supreme Court's problem in delineating pornography. One of the justices noted that though he could not define the term, he was sure he would recognize pornography when he saw it.[3] To help you gain a better understanding of the equally elusive concept of leadership, we will briefly examine influence as an important

1. See Bobby J. Calder, "An Attribution Theory of Leadership," in *New Directions in Organizational Behavior,* ed. Barry M. Staw and Gerald R. Salancik (Chicago: St. Clair Press, 1977), pp. 178–204; Dennis S. Gouran, *Making Decisions in Groups: Choices and Consequences* (Glenview, Ill.: Scott, Foresman and Co., 1982), chap. 7.
2. For a brief review of leadership theories and research, see Patricia Hayes Bradley and John E. Baird, Jr., *Communication for Business and the Professions* (Dubuque, Iowa: Wm. C. Brown, 1980), pp. 192–202.
3. *Jacobellis* v. *State of Ohio,* U.S. Supreme Court, 1964, concurring opinion by Justice Potter Stewart.

factor in leadership and the formal and informal leadership that occurs in groups.

LEADERSHIP AS INFLUENCE

The term *leadership* emphasizes the influencing of other people to accomplish some goal. Leaders direct, control, guide, induce, and sometimes coerce. The concept of leadership as involving *influence* raises some important ethical issues. What responsibilities, for example, does the leader have to provide people with "adequate information, diversity of views, and knowledge of alternative choices and their possible consequences"? What can leaders in the business and professional world do to encourage "significant debate," "freedom of expression," and "constructive criticism"? To what extent should the professional "preserve the dignity and integrity" of others, allow for "optimum sharing of thought and feeling," make possible "the experience of belonging and acceptance," and foster "cooperation and mutual respect"?[4] Keep these questions in mind as you explore the various approaches to leadership described in this chapter.

FORMAL AND INFORMAL LEADERSHIP

We often associate leadership with the person who has formal responsibility for the group. Individuals become *formal* group leaders either by appointment or because of their position in an organization. Groups may not have a voice about the appointment of their formal leaders. Sometimes they may even resist or reject these people and look to group members for *informal* direction. In other words, designated leaders may have *responsibility* and *authority* for leading groups, but they may need to gain the support of members if they are to accomplish their goals.

This chapter provides some specific and practical suggestions (not hard and fast rules) for improving your *skill* in leading meetings. These suggestions reflect our belief that leaders who wish to be more effective must be aware of the interrelation of at least four variables: *personal characteristics, leadership style, adaptability to different situations or contexts,* and *skill in carrying out appropriate leadership functions and responsibilities.*

Personal Characteristics

One way to improve your leadership skills is to *identify the personal characteristics that leaders share and then work to develop those traits.* On the basis of a comprehensive review of trait research, Ralph Stogdill provides the following profile of leaders: intelligence, achievement, dependability, participation, and sta-

4. See Thomas R. Nilsen, *Ethics of Speech Communication,* 2nd ed. (New York: Bobbs-Merrill Co., 1974), pp. 18–19, for a discussion of ethical requirements of speech communication.

tus.[5] Chapter 7 describes the influence of *status* in group work. The following discussion examines the remaining four personal characteristics identified by Stogdill.

INTELLIGENCE

People tend to choose as their leaders individuals they believe have common sense and good judgment. Organizations usually designate as leaders those who understand the broad implications of problems, ask insightful questions, and cut through irrelevant material to draw together main ideas and suggestions. Such leaders usually think and reason well and have good verbal facility. This description does not suggest that to be an effective leader you must have a high IQ. What it does imply is that you can improve your effectiveness in groups by *behaving* intelligently—being alert and rational, offering original ideas and well-reasoned judgments.

Knowledge is particularly important in achieving group goals in organizations. As a leader, learn as much as possible about the subject your group is considering. Bring useful information to the meeting, and tap the expertise of group members. Insist, moreover, that information be communicated clearly and concisely.

ACHIEVEMENT

Most successful group leaders are high achievers. If you have a past record of superior performance (academic excellence, meritorious service, athletic prowess), you recognize the need to *set goals and focus your resources on accomplishing them.* The same holds true for leadership. Whether the goal of a meeting is set by the organization, the leader, or the group itself, the goal must be clarified in such a way that the group is committed to the task. Later in this chapter you will find a discussion of specific leader and participant responsibilities that will help you accomplish meeting goals.

DEPENDABILITY

If you are to be a successful leader, others must be able to depend on you to help them accomplish their assigned tasks. In a group setting such as a meeting, they will depend on you to guide, direct, and sometimes control the group's work. Being dependable and reliable in meeting your leadership responsibilities requires self-confidence, initiative, and persistence.

Self-confidence. If you are confident you can do the job, you will communicate your self-assurance both verbally (language such as "we can") and nonverbally (cues such as good eye contact). A positive attitude tends to rub off on groups and results in greater effort and commitment to the goal. As a leader, ban from your

5. Ralph M. Stogdill, *Handbook of Leadership: A Survey of Theory and Research* (New York: The Free Press, 1974).

vocabulary such negative words as *can't, never, impossible*. Greet people with a firm handshake, sit or stand straight in the meeting, and speak loudly enough to be clearly heard. When you are confident in yourself, you tend to be perceived as a person capable of being depended on.

Initiative.   As a leader, you will be an initiator, setting the group in motion and intervening when necessary to offer direction, order, and focus. Rather than dominate discussion, however, provide a stimulus and direction for group interaction. Your initiative will not be without its risks. To step out front, to make the first move, to commit yourself to a new (and perhaps controversial) position may result in a loss of leadership.

Persistence.   To be successful as a leader, you also have to be persistent. Since you are committed to finishing the task, you will not let most obstacles prevent you from moving toward your goal. Rather, you will use diversity to push yourself and others to meet the challenge. That pushing, directing, and controlling can sometimes undermine interpersonal relations in the group. Be careful not to allow your persistence to polarize you from group members. They must be able to depend on you for leadership.

PARTICIPATION

Participation means *active involvement* in the group's work. Most leaders are not passive observers of the groups for which they have responsibility. Instead, they tend to be dynamic individuals who participate actively in the group process. They contribute to group movement through diffusing tension with humor; giving direction through questions, restatement, and summary; and reinforcing individuals and the group.

Although traditional research on leadership has focused primarily on personal characteristics or traits such as those we have just described, this approach has some obvious limitations. For one thing, no single trait is always present in effective leaders. Researchers also have compiled differing lists of characteristics. Nonleaders, moreover, seem to have many of the same characteristics that leaders do. Finally, the approach does not account for the fact that a leader in one situation may not be a leader in another. Simply identifying personal characteristics, therefore, has not provided an adequate explanation of leadership. Rather, how specific personal characteristics affect leadership seems to be contingent on other factors that are operating, such as interpersonal relationships and the situation itself.[6]

6. Some relatively recent leadership research focuses on personal characteristics within a contingency framework. See R. J. House, "A Theory of Charismatic Leadership," in *Leadership: The Cutting Edge,* ed. J. G. Hunt and L. L. Larson (Carbondale: Southern Illinois University Press,

Figure 8.1

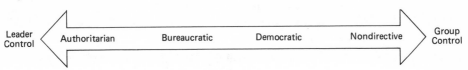

Leader Control ⟨ Authoritarian   Bureaucratic   Democratic   Nondirective ⟩ Group Control

Another way of describing leadership is to identify the different *styles* people use. A traditional and still useful way of looking at leadership styles is to plot them on a continuum that ranges from leader control of the decision to group control.[7] (See Fig. 8.1.) Four positions along that continuum include the authoritarian, bureaucratic, democratic, and nondirective leadership styles. The following discussion describes these styles and suggests situations where they are most useful.

AUTHORITARIAN STYLE

If you are extremely task-oriented, do not like a lot of foolishness in meetings, and prefer to be in control of the situation and make the decisions for which you will ultimately be responsible, then you are probably comfortable using an authoritarian style of leadership. Authoritarian leaders do most of the talking in their groups; they control and direct the flow of information and retain control over decision making.

The authoritarian leader's group will be well organized and is often productive, though sometimes at the expense of human relationships. In fact, an authoritarian style can foster rebellion and be counterproductive to reaching the desired results. The authoritarian style is most useful for giving information (explaining a new management plan). It is less appropriate for problem-solving meetings (setting resource priorities for the coming year), since it restricts potential influence of group members.

BUREAUCRATIC STYLE

If you are not much of a risk-taker, prefer to follow existing rules, and see the leader's role as primarily a coordinator or administrator, the bureaucratic style may be most normal and natural for you. Here the rules dominate. The regulations or directives control. Though the bureaucratic style usually accomplishes

1976), pp. 189–207; F. E. Fiedler, E. H. Potter III, M. M. Zais, and W. H. Knowlton, Jr., "Organizational Stress and the Use and Misuse of Managerial Intelligence and Experience," *Journal of Applied Psychology* 64 (1979): 635–47.

7. See McGregor's Theory X and Theory Y, which draws a theoretical distinction between authoritarian and permissive leadership styles. D. McGregor, *The Human Side of Enterprise* (New York: McGraw-Hill 1960).

the task, it often results in sterile solutions, since individual creativity can be stifled.

You may find the bureaucratic (or structured) style useful when you want to consult group members but retain control of a decision, such as taking a controversial product off the market. You will also find it appropriate for handling high-risk situations in which you prefer to rely on precedent. Any decisions involving government regulations (pollution control, hiring practices) would fall into this category.

DEMOCRATIC STYLE

If your natural tendency is to consult others and allow their ideas to influence your course of action, then you probably are happy with a participatory or democratic style of leadership. This style may not be particularly useful, however, when your goal is to share information such as a negative report on investment yields. It is more appropriate for problem-solving situations (determining a strategy for increasing yields) because it does not rest on preconceived ideas about the "best" solution or decision.

The democratic style has a number of advantages, particularly in problem-solving groups.[8] First, it contributes to group cohesiveness and therefore helps build a more positive interpersonal climate. Second, it usually results in better solutions than those reached by individual effort alone. In addition, the group members will probably be committed to implementing their solution, since they participated in reaching that decision.

If you choose to use a democratic leadership style, concentrate on your listening skills. Your sensitivity and responsiveness to the feedback you receive will be important to the style's success.

NONDIRECTIVE STYLE

If you prefer a very informal leadership style with minimal control by the leader, then a laissez-faire style may be most comfortable for you. The nondirective leader offers little or no guidance to the group and essentially turns the task over to group members to accomplish. This does not mean, however, that the leader withdraws from the group. Rather, the leader simply expects self-direction from the group.

Groups that have functioned over a long period of time (partners in an accounting firm) may respond well to the nondirective leadership style. These groups usually have the cohesiveness necessary to set goals and reach them. Such groups tend to treat the leader (the managing partner) as a group member and would resist a more authoritarian approach.

8. See Ralph K. White and Ronald Lippin, *Autocracy and Democracy: An Experimental Inquiry* (New York: Harper & Row, 1960).

The preceding discussion indicates that no leadership style is necessarily good or bad. The "best" leadership style depends on the situation. In some instances, organizations will try to *match a leader's style with the demands of the situation.*[9] Sometimes they encourage and train leaders to *change the setting* to make it more compatible with their natural style.[10] Still another approach suggests that leaders should adjust their style of leading according to the demands of the situation. That is, leaders should adapt and react to contingencies.[11] How do leaders who wish to adapt know which approach is most useful in a given situation? By asking the following questions, you should have a better understanding of which leadership style to use.

1. What is the purpose of the meeting?

   PRINCIPLE: Directive styles are normally more appropriate for giving information; nondirective styles for problem solving.

   EXAMPLE: A sales manager explaining a new product line to sales personnel will probably need to be more directive (authoritarian) than an engineering team designing a solar power unit.

2. What is my normal or natural style?

   PRINCIPLE: Do not try to come across as someone you are not. If you are uncomfortable with the leadership style needed in the situation, then enlist the aid of another member of the group.

   EXAMPLE: As an advertising executive, you prefer a democratic approach to group work. Yet the layout deadline is approaching, and your group has not even agreed on a theme. Ask Mary, an authoritative, task-oriented group member, to help get your work completed.

3. What is the maturity of the group?

   PRINCIPLE: Groups that have been together a long time generally need less direction from a designated leader than recently formed or one-time groups.

   EXAMPLE: Your office staff will probably work more independently than a committee you form to solicit funds for the Red Cross.

9. Fred E. Fiedler, *A Theory of Leadership Effectiveness* (New York: McGraw-Hill, 1967); R. J. House and T. R. Mitchell, "Path Goal Theory of Leadership," *Journal of Contemporary Business* 3 (1974): 81–89.
10. F. E. Fiedler and L. Mahar, "The Effectiveness of Contingency Model Training: A Review of the Validation of Leader Match," *Personnel Psychology* 32 (1979): 45–62.
11. See R. M. Osborn and J. G. Hunt, "An Adaptive-Reactive Theory of Leadership: Macro Variables in Leadership Research," in *Leadership Frontiers,* ed. J. G. Hunt and L. L. Larson (Kent, Ohio: Kent State University Press, 1975), pp. 27–49.

4. What are the time constraints?

   PRINCIPLE: In general, the tighter the time frame, the greater the need for an authoritarian approach to leadership.

   EXAMPLE: As director of your local rescue unit, you are more likely to give orders when evacuating flood victims than in a weekly staff meeting.

5. What is the knowledge level or the expertise of the group?

   PRINCIPLE: The members' knowledge about an issue will suggest what their legitimate influence and value should be in organizational decisions.

   EXAMPLE: Though a hospital board has the authority to purchase sophisticated medical equipment, many board members may not have the expertise to make wise buying decisions. In a board meeting, health care professionals or equipment specialists will likely "take charge" of the discussion and thus of the decision.

6. What is the trust level in the group?

   PRINCIPLE: The lower the level of trust, the greater the need will be for the democratic style or wide participation by group members.

   EXAMPLE: Management and labor are negotiating a new contract. An authoritarian leadership style will probably heighten tension even further. You will want to use a more participative leadership style.

7. Is the group cohesive?

   PRINCIPLE: A cohesive group usually functions more efficiently than a noncohesive group.

   EXAMPLE: A publishing staff that works well together will probably need less direction from the editor than a fragmented staff that has poor interpersonal relationships.

8. Who is ultimately responsible for the group outcome?

   PRINCIPLE: Leaders may wish to exert control over decisions to the extent they are ultimately responsible for those decisions.

   EXAMPLE: As director of research for a pharmaceutical company, you are under pressure from your research team to introduce a new cream for baldness. Though preliminary testing indicates your drug is "safe," you are not convinced. Your job is on the line. You may prefer to make the final decision.

9. Who will implement the decision?

   PRINCIPLE: Groups are more likely to be committed to decisions over which they have some control.

   EXAMPLE: A company reorganization will probably go more smoothly if those individuals who are affected have been consulted. This calls for participative leadership.

10. What *legitimate* influence can the group have?

    PRINCIPLE: Organizational constraints, policies, and procedures sometimes remove a decision from a group's legitimate influence.

    EXAMPLE: Though your production line would prefer flexitime work schedules, the manufacturing process requires a constant work force. You should make those constraints clear. This is likely to call for an authoritarian or bureaucratic style.

Whatever leadership style you use, you are charged with accomplishing the goal of the meeting. To do that and to fulfill your ethical responsibilities toward those you work with, you need to be sensitive to the "people dimension" in groups. Put simply, you have responsibilities that are primarily *task-related* and responsibilities to *maintain positive human relationships* in your group. Some writers refer to these as the task role and the maintenance or social role.[12] Leaders fulfill these roles through their planning and conducting of meetings.

RESPONSIBILITIES FOR PLANNING

Most planning responsibilities relate directly to accomplishing the meeting goal (task function). The following discussion focuses on specific things a leader should do when planning for a meeting. (See Fig. 8.2.)

Figure 8.2 Planning Responsibilities

1. Determine meeting goal.
2. Determine participants.
3. Prepare and distribute an agenda.
4. Arrange facilities.
5. Distribute materials.
6. Provide for a record.
7. Provide for evaluation.

Determine meeting goal. Do not plan to have a meeting; plan to accomplish something. For example, you may use a staff meeting as an occasion for a problem-solving discussion on working out ways to reduce energy costs. Sometimes, the organizational goals will dictate the work to be done. Your company may require an annual safety program, and you have the task of arranging a symposium on safety. On occasions, groups set their own goals, as when members of an office get together to coordinate vacation

12. See D. Cartwright and A. Zander (eds.), *Group Dynamics: Research and Theory,* 3rd ed. (New York: Holt, Rinehart and Winston, 1958).

schedules. The important thing is to (1) *have a goal* and (2) *have a clear understanding of what the goal is.*

Determine participants.   The nature of the group will largely determine who participates in the meetings. Obviously, staff members attend staff meetings, team members attend team meetings, and committee members attend committee meetings. Conference and convention rules, moreover, prescribe who participants should be. You may need to invite people other than those designated. The following questions will indicate additional people to invite: Who has information you need? Who will keep the "people" relationships operating smoothly? Who are the major persons on the organizational grapevine? Who should be invited for status reasons?

You may need to find out as much as possible about the participants before the meeting. What do they already know about the subject? What can they add? What attitudes do they have that might hamper getting the group work done? How do they get along with others in the group? Are they risk-takers? What agenda or other changes need to be made on the basis of answering these questions?

Prepare and distribute an agenda.   The agenda is a written plan for the meeting. Though the leader has the primary responsibility for preparing that plan, participants need an opportunity to contribute agenda items.

The meeting leader should distribute the agenda *before the meeting.* Sometimes one or two days is sufficient time; however, if participants are expected to prepare lengthy reports or read long documents, the agenda may need to reach them a week or two in advance.

As Figures 8.3 and 8.4 show, typical agendas set out the topics the meeting will cover, the order, and in some cases the amount of time allotted to each topic. Finally, they sometimes designate individual member responsibilities: "*Report on Resources* (Joe Jones)."

Figure 8.3 Agenda: Happy Homes Realty
April 3 Sales Meeting

1. Call to order
2. Approve record of March 6 meeting
3. Report on March sales (Sam—15 min.)
4. Alternative methods of financing mortgages (nominal group—30 min.)
5. Announcements (5 min.)
6. Agenda items for May 8 meeting (5 min.)
7. Adjournment

> **Figure 8.4 Agenda: Northwood Hospital Board**
> **January 22**
>
> 1. Call to order
> 2. Approve record of December 19 meeting
> 3. Financial report (Karen Thomas—5 min.)
> 4. Develop resource priorities (45 min.)
>   - Problem (needs great; funds limited)
>   - Facts
>   - What criteria do we use in setting priorities?
>   - Specific needs
>   - How needs stack up against the criteria
>   - Set priorities
> 5. Evaluation of meeting (5 min.)
> 6. Adjournment

The leader may wish to "flesh out" the agenda by incorporating questions to be asked, points to be made, or particular group members to call on. This more detailed outline can help the leader make the meeting as complete as possible and keep it on track. A comprehensive discussion outline can also help the recorder when preparing minutes.

Arrange facilities.   The meeting leader should try to control the physical climate within which a meeting takes place. Specific factors to be "managed" include the following.

Equipment.

Determine whether you need a microphone, and test it before the meeting. (See Chapter 13, "Delivering a Message.") Arrange for the necessary visual aids such as slide projectors, chalkboards, or flip charts. Bring along an extension cord and an extra projector bulb. (See Chapter 12, "Visual Aids.")

Size of Room and Seating Arrangements.

Ideally, room size should be influenced by the size of the group. A "packed" room with participants in close proximity can reinforce the importance or urgency of the issue; it can heighten tensions when participants have no space in which to maneuver. A very large room with few participants can undermine cohesiveness. If possible, choose a room that will comfortably seat your participants but will not leave a lot of empty space. (Use the seating arrangements suggested in Chapter 3 to encourage the amount of interaction or the amount of authority and control you need.)

Meeting Length.

As a rule of thumb, limit meetings to one hour. Begin on time and end on time. Carry unfinished business to the next agenda or, if necessary, schedule an additional meeting.

Distribute materials. The manager is responsible for preparing, duplicating, and distributing any materials necessary for the meeting. Recognize, however, that materials distributed during a meeting will detract from the discussion unless they directly relate to it.

Provide for a record. The manager should appoint a group member as recorder, request a secretary, or in some other way provide for a record of the meeting. The record documents the work of the group both for its own use and for the organization's review.

Provide for evaluation. One important leadership tool that people tend to overlook or resist is evaluation of meetings. They do not seek adequate feedback about the meetings they hold for a number of reasons. First, they are afraid of what they might hear—that others consider the meetings a waste of time or otherwise counterproductive. Second, they are not willing to use the time necessary for evaluation. Finally, they do not know how to evaluate meetings effectively.

No one evaluation method will work for all leaders and all groups. The following list includes some of the more common *evaluation methods.*

Checklist.

You may distribute a list of questions designed to evaluate leadership, individual participation, and group process. The following sample listing suggests some of the areas the evaluator may wish to assess.

> Was the purpose clear?
> Were group members adequately prepared?
> Did the social climate allow free participation?
> Was feedback encouraged?
> Did the group stay on the topic?
> Was the degree of leader control appropriate?
> How well did the leader handle difficult
>   situations?
> Did the group accomplish its goal?

General Discussion.

Sometimes group leaders reserve the last five minutes of a meeting for general evaluation of the strengths and weaknesses of the meeting. The leader may chair this discussion or turn it over to a group member.

Written Feedback.

A leader may ask group members to prepare a written evaluation of the meeting. A more structured approach is to hand out 3 × 5 cards at the end of the meeting and ask participants to list in order the three things that would most improve the next meeting.

The important point to remember when evaluating meetings is this: do not ask for feedback unless you are willing to consider it seriously and respond to it. That does not mean you have to do everything your group members suggest, but you should explain your reasons for accepting or rejecting those ideas.

RESPONSIBILITIES FOR CONDUCTING MEETINGS

Whereas planning functions are primarily associated with accomplishing the task, responsibilities for conducting meetings involve both task and maintenance or social functions. (See Fig. 8.5.) The following discussion describes some specific leader responsibilities for conducting meetings.

Figure 8.5 Responsibilities for Conducting Meeting

Task Functions

1. State the goal for the meeting.
2. Clarify the procedures.
3. Provide ideas, information, and suggestions.
4. Seek and respond to feedback.
5. Clarify, summarize, and evaluate.
6. Draw consensus.

Maintenance or Social Functions

1. Provide a supportive climate.
2. Encourage participation.
3. Encourage diversity of opinion.
4. Manage conflict.
5. Control disruptive behavior.

Task Functions

State the meeting goal. In the planning stages, you determined your goal. You also need to specify in the meeting exactly what you expect to accomplish. If you have several agenda items, you may have several goals. For example, you may wish to explain a new company policy, set up a procedure for United Way solicitations, gain approval for or amend a personnel procedure, and formulate a new parking policy for employees. You may also need to motivate the group to reach these goals.

Clarify meeting procedures. Group members need to know the rules of the game—what norms will be enforced—but they may resist having those rules dictated by the group leader. Some leaders find it useful to spend the first few minutes of a meeting discussing specific meeting procedures (such as the reflective thinking or nominal group models). Be careful, however, not to spend your whole allotted time talking about procedures. Depending on the nature and purpose of your group, you may wish to follow parliamentary procedure as a means of introducing ideas, debating them, and reaching a decision. The Appendix provides basic rules of parliamentary procedure.

One important matter that should be clarified early in the meeting is any limitations such as lack of resources or the lack of decision-making authority. If the group is to act only in an advisory capacity, state this. Also, any rules about participation—who speaks when—should be clearly stated. Problem-solving and nominal group methods should be explained when needed.

Provide ideas, information, and suggestions. The leader is often the primary resource person in a group. Managers should recognize, however, that when they start the meeting with their own ideas, they necessarily influence—if they do not restrict—the participation of subordinates. Because of their possible status influence, managers often choose to restrict their early comments to providing information and hold their own ideas and suggestions for the end of the discussion.

Seek and respond to feedback from group members. One of the purposes of meeting in groups is to get the ideas of all the people. When members do not volunteer information and opinions, the leader may need to ask for them.

Clarify, summarize, and evaluate contributions of group members. The leader must move the group toward its goal. Clarifying vague or confusing contributions and summarizing the discussion can help do that. Further, leaders may find it necessary to make some judgments about contributions of group members. Is the information irrelevant or to the point? Is it accurate? Are there exceptions to the conclusions drawn?

Draw consensus. Often groups "talk around" a subject without reaching any common agreement, or consensus, on what should be done. A meeting leader can help a group formulate consensus by restating general areas of agreement. If a summary statement does not accurately represent the thinking of the group, someone will say so. Summarizing to see if consensus has been reached provides for several things: a summary for the record; a starting point for subsequent discussions; and, for participants, a sense that they accomplished something in the meeting.

Maintenance or Social Functions

Provide a supportive climate. Supporting group members does not necessarily mean agreeing with everything they say. Support means that group members are accepted, respected, and allowed to have opinions that differ from those of the rest of the group. (See Chapter 4 for other ways to provide a supportive atmosphere.) Insist that conflict be restricted to controversy over ideas and never be allowed to develop about the participants. Minimize your own evaluation of participants' contributions—that is, avoid such language as "I agree," "I disagree," "You're right," or "You're wrong." Further, group leaders can offer positive reinforcement: "That shows a lot of thought"; "Thanks for adding to the discussion"; "That's an idea we'll have to consider."

Encourage participation. Group members need to feel that they are a part of the group. The group, in turn, needs the ideas of all its members. Some managers fail to recognize and use the individual strengths of their group members. As a leader, you need all the resources you can muster. Who is the idea person in your group? Who is the technical expert? Who knows about budgeting? Who can handle conflict? Once you determine what your group members have to offer, use their talents.

Leaders who wish broad participation by group members can increase that participation in a number of ways. The most obvious way is to ask for it. *Open-ended questions* to members who have not previously contributed are particularly useful. "How would you respond to Jerry's comment?" is an example of an open-ended question. "Do you agree?" would be closed (the possible answers are *limited* to either "yes" or "no") and not likely to get much information from the group member. A word of caution: beware of embarrassing a shy, unprepared person through the questions you ask. Make your questions broad enough that even an unprepared participant can respond.

You also encourage participation from group members by listening to their contributions and by the nonverbal communication that says "I'm willing to listen." Sometimes you may need to insist that everyone has an opportunity to speak on an issue before an individual may speak a second time.

Another way to increase the participation of group members is to ask individuals to come to the meeting prepared to discuss a specific issue or provide information on a given project or proposal. By giving them advance notice, you give them an opportunity to do their homework and organize their thoughts.

Finally, you can increase participation by minimizing your own status in the group. Where you—as leader—sit, the number and kinds of comments you make, your willingness to allow disagreement, and your praise or censure of the ideas and opinions of others will affect the extent to which group members participate and whether their contributions reflect their true position on the issues.

Encourage diversity of opinion. Only through examining a wide range of options can a group make an informed decision. You must be careful to provide opportunities for disagreement as well as agreement. Questions are sometimes useful in getting diverse opinions.

Manage conflict. Sometimes disagreements arise in groups because of personal differences; at other times they grow out of conflict on substantive issues such as organizational goals, policies and procedures, or resource allocation. Not all conflict is necessarily bad, however. It can sometimes stimulate a group toward greater productivity. The challenge is to manage the conflict toward accomplishing the group's goals.

People typically deal with conflict in several different ways. Some prefer to ignore it or deny its legitimacy. When conflict arises, they use stopgap measures such as changing the subject, introducing humor, or adjourning the meeting. These methods resolve few problems. Other common ways to handle conflict include the power play and compromise. In the first alternative, either the leader or another high-status figure makes a unilateral decision in favor of one of the conflicting parties: "Joe's plan is best." This action can result in the withdrawal of the "losing" side from any further discussions or meetings. Compromise, on the other hand, may result in neither side's being satisfied. If production wants to paint the safety equipment white and management wants to paint it red, neither is likely to be happy with a shocking pink.

A useful strategy for handling conflict in a meeting is to take time to clarify the points at issue and work toward some common agreement among participants. The following strategies will not guarantee a resolution to all conflicts, but they will give you some ideas about ways to make the situation better.

Strategies for Handling Conflict

- Openly recognize that a conflict exists.
- Summarize points on all sides. Summary will help clarify the major points at issue.
- Begin with the areas in which participants agree.
- Restrict the discussion to one point of conflict at a time.
- Insist that discussion be issue-centered and not person-centered.
- Demand respectful responses.
- Ask other participants for opinions, but do not encourage them to choose sides.
- Work toward a resolution that enables all sides to "win" and maintain a sense of pride.
- Do not, as the leader, take a position unless it is to point out a policy or precedent.

Control disruptive behavior. When one or more group members continually dominate the discussion, interrupt others who are talking, demonstrate aggressive behavior, or persist in making irrelevant comments, the leader must step in and get the discussion on track. Sometimes leaders are more effective dealing with disrupters *outside* the group setting. You may, for example, have a frank talk with the disrupter about the behavior and its impact on the group; or you may have the person listen to an audio tape of the meeting. If possible, a video tape is even better since it shows the reactions of other participants. Most often, however, leaders find it necessary to handle disruptive behavior *during* the meeting. If your persuasive tactics are ineffective, you may find the following strategies for controlling disruptive behavior useful:

Strategies for Controlling Disruptive Behavior

- Give a "stop signal" either verbally ("Thank you for that point; now let's move to the next item on the agenda") or nonverbally (hold up your hand as a stop sign).
- Put the disrupter on your immediate right and recognize him or her minimally.
- Give the disrupter a job to do—minutes to keep, a subcommittee to chair. Often disrupters need status.
- Reinforce positive contributions by disrupters. Give recognition to their ideas when those ideas add to the discussion; ignore them when they detract. Cut into overlong or irrelevant discussions as tactfully as possible and suggest holding the comments for later.

Whatever approach you use, remember your responsibility to be respectful and courteous. You must control the disruption, but handle it in as nonthreatening a way as possible for the person involved.

The Role of the Participant

Participants have ethical as well as job-related responsibilities in meetings to accomplish the task and to contribute to a positive interpersonal climate. Sometimes, particularly in nondirective groups, they also assume leadership responsibilities. Therefore, the principles of leadership frequently apply to the participants. Specific *member responsibilities* include the following.

Complete the Task.

Participants have as great an obligation as the leader to accomplish the group task. Group members should be on time to meetings, follow procedures, seek consensus, share leadership functions when appropriate, and contribute to the supportive interpersonal climate necessary for completing the task.

Be Prepared.

Participants should come to meetings with the information they need for accomplishing the task. Sometimes this preparation means reading reports; sometimes it means systematizing records; sometimes it means running computer programs and preparing comprehensive projections. Preparation done before the meeting usually affects the quality of the decision made in the meeting.

Participate Meaningfully.

Group members not only have an obligation to do their homework; they also need to share their information, ideas, and opinions in the group. Group members should actively encourage others to contribute thoughtful and relevant information and ideas that will move the discussion forward.

Be Open-Minded.

Sometimes, as a result of preparation, position in the organization, or the need to protect their own territory, participants close their minds to the ideas of others. The dogmatic participant can undermine a meeting's effectiveness as surely as the dogmatic leader. An unwillingness to be open-minded toward others' positions often reflects a general unwillingness to listen. Meeting participants should practice active listening skills and work toward understanding others' positions.

Be Issue-Oriented.

Sometimes a participant's lack of knowledge hampers effective group work; more often, it is interpersonal conflict that undermines the group's goals. If participants are committed to staying on the subject, restricting their disagreements to the issues, and letting their own personal grievances and agendas play a secondary role in the meeting, then they will be more productive group members.

SUMMARY

This chapter has suggested that both the designated meeting leader and the participants have responsibilities for managing the meetings they attend. Specifically, the chapter has focused on leadership styles and on responsibilities of both leader and participants in meetings.

Though personal traits are by themselves inadequate as an indicator of leadership, there are some common indentifiable characteristics that most leaders share, including intelligence, achievement, dependability, participation, and status. Just as all leaders do not have all of the same personal characteristics, they manage the groups for which they are responsible in different ways. For one thing, the leadership styles vary widely. Some managers demand a high degree of group control and are usually most comfortable with an authoritative or bureaucratic leadership style. Others, who like more group involvement, prefer a participative or nondirective approach. Good leaders are able to adapt their management style *to the situation,* or they choose to work in environments conducive to their preferred style of leading.

Leaders have responsibility for planning and conducting the meeting. Planning includes determining the meeting goal; determining participants; preparing and distributing the agenda and other relevant materials; arranging facilities; and providing for the record and for evaluation.

In conducting meetings, leaders have some responsibilities that relate directly to the task and some that are more socially oriented. Task responsibilities are to state meeting goal; clarify procedure; provide information, ideas, suggestions; seek and respond to feedback; clarify, summarize, evaluate; and draw consensus. Social or maintenance functions are to provide a supportive climate; encourage participation; encourage diversity of opinion; manage conflict; and control disruptive behavior.

Participants also have an obligation to make the meetings they attend successful. Group members should be prepared, participate meaningfully, be open-minded, and focus on the issues, not people. Leaders and group members who wish to improve their meetings must diagnose the major problem areas and set out an action plan for dealing with them. This chapter has provided some practical suggestions they may use.

EXERCISES

1. On a scale of 1 to 5 (5 being the highest), how do you rate yourself on the personal characteristics of intelligence, achievement, dependability, participation, and status? Ask three people who know you well to rate you on those areas. What are your strengths? Weaknesses? What can you do in groups to improve your leadership potential?

2. Using the descriptions of the four leadership styles, are you most comfortable with the authoritarian, bureaucratic, democratic, or nondirective approach? Ask three people who know you well how they would characterize your leadership. What can you do to overcome the weaknesses of your "typical" style? How can you build on its strengths?

3. Using the description of the four leadership styles, which style of leader would you *not* like to work with? Why? (You have probably just described your own typical style and its major weaknesses.)

4. Prepare a form that you might use for evaluating leadership, participation, and group process in the meetings you attend.

5. Using the form you have prepared, evaluate a meeting you participate in.

6. Based on your evaluation, prepare an action plan for improving future meetings.

7. Conduct a problem-solving meeting in class. (See Chapter 7 for problem-solving model.) Use a current event topic or a school-related problem. Designate the topic and the leader at least one week in advance of the meeting. The leader should fulfill all the responsibilities for planning and conducting the meeting described in this chapter. The participants should also fulfill their responsibilities. Student observers and/or the instructor should evaluate the meeting (see Exercise 4).

Suggested Readings

Bass, Bernard M. *Stogdill's Handbook of Leadership: A Survey of Theory and Research,* rev. ed. New York: Free Press, 1981.

A comprehensive survey of leadership theory and research, this revised edition of the standard reference work on leadership goes beyond a review to synthesize research findings.

Hersey, Paul, and Ken Blanchard. *Management of Organizational Behavior,* 4th ed. Englewood Cliffs, N.J.: Prentice-Hall, 1982.

The Hersey-Blanchard model is widely used in management training programs. See Chapter 4 for a short though excellent review of leadership theory and research.

Hunt, James G., and Lars L. Larson (eds.). *Leadership: The Cutting Edge.* Carbondale, Ill.: Southern Illinois University Press, 1977.

This compilation of papers from a 1976 Southern Illinois University symposium examines both theoretical and empirical directions in leadership. See Chapter 2, "Theories and Measures of Leadership: A Critical Appraisal of Current and Future Directions," by Chester A. Schriesheim and Steven Kerr for a critique of the contingency model, Fred E. Fiedler's rejoinder, and Schriesheim and Kerr's response.

Kanter, Rosabeth Moss. "Dilemmas of Participation." *National Forum* (Spring 1982): 16–23.

The author gives insight into the issues involved in implementing participatory management. She offers helpful lessons founded on documented theory.

Pagel, Larry. "Parliamentary Procedure for Office Personnel." *Journal of Business Education* (March 1982): 240–42.

The author gives a brief list of what should be included in the minutes and the usual order of business in most meetings. A sample of minutes is included.

Tuttle, Thomas C. "Measuring Productivity and Quality of Working Life." *National Forum* (Spring 1982): 5–7.

This article discusses the use of employee participation to produce better decisions and an improvement in the quality of the working life. Such improvements affect productivity. The article is documented for additional sources.

Zelko, Harold P. *The Business Conference: Leadership and Participation.* New York: McGraw-Hill, 1969.

This is an excellent book, with useful suggestions for conference leaders in improving the meetings they hold.

CORPORATE SPEECHES AND PRESENTATIONS

4

Public Relations and Corporate Advocacy

9

Whether you are a lawyer, a physician, a teacher, or a businessperson, part of your job will be public relations. Even if your organization has a public relations department, you will have an obligation to establish and maintain goodwill for your business or profession. *In your public relations role, you try to communicate a positive image of your organization or profession.*

In addition to public relations responsibilities, you sometimes need to be an advocate; that is, you may be called on to (1) make a case for your organization's (or profession's) policies, and/or (2) debate public policy issues that affect your organization (such as nuclear energy, environmental issues, or government regulations). *As an advocate, you confront your organization's critics with argument.*

This chapter focuses on public relations and advocacy as they apply to the corporation. Specifically, it describes the public's generally negative view of American business, the multiple audiences corporations must address, and the media and the communication strategies useful for public relations and advocacy. Most of the material presented here also applies to not-for-profit organizations and to the professions.

The Corporate Image

Public opinion surveys show that confidence in big business has declined dramatically in the last two decades. Whereas over half the American people had a positive image of business in the 1960s, by the 1980s that number dropped to approximately 25 percent.[1]

The loss of credibility reflects a growing debate over whether or not American business policies and practices are ethically responsible—that is, do they serve the public good? Media coverage of offshore oil spills, nuclear plant accidents, and strip mining in scenic mountain ranges has raised public awareness of the impact of business practices on the quality of life in the United States. The sheer size of the larger companies has bred skepticism and distrust of corporate motives. A growing consumerism movement has

---

1. The Opinion Research Corporation, cited in David M. Liff, Mary O'Connor, and Clarke Bruno, *Corporate Advertising: The Business Response to Changing Public Attitudes* (Washington, D.C.: Investor Responsibility Research Center, October, 1980), pp. 3–4.

encouraged strong reactions to shoddy products and misleading advertising. Robert E. Kirby, chairman of Westinghouse Electric Corporation, described the image problem this way:

> This hostility is real. College professors don't love us. The news media don't trust us. The government doesn't help us. Some special interest groups wish we weren't around. And each of these creates an ever expanding ripple of hostility—professors to their students, citizens' groups to the government, government to the news media and the media to the general public.[2]

Organizations that wish to build a positive image need to do two things. First, they must make sure their policies and practices are sound *(actions)*. Next, they need to develop public relations and advocacy campaigns designed to influence public perception of who and what they are *(messages)*. Sometimes these campaigns simply provide information. At other times, they seek to correct public misconceptions about the corporation. In either case, they should not mislead. We believe that both public relations personnel and corporate spokespersons have a responsibility to be fair and honest. Communication that misrepresents is unethical, and we neither advocate nor condone it.

Johnson and Johnson's handling of the 1982 Tylenol poisonings provides a useful example—it has generally been perceived as a socially responsible and highly credible corporate response to an image problem. As Jerry Knight of the *Washington Post* put it, "Johnson and Johnson has effectively demonstrated how a major business ought to handle a disaster."[3] To preserve what the *Wall Street Journal* called its "carefully nurtured image of responsibility and quality," Johnson and Johnson followed the action-message model described above. Their actions included reviewing the Tylenol capsule's manufacture and distribution, taking the capsule off the market, and offering to substitute Tylenol tablets for capsules already purchased. Their message, which made no attempt to disguise the seriousness of the problem, cast the product and the company as victims. James E. Burke, Johnson and Johnson Chairman, summarized the argument: "People just don't blame us. They feel we are being victimized just like anyone else. It could have been anyone else."[4]

Johnson and Johnson's strategy is not the one every corporation under attack should necessarily follow. Public relations personnel and corporate advocates can learn, however, from the Tylenol example. First, an action-message strategy is useful *if* actions and messages are perceived to be consistent with each other. Second, a

2. Cited in Liff, O'Connor, and Bruno, *Corporate Advertising,* p. 13.
3. Jerry Knight, "How to Cope with a Crisis," in the *Boston Globe,* October 12, 1982.
4. "Growing Headache: Tylenol's Maker Tries to Regain Good Image in Wake of Tragedy," *Wall Street Journal,* October 8, 1982.

candid, compassionate approach helps build credibility for the company and its message. Third, the situation, and also the audience and media, will influence the choice of the most useful approach. Finally, a knowledge of available communication strategies and their advantages and disadvantages will be helpful in making wise public relations and advocacy decisions. We will now turn our attention to those issues.

Effective public relations and advocacy require special attention to audience analysis. Who are the various internal and external publics to be addressed? What are their attitudes toward the organization and its activities? The following discussion identifies who the corporation's publics are and suggests problems peculiar to dealing with each of them.

CUSTOMERS

Every corporation has customers or clients. Though they differ widely (depending on the product or service the corporation is offering), most customers are looking for the same thing: the highest quality at the best possible price. They also expect to be treated fairly, kindly, and pleasantly.

The public relations task in dealing with customers is to create as positive an image as possible of the corporation and its products and services. The advocate must defend the organization's policies. Customers are particularly sensitive to any conflict between corporate profits and their own benefit. Therefore, both public relations and advocacy need to focus on customer satisfaction, product quality, and corporate responsibility. Sears's slogan, "Satisfaction Guaranteed," is a direct customer appeal. Similarly, in television commercials for his company, Chrysler president Lee Iacocca has stressed the automotive industry's renewed interest in product quality. An example of an emphasis on corporate responsibility is Arco's miniparks program in urban ghettos, which its former president, Thornton Bradshaw, widely publicized.[5]

STOCKHOLDERS

Stockholders naturally have a primary interest in a corporation's profits. Some, however, are also concerned about ethical implications of corporate decisions. At least one major university has formed a faculty and administration committee to investigate ethical issues and make recommendations for acquiring, selling, and voting corporate stocks. An advertisement that appeared in a

5. See Thornton F. Bradshaw, "Corporate Social Concern: Measurements and Priorities," speech delivered to American Marketing Association's International Conference, Los Angeles, Calif., June 9, 1976 (reprint available from Atlantic Richfield Company).

Figure 9.1

Annually, Georgetown University is asked to exercise its proxy at the stockholders' meetings of corporations in which the University has an investment. In order to advise the University in this matter, the Board of Directors established the University Committee on Investments and Social Responsibility. Anyone wishing to express an opinion on voting of the University's proxies is invited to state their position(s) in a letter addressed to the Committee, in care of George R. Houston, Jr., Vice President and Treasurer, Ryan Administration Building, Georgetown University, Washington, D.C. 20057.

A list of the corporations in which the University held investments, along with the issues identified by the Investor Responsibility Research Center and the dates of the annual meeting, are as follows:

CORPORATION	ISSUE	DATE
AT&T	Nuclear weapons production Political contributions	April 21
American Cyanamid	Drug sales abroad Pesticide exports	April 20
American Home Products	Drug sales abroad Secret ballot Implement infant formula code	April 21
Atlantic Richfield	Disclose Chilean investment Plant closings	May 4
Chase Manhattan	Energy loan program	April 20
Citicorp	No loans to South Africa	April 20
Consolidated Edison	No nuclear plants Lifeline rates	May 17
Du Pont	Nuclear weapons production	May 3
Exxon	Disclose Chilean investment	May 13
General Electric	Plant closings Genetic engineering Nuclear weapons production Nuclear exports Nuclear weapons	April 28
General Motors	Plant closings	May 21
Gulf	No new investment in Angola Stop funds to Angolan government for SWAPO support	May 11
IBM	Withdraw from South Africa EEO Report	April 26
Lockheed	No trade with Communists	May 11
McDonnell Douglas	Secret Ballot	April 26
Marathon Oil	Corporate takeovers	May 6
Merck	Drug sales abroad	April 27
Mobil	Overseas investment criteria Corporate takeovers	May 6
Monsanto	Economic conversion	April 26
Northern States Power	Renewable energy sources	May 26
Pfizer	Drug sales abroad	April 22
Philip Morris	Tobacco sales abroad	April 28
Phillips Petroleum	Get out of uranium business	April 27
RCA	EEO report Appoint ombudsman	May 4
R. J. Reynolds	Tobacco sales abroad	April 28
Sears	No loans to South Africa	May 17
Shearson American Express	No loans to South Africa	withdrawn
Squibb	Drug sales abroad Comply with Sullivan principles	April 28
Standard Oil of California	Get out of uranium business	May 4
Superior Oil	No investment in Namibia	withdrawn
Union Carbide	Pesticide exports	April 28

campus newspaper (see Fig. 9.1) indicates the issues these stockholders are raising. As an advocate, therefore, you may need to justify your organization's investments and activities to stockholders.

Stockholders need and demand accurate information. Yet they want to hear good news. Both public relations and advocacy messages, which aim at encouraging future investment, must adapt to these potentially conflicting demands.

EMPLOYEES

Employees are interested in all kinds of things. They *want* company news—who is being promoted, how the company is doing financially, what new products or services are being marketed. Employees also *need* information from the organization: What are their sick leave, retirement, and insurance benefits? What additional benefits or services such as day care, housing subsidies, or transportation pools are available? What procedures do they follow to do their work, file grievances, or make suggestions? Employers have a legal responsibility to communicate certain information to employees. They can also improve both productivity and morale through sharing task-related and personal information.

Both public relations and advocacy problems may arise because some of the information you send will be negative. Particularly when your company cuts back production, lays off workers, or freezes wages and benefits, your messages will not be welcome. The challenge for public relations is to present bad news credibly. While you stress employee benefits in internal communication, an effort to conceal or ignore facts will fail. Eventually the employees will discover the bad news, and your credibility will have been destroyed.

In your role as advocate, you must do your best to emphasize positive aspects of a situation. What opportunities exist for employees in the changes that are being made? What benefits can they realize from a potentially negative situation? The advocate faces the challenge of fairly justifying the company's changes in policy.

MASS MEDIA

The mass media (radio, television, newspapers) focus on news. What they most often consider newsworthy about business, however, is usually controversial (layoffs, mergers, profits) or disastrous for someone (mine explosions, nuclear leaks, oil spills). Since the mass media play a large part in determining the opinion of the general public, the resulting image for business is often negative. The public relations task is to improve this negative image. The corporate advocate counters or disproves charges, or defends the organization's position.

In your public relations dealings with the mass media, you try to build a positive image for your company by (1) *initiating news stories that reflect favorably on the company,* (2) *making the facts about your company available to the media* (except for confidential data such as the formula for a product), and (3) *clarifying distortions of information reported.* One way to get favorable attention for your corporation is to prepare press releases and ask for coverage of human-interest items and events. Special talents, achievements, or interests of employees may fill an empty spot on the local television news or in the daily newspaper. Information on new products (especially if you stress their innovativeness or consumer benefits) may also get mass media attention.

In addition to getting favorable attention for the corporation, your public relations job is to provide information that will clarify distortions or counter misrepresentations in mass media reporting. The best approach is preventive. Provide reporters with complete information *before* news stories are written. When stories about your corporation are published or aired, *follow them up.* Provide additional material to clarify any distortions and, when necessary, ask for corrections or retractions. Figure 9.2 provides an excellent example of countering media news with information. Examine the statement carefully. What major point is it trying to make? How do you respond? Do the "facts" cited adequately refute the television station's claims ("hatchet job")? What does the term "hatchet job" mean to you? Is that an effective approach to use? Is it an ethical approach to use?

UNIONS

Union/company confrontation is rooted in conflicting views of how to achieve the corporate goal of profit and the employees' goals of higher wages and better benefits. When formally bargaining with unions, the corporate advocate must build a case for the company position and counter arguments made by the union. In large organizations, special negotiators (often attorneys) present that case. In smaller companies, the president or another administrative officer may have the responsibility to represent the company in formal negotiations.

SPECIAL-INTEREST GROUPS

Groups that have special interests (religious activists, environmentalists, etc.) will sometimes be your "public." Because these groups are usually very vocal about their likes and dislikes, and often get good media coverage, they can influence the general public's image of your corporation. You may not need to make any special public relations or advocacy efforts with those groups that like your company. When special-interest groups do not like it, however, you should try to minimize press attention. One strategy some companies use is to keep a low profile; they publicly ignore the charges made against them. That strategy can be very risky,

Figure 9.2 This ad appeared in the *New York Times* on March 3, 1976.

What ever happened to fair play?

WNBC-TV's recent series on gasoline prices was inaccurate, unfair, and a disservice to the people.

Like a lot of folks in the New York Channel 4 viewing area, we tuned in the local news show a few days ago to catch Liz Trotta's highly promoted five-part series on the price of gasoline. The show—it was hardly news—left us dismayed, concerned, and angry.

For many years now, we've engaged in a running commentary on how energy news is reported, especially on television. Generally, we've given the media credit for objectively attempting to tell a complicated story, and we've said so publicly on occasion. Sometimes they made mistakes, which we tried to correct. Fair enough.

But what we saw on the Liz Trotta segment of the WNBC-TV Evening News for five nights running really shook our confidence that objectivity is of paramount concern to some journalists. We saw a parade of warmed-over distortions, half-truths, and downright untruths marching across the screen like an army of tired ghosts—ghosts we thought had been laid to rest two years ago. Ghosts that made us wonder whether, in an election year and with various proposals to break up the oil companies rapidly becoming a campaign issue, WNBC-TV hadn't made a conscious decision to actively help those politicians who are busily running against the oil industry.

On a show-by-show basis, let's compare the facts with what Liz Trotta, her script writers, and WNBC-TV sent into your living room.

Monday: *The embargo through a dirty looking glass.*

HATCHET JOB: **At the outset, Ms. Trotta referred to "the rather vague circumstances that surrounded the Arab oil embargo back in 1973."**

FACT: There wasn't anything "vague" about the embargo. The Arab nations made a simple, straightforward decision to use oil as a political weapon and they cut off supplies to certain countries, including the U.S. We hope Liz Trotta knew this. If she didn't, her research was shoddy. Apparently she preferred to create an aura of mystery and conspiracy around a straightforward set of circumstances.

HATCHET JOB: **After stock footage of the gasoline lines that followed the embargo, Ms. Trotta asked: "How did we ever get into such a bind?" Her answer: "It all started in October of 1973."**

FACT: Sorry, Ms. Trotta, but it all started well before 1973. On August 7, 1967, for example, Mobil told Interior Secretary Udall, in the context of an oil import program then under discussion, that domestic production would become increasingly important . . . "not only for national security reasons . . . but also as a deterrent against potentially irresponsible price demands on the part of foreign producing governments." On May 11, 1972, in a message in *The New York Times*, Mobil said: "By 1985, Americans will be consuming twice as much energy as they do today, according to government forecasts . . . The problem is, no one can be sure how the U.S. will be able to get the additional energy needed . . ."

The oil companies didn't delay the Alaska pipeline, or set the policies that crimped natural gas supply, or prohibit drilling off the East Coast, or decree a moratorium on production off the West Coast. The government did. And all these things happened well before 1973. And the oil companies warned that, taken together, they could prove disastrous.

HATCHET JOB: **One of Ms. Trotta's guests stated that the crisis was a "rip-off," and that the oil companies "taught" the Organization of Petroleum Exporting Countries how to raise their prices.**

FACT: Aside from the fact that no oil company spokesman on the show was asked to rebut this particularly nasty attack, the fact remains that a few years ago, when Mideast oil sold for about $2.00 a barrel, the oil companies earned about 35 cents on each barrel produced. Today, with Middle East oil selling for over $11.50 a barrel, industry profits on this oil are averaging just under 20 cents a barrel. Since when is a 15-cent-a-barrel profit reduction a rip-off?

The truth is that OPEC—sovereign nations, not companies—unilaterally raised the price of crude oil.

HATCHET JOB: **"There were reports," said Ms. Trotta, "that tankers loaded with millions of gallons of oil were waiting offshore in New York Harbor." This statement was accompanied by pictures of tankers at sea, leaving the inference that these tankers were among the ones doing the "waiting"—for higher prices, presumably.**

FACT: Of all the embargo-spawned nonsense, the tanker rumor was the most vicious and ridiculous. But it keeps popping up, in spite of the documentation provided by the Coast Guard, the captain of New York Harbor, and William Simon, who was head of the Federal Energy Office at the time. All conducted investigations and stated on the record that tanker traffic was normal for that time of year. WNBC-TV must have been aware that this whole tanker story was false.

HATCHET JOB: **Another of Ms. Trotta's visiting "experts" opined that if the oil industry had produced more gasoline in the first six months of 1972, the embargo could have been avoided.**

FACT: The truth is, there is absolutely no correlation between gasoline production in early 1972 and events a year and a half later. As we've already pointed out, made-in-Washington energy decisions *really* made the embargo as effective as it was.

If the Alaska pipeline had been built on schedule, it would have been moving 1.2 million barrels of oil a day into the American market during the embargo. If we had been allowed to develop the Santa Barbara leases, and if there hadn't been a virtual moratorium on offshore leasing for about two years, U.S. production could have been higher by about 400,000 barrels a day. If nuclear power plants had been built, and if coal hadn't been restrained as a fuel for power plants, there would have been a saving of 700,000 barrels a day of liquid fuels used to generate electricity. These factors, when coupled with the auto emission control devices that increased gasoline consumption by about 300,000 barrels a day, added up to about the number of barrels this country was short during the embargo.

Tuesday: *Confusing the past with the present.*

In her "opening monologue," Ms. Trotta rightly pointed out that a dealer's price reflects his rent, his federal taxes, his local taxes. These factors were never mentioned again, as she went into a pitch about the oil industry's "generous tax benefits and tremendous government influence, not only in Washington but in most capitals of the world."

FACT: The show kept harking back to 1911, and the days of John D. Rockefeller. Even when Ms. Trotta purported to be reporting in the present tense, she came on like ancient history. How can one reconcile "generous tax benefits" with major oil companies' loss of the depletion allowance—still permitted *other* extractive industries? Or with the cutback in foreign tax credits—again, only for oil companies? Moreover, the oil industry is the only one in the nation still under the price controls initiated back in 1971—another fact Ms. Trotta never mentioned. And where's the vaunted political clout of an industry that's had its prices rolled back, is fighting divestiture at home, and watching its properties become nationalized overseas?

HATCHET JOB: **In the same rapid-fire monologue, Ms. Trotta listed the profits earned by Mobil and other companies in the last quarter of 1975.**

FACT: Ms. Trotta didn't even attempt to explain what those numbers represented, either as a rate of return on invested capital, or as a return on the shareholders' investment. She simply implied they were too high. (In Mobil's case, profits represent 1.5 cents on every gallon of petroleum sold in our worldwide operations.) Reciting numbers alone, we submit, is an exercise in deliberate distortion, unless they're put into context. She didn't mention that in 1975, the aggregate earnings of 25 leading oil companies fell 23.6 percent from 1974 levels.

HATCHET JOB: **Ms. Trotta said that the *seven* largest oil companies produce "39.8 percent of all domestic crude oil. They account for 44 percent of the oil refined domestically, and they market 44.8 percent of all gasoline sold in this country. Critics say the consumer pays for all that concentration . . ."**

FACT: All what concentration, Ms. Trotta? You counted up to seven, and you still didn't reach 50 percent of any single market. Last time we looked, there were only *three* major television networks, and they controlled about 75 percent of their market. However, we would be the first to admit that the television viewer would be worse off if every local station had to produce its own TV shows.

The truth is, there are more than 8,000 companies engaged in oil production, some 130 in refining, and about 15,000 in wholesale marketing.

HATCHET JOB: **Ms. Trotta asked several motorists why gasoline prices varied from place to place. While most of those shown said they didn't know, one asked her if *she* did.**

FACT: Point is, Ms. Trotta *does* know. She herself had cited the big reasons for differing prices when she opened the show: different tax structures in different communities, different rents, and different competitive situations. And, in some cases, distances from a refinery. But Ms. Trotta chose to treat the subject like a deep, wicked conspiracy.

HATCHET JOB: **Asked Ms. Trotta: "If there's a surplus of oil, then why hasn't the price of gasoline gone down?"**

FACT: It has, by about two cents a gallon in recent months. This reflects competition in the marketplace, plus the rollback of the average price of domestic crude, and the disappearance of the $2 import duty. Besides, gasoline is selling today at below government-set ceiling prices, because of competitive conditions in the marketplace.

Interestingly enough, in reeling off the prices, she cited an "independent" as being the lowest of all. Weren't they the fellows the "majors" were driving out of business? If so, how come the independents have substantially *increased* their share of the market over the last eight years, largely at the expense of the majors? And why didn't Ms. Trotta point out that fact? Besides, under federal law, it's impossible to unilaterally stop supplying any independent.

Of course, no discussion of pricing can overlook, as Ms. Trotta did, the fact that almost 40 percent of America's oil comes from foreign sources, at prices set by foreign governments.

HATCHET JOB: **Said Ms. Trotta: "The objective, then, is to sell as much gasoline as possible to keep the high-profit refining operation going."**

FACT: What high profit? Mobil's U.S. refining and marketing operations actually *lost* money in 1974 and only began to break even in 1975.

Wednesday: *Two sides to every story?*

HATCHET JOB: **In this segment, Ms. Trotta attempted to show that the big companies are pushing their dealers around—she calls the gasoline dealer "a small businessman under siege." After talking to two of them, including a Mobil dealer, she concludes that one hears "the same sorry complaints throughout the metropolitan area. Dealers aren't making it. The major oil companies . . . simply won't allow them to make a decent profit. The dealers say they are caught in a vise controlled by the oil companies."**

FACT: There are thousands of dealers in the Channel 4 viewing area. Certainly, some of them must be making a decent living. But there's no way to find out from Liz Trotta's show. She talked to a few dealers with gripes, and from her tiny sampling—apparently hand-fed to her by various dealer "spokesmen"—she came up with a sweeping generalization. Why didn't she interview some of the dealers who are satisfied with their company arrangements? If she can't find any, we can and will.

According to Platt's Pricing Service, the average dealer mark-up in New York City in February 1976, was 12.2 cents a gallon. In March of 1973, it had been 9.8 cents a gallon.

HATCHET JOB: **Ms. Trotta said that a Mobil dealer claimed he was promised $25,000 to sell Mobil gasoline but the company never came up with the money or signed the contract.**

FACT: Mobil never made such an offer. The money in question was the amount the dealer said competing companies offered him to join them in 1973. (How's that for competition, Ms. Trotta?) In any event, Mobil specifically told him that we had no intention of meeting these offers and that he was free to accept them. The dealer didn't. Moreover, in 1975, he accepted a new Mobil contract, and just recently, that contract was renewed.

Thursday: *More of the same.*

HATCHET JOB: **This one is a beauty, because it involves TV production technique, rather than words alone. Says a dealer: "The only difference between them [oil companies] and the hoodlums in the street is that they don't get caught. They're too big." Then the camera flashes back to an oil company executive, obviously in the midst of a pre-recorded interview, and the first words allowed to come out of his mouth are: "It is true, we're not willing to subsidize an economic loss at a marginal station . . ."**

FACT: The implication is clear. The oil man is made to appear in agreement with the line about "hoodlums." Frankly, nothing in the show made us as angry as that cheap distortion, because it was so patently contrived.

Friday: *Beating the drum for divestiture.*

HATCHET JOB: **At the start of her grand finale, Ms. Trotta said "reformers are trying to pass laws that would break up the big oil companies into smaller units in hopes of making them more competitive and more responsive to consumers."**

FACT: Sure, they're trying to break up oil companies but to call it "reform" is pure bias. What gives her the idea it would in any way help the consumer to break America's large oil companies into small firms limited to exploration and production, or transportation, or refining, or marketing?

The consumer would end up paying more, not less. Suppose, for example, our refineries had to stand alone, as a separate company. Does Liz Trotta really believe that whoever operates them would be content to lose money, or just break even? Obviously, any such operator would have to raise prices.

Happily, not all TV stations subscribe to this view. KNXT-TV, for example, a CBS-owned station in Los Angeles, had this to say in an editorial—which was labeled as such, by the way: "Several of the biggest campaigners have decided to take on the oil companies and preach the gospel that the companies are monopolistic and ought to be broken up. If they're sincere, they're misguided . . . The complaint about monopoly is a joke. You can't find much more intense competition anywhere than when the oil companies bid for leases or bid for retail dollars. The customer benefits. The biggest oil company has less than 10% of the market."

HATCHET JOB: **"The decision on divestiture," Ms. Trotta intones, "will be made in Washington. But legislators find it difficult to obtain information especially since most of it comes from the oil companies themselves." As "proof", the camera showed a hearing conducted by Senator Jackson, in which he roasted an oil company executive who couldn't recite his company's per-share dividends in 1972 and 1973.**

FACT: First, that particular hearing had nothing to do with divestiture. Second, it took place in early 1974 as an outgrowth of the embargo-induced gasoline shortage. Third, many thoughtful people (including some Senators) felt Senator Jackson's inquisitorial grandstanding deplorable, and said so. Fourth, the figures the Senator requested were easily available public information. Moreover, Ms. Trotta didn't see fit to mention the recent hearings held precisely on the divestiture proposals. Mobil's president was just one of many who testified, on all aspects of the issue. But their reasoned words weren't as dramatic, apparently, as Jackson's ancient and unrelated diatribe.

HATCHET JOB: **Said Ms. Trotta: "To several Senate and House committees, the idea of vertical integration has all the earmarks of a conspiracy to monopolize the industry."**

FACT: Never, to our knowledge, has any Senate or House committee stated or claimed what Ms. Trotta alleges. Now, would you believe this: we made several requests to WNBC-TV for documentation as to which committee-adopted reports this charge was supposed to have come from, and we were told by a station spokesperson that it is "official NBC policy *not* to provide any documentation on news items."

HATCHET JOB: **Much of this final segment presented in a most laudatory light a spokesman for a self-styled public interest group, which favors divestiture. Said Ms. Trotta of the group, whose spokesman in a recent Congressional hearing was movie actor Paul Newman: "This is a new and energetic group of young lobbyists, who are determined to take on the powerful oil lobby."**

FACT: Does youthful energy make the difference between a "good" lobbyist and an "evil" one? Come on, Ms. Trotta. Everybody has the right to present his views in Washington, oil companies as well as movie stars. But do Americans *really* want energy policy made in Hollywood?

In fairness to WNBC-TV, we will say that they asked to interview a Mobil spokesman for the Trotta series. In fairness to ourselves, we didn't participate. Experience has shown us how what we say on pre-recorded TV, as contrasted to live, is edited out or watered down. And the treatment accorded to the oil people who *did* appear makes us doubly glad we weren't there. We didn't want to be the ones to appear to "agree" we're hoodlums.

We've written to WNBC-TV about our objections to the Liz Trotta energy series, and we've offered to buy 30 minutes of air time in which to present our side of the story, without any editing. So far, we haven't had any reply. Based on the record, we aren't holding our breath.

What official sources have said about us.

In Liz Trotta's words, "some critics" saw "the look of conspiracy" in the companies' dealings with Arab oil-producing nations.

Well, the oil industry's conduct during the Arab embargo has been looked at microscopically by experts, and in our view, it's Liz Trotta who has tunnel vision. Here's what some official sources had to say after examining our business:

- **From a January 2, 1975, report of the Senate Foreign Relations Subcommittee on Multinational Corporations: "While the Arabs provided explicit instructions on the allocation of their production, the consuming nations provided no coordinated guidance . . . Essentially, U.S. companies decided that 'the pain should be evenly spread' to all major consuming regions . . . During the embargo, the international oil companies acted as a buffer between producer and consumer nations."**
- **From a January 27, 1975, report of the Federal Energy Administration: "U.S. companies helped to blunt the edge of the Arab oil weapon by redistributing global supplies so that the constriction of supplies was fairly evenly allocated."**
- **From a report by independent consultants to the FEA: "Although the Arab production cutbacks were eventually increased to 25%, the impact of the embargo was ameliorated by increased production in non-Arab countries and by the skillful and evenly balanced distribution of available supplies by the major petroleum companies."**
- **From a special report of the Commission of the European Communities (The Common Market): "Thanks to the oil companies, neither Denmark nor Holland suffered any serious supply shortage."**

Mobil

© 1976 Mobil Oil Corporation

however, because people may assume that failing to answer charges is an indication of guilt. If you do decide to confront the special-interest group, build your case on indisputable facts and choose media that will reach both those who have challenged your position and others they may have influenced.

GENERAL PUBLIC

Sometimes you need to build goodwill through the corporate image you present to the general public. At other times you need to argue the company's case. That case may be a defense of controversial policies, or you may seek a change in public policy.

A problem in reaching the larger public is the corporation's limited access to the mass media. Though you may buy advertising space in newspapers and magazines to present the corporation's case, you will have limited opportunity to get your message on radio or television. Because of the constraints imposed by the Fairness Doctrine, which requires balanced programming on public issues, none of the three major networks accept *any* advertising that relates to public policy issues. As demonstrated by the Mobil ad asking for readers' opinions (Fig. 9.3), however, the networks do not always agree on what constitutes public policy advertising.

Media for Corporate Messages

Corporations frequently use media over which they have direct control. Some of these media are appropriate for communication within the organization, others for communicating with people outside the organization.

INTERNAL MEDIA

Organizations use internal media to communicate with their employees. Occasionally, these media also allow employees to communicate upward. Internal media include the following.

Newsletters. The content and layout of newsletters vary widely among organizations. Some newsletters are primarily job-related and focus on such things as work schedules, pension plans, and safety records. Others give attention to items of personal interest such as birthdays, travel plans, and retirements. Many include diverse information ranging from poems by employees to CPR lifesaving techniques.

A company's newsletter is successful to the extent that it accomplishes the purpose for which it is published. Some legitimate purposes are building cohesiveness in the organization, increasing productivity, and stimulating employee investment.

Bulletin boards. Work-related or personal information can be quickly and economically disseminated by means of bulletin boards. They allow organizations to get repeated attention for messages they need to reinforce. Safety campaigns, for example, typically use posters to call attention to the disasters that can result if procedures are ignored. Diagrams of fire escape routes are generally posted.

Bulletin boards are probably successful communication media, when they are read. Managers can increase the probability that subordinates will read posted information by (1) changing the information regularly, (2) keeping the boards uncluttered, (3) including messages that are positive, and (4) posting personal as well as work-related messages.

Figure 9.3 This ad appeared in the *New York Times* on July 17, 1974.

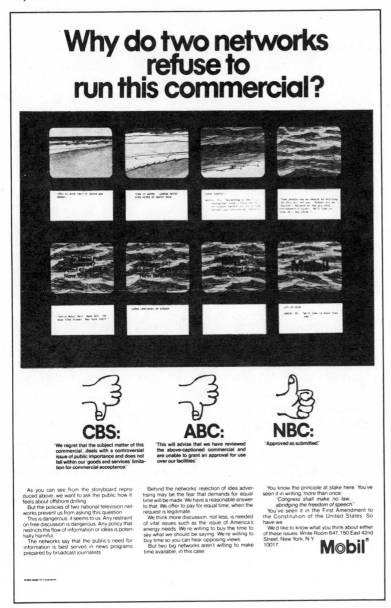

Brochures and flyers. Brochures contain standard information the organization needs to give employees. This information may relate to employee benefits, career development tips, training opportunities, or specific organizational policies. Brochures should be accessible to those who need them.

Flyers are minibrochures enclosed in wage statements or distributed in employee mailboxes. To get attention, flyers should be visually interesting and simply written. They should be distributed only to those who will need or want the information. Otherwise, important messages may be considered "junk mail" and remain unread.

Telephone "hotlines." Most employee communication is initiated by the organization. Someone in management decides what information employees should receive and authorizes brochures, newsletters, or other media to make that information available.

Some companies, however, have installed telephone hotlines that allow employees to ask specific questions about company policy or benefits. These information hotlines are successful to the extent that employees receive precise, accurate, understandable answers quickly.

Some company hotlines also allow employees to bypass formal grievance procedures and make complaints directly to management. This practice is useful when the complaints are forwarded to someone who can take action and when confidentiality is preserved.

EXTERNAL MEDIA

External media allow organizations to send messages to customers, stockholders, and the larger public. Common external media corporations use include the following.

Annual reports. Annual reports differ in content and format from organization to organization. In general, however, they contain a balance sheet, a statement of earnings and expenses, and a discussion of operations.

Originally designed as financial statements for stockholders, annual reports are increasingly read by a larger audience. Accordingly, they are becoming an important public relations tool in many organizations, emphasizing good news—positive sales trends, new products, and happy employees. That strategy not only promotes a positive company image, but may also encourage investment in the company.

Speakers bureaus. One way to get the corporate message to the larger public is to send speakers to civic clubs, college organizations, radio and television talk shows, and other public forums. Some organizations have sophisticated speakers bureaus that identify company spokespersons, investigate speaking opportunities, supply speech materials, provide speaker training, and coordinate speaking engagements. Other speakers bureaus do little more than assign speaking engagements to a few hand-picked executives.

Letters. Letters are a major way organizations communicate with their various external publics. Most often, letters are a means of transmitting information. However, they also serve public relations and advocacy functions. Specifically, companies use personal letters and letters to the editor to explain, defend, and persuade others to accept their positions. They also use them to sell their products and services through direct mail.

All correspondence has a public relations dimension. That is, the material you choose to include in your letters and the way you present that material will either improve the company image or make it worse. Further, you will write some letters specifically for public relations purposes. For example, when you send a congratulatory note to a customer and enclose a favorable news clipping, you are trying to build goodwill. Your long-range goal, however, is probably future sales. You help maintain goodwill with customers through follow-up letters that offer service.

Press releases.   Press releases are one way to gain access to the mass media. To get your press release read and to increase the probability that it will be used, put it in an acceptable form and provide complete information. Proper form means typed, double-spaced material with a heading that includes company name, address, phone number, contact name, and release date. Be sure your material includes what you want to say and what the press will want to know. In other words, answer the traditional journalistic questions (the 5 Ws and H): Who, What, Why, When, Where, and How. Figure 9.4 illustrates a press release.

Figure 9.4. Sample Press Release

```
            CHEMICAL COMPANY OF THE U.S.
                4323 South Plum Street
                Spring Grove, MN 20003
                   (401) 236-2780


Contact: Rea Johnson, Public Affairs        June 30, 1984
------------------------------------------------------------
                 FOR IMMEDIATE RELEASE
------------------------------------------------------------
      Chemical Company of the U.S. announces an $8
billion expansion to its Hollow Ridge plant, scheduled for
completion January 1, 1986.
      Chemical's expansion will make the company the
largest industrial employer in the lakes region. The
expansion will provide jobs for 500 additional skilled
workers and increase the area's annual payroll by $12.5
million.
      Martha Jones, Company President, explained the
decision to expand the Hollow Ridge plant. "We've had
good labor relations here," she said. "Many other cities
actively competed for our new facility, but we have been
pleased with our past performance in Hollow Ridge. We
look forward to many years of continued prosperity in
the lakes region."
```

Be sure to clear your material with the appropriate people within your organization before releasing it to the press. Has the company president or another executive officer cleared the copy? Has the legal department seen it? Is the material consistent with other information the company has distributed? What are the public policy implications of your statement? Is the material timely? Will you cause more or fewer problems by releasing it? Will the press be interested?

Press conferences. At some point in your career, you may represent your organization in a press conference. Or you may be hired to "coach" others to perform well. The following information should help you in either situation.

The press conference is a public interview. The person being interviewed may begin with a short prepared statement, but the focus of the press conference is always on questions and answers. Sometimes press conferences are aired live, as when the president of the United States holds a televised conference or when a public figure is interviewed on "Meet the Press." More often, the press conference is video-taped or covered by print journalists who include segments of the conference or specific quotations in their news stories.

How you present yourself, and the press's choice about what is printed or aired, will reflect on your corporation's image and its position. To increase your effectiveness in press conferences, you need to plan carefully for the interview and pay careful attention to what you do and say in the interview itself.

In planning for the press conference, you should use the following steps. First, write down in a one-sentence statement what you want to accomplish. Second, determine the one point you need to emphasize to accomplish your purpose. That is your message. Third, analyze your two audiences, the press and the public. What kind of story is the press looking for? How can you present your message so that it will make a good story that will "sell"? Are your interviewers likely to agree or disagree with your position? What questions are they likely to ask? What will they *not* ask that you need to talk about? How will the reporter present your message to the public? How will they respond? The fourth step is to set ground rules about appropriate lines of questioning. If that is not possible or desirable, determine which questions you will not answer, and plan an alternative to "No comment." Explain your reasons for not addressing the particular issues raised (they are not germane; the material has legal implications; national security is at stake). The final planning step is to determine which strategies will be most appropriate to get the kind of coverage you want for your message. Should you ignore controversial issues, defend the corporation, or take the offensive? See the following sections on communication strategies for help in determining specific methods to use.

What you say and do *in* the press conference is what ultimately counts. Your planning should have given you some preparation for what to say. Koehler and Sisco have provided the following guidelines.[6]

1. *Begin with the news, then explain:* (a) This is what we have done; (b) this is why we did it.
2. *Answer direct questions directly.* Avoid hedging and evasiveness at all costs.
3. *Don't lie or exaggerate.*
4. *Don't argue with the reporter.* You lose, even if you win. The reporter is going to have the last word where it counts—with the public you are trying to reach.
5. *Don't let the reporter put words in your mouth.* State the case objectively; or deal frankly with the difficulty of answering insinuating or loaded questions.
6. *Don't talk off-the-record.*
7. *Put everything you can in the public context.* A public audience is really interested in the effect of your company's ideas and actions on the public.
8. *Follow up.* Give the reporter a call after the interview to provide the additional information you promised or to clarify a point that may have been slighted in the interview.

Educational materials. A number of organizations counter negative publicity by preparing and distributing educational materials about their company or industry. Some materials are made available to the general public; others are sent to teachers in elementary and secondary schools. Though the practice of distributing corporate materials in the classroom has raised ethical questions among educators and the public alike, companies continue to use the method as a way to gain a hearing for their positions.

Advertising. Probably the most effective way to reach a large audience is through mass media advertising. When the mass media run news stories on your corporation or industry, you have relatively little control over the message. By purchasing advertising time and space, however, you can influence what will be published or aired. Much of your advertising will be to improve the corporation's image. Sometimes, you will buy advertising to defend your corporation's policies, correct misinformation, or protest media treatment of your organization. Kaiser Aluminum's ad "Trial by Television" attempted to do all three things. (See Fig. 9.5.)

If you are debating public policy issues, you will be limited to print media and to "journalistic" interviews on radio and televi-

6. Condensed from Jerry W. Koehler and John I. Sisco, *Public Communication in Business and the Professions* (St. Paul, Minn.: West Publishing Co., 1981), pp. 178–79.

Figure 9.5

Trial by Television

The American system of justice is founded on a simple principle: The accused has the right to be fairly heard in his own defense, and to confront and cross examine his accuser.

This principle, more than any other, defines the difference between freedom and tyranny.

Yet today, here in America, charges are aired before tens of millions of people without fair opportunity for the accused to respond.

They call it "investigative" television journalism. We call it "Trial by Television."

Much of investigative television journalism is solid and responsible reporting—but much is not. Many producers of "news magazine" programs too frequently select story segments with their minds already made up about the points they want to make. Then they proceed to select the facts and quotes which support their case. "Interview" opportunities are sometimes provided the "accused." But the edited "interview" format puts the producer (i.e. the accuser) in full control of deciding what portions, and how much of, the accused's defense the public will be allowed to see.

Rarely does this result in balanced and objective coverage.

The television production team becomes the accuser, judge, and jury. With no real recourse for the accused to get a fair hearing in the court of public opinion. Yet the viewing public is led to believe that the coverage is balanced and objective. This is a deceptive and very dangerous practice.

"Trial by Television," like the kangaroo courts and star chambers of old, needs to be examined. If we decide, as a society, that we are going to try issues, individuals, and institutions on television, then some way must be found to introduce fairness and balance.

Here's what we're doing about it.

Recently, Kaiser Aluminum was the victim of grossly misleading and inaccurate statements on a segment of ABC's "20/20" program. On its "20/20" segment of Thursday, April 3, the announcer accused aluminum house wiring of being unsafe, and Kaiser Aluminum of intentionally marketing an unsafe product. These accusations are blatantly wrong.

Although we were offered an opportunity to be "interviewed," "20/20" reserved the privilege of editing any part of our statement. Any defense we might have made would be subject to their sophisticated editing techniques, and to their commentary. Since it was evident to us that the producers had already formed their opinions, we declined their offer. How can a defense be fair if it is subject to censorship by the accuser?

We have been advised by many to ignore the "20/20" attack on the basis that you can't fight the network, and to prevent further harassment. We will not allow ourselves to be maligned or misrepresented by any group—even television.

Here is what we are doing:
1. We have demanded a satisfactory retraction from ABC-TV.
2. We are asking the Federal Communications Commission, under their "Personal Attack" doctrine, to order ABC-TV to provide us with time and facilities to present our side of the story to the same size audience in a prime time segment.
3. We have asked Congressman Lionel Van Deerlin (D-California), Chairman of the House Sub-Committee on Communications to consider Congressional hearings to examine the implications of this increasingly insidious and dangerous practice.

Here's what you can do about it.

Unfortunately, not all victims of "Trial by Television" have the resources to defend themselves, as we are trying to do. Their only defense is you.

If you believe the rights of the accused to fairly defend themselves are more important than sensational attempts to increase TV ratings; if you believe the right of the public to get balanced and objective information on issues of importance is as important as it has ever been, please speak out and let your elected representatives know.

America was conceived to prevent tyranny by providing checks on the power of any institution. Today, a new power is dispensing its own brand of justice—television. There's only one check against it. You.

If you are upset by the unfairness of "Trial by Television," write your elected representatives, or us at Kaiser Aluminum, Room 1137KB, Lakeside Drive, Oakland, CA 94643.

KAISER ALUMINUM & CHEMICAL CORPORATION

One person can make a difference

WASHINGTON POST
MAY 20, 1980

sion. Such television programs as local talk shows, "Meet the Press," "Sixty Minutes," and "The Today Show" treat policy issues, but whether or not your corporation will be invited to participate is at the discretion of the network or local station. Therefore, corporate advertising in newspapers or magazines may be the only way to get your message to the larger public.

Your public relations problem may be to create an image for a new company or a new product. More often, it is to change the organization's image to a more positive one. Sometimes that means actually renaming the company or product. Usually, however, you develop an information campaign that (1) provides facts about the industry or product, (2) fills a consumer need, or (3) identifies the corporation with something the public regards as positive.

PROVIDING FACTS ABOUT THE INDUSTRY OR PRODUCT

The "providing facts" approach is usually based on one of the following four assumptions:

1. Business has an ethical responsibility to report corporate information to the people whose lives it influences.
2. Providing information gives the corporation a measure of control over its image.
3. Providing information decreases distortion in mass media reporting.
4. If the public has sufficient understandable information, it will revise its negative opinion of your business.

Corporations often use the "providing facts" strategy to confront a negative image problem head-on. Specifically, they release information that disputes or gives a different perspective to the claims of their opponents so as to improve their public image. For example, after the widely publicized chemical seepage at Love Canal, New York, Hooker Chemical president, Donald L. Baeder, made a speech to the Commonwealth Club of California clarifying "facts versus perceptions concerning chemical wastes and chemical waste disposal."[7] Though Proctor and Gamble took Rely tampons off the market after their use had been linked to the deaths of young women, the company continued to wage an information campaign about how the product had been safety-tested. In justifying large profits in a time of energy shortages, oil companies attempted to educate the public about profit margins, oil depletion, and exploration costs.

FILLING A CONSUMER NEED

The second public relations strategy, filling a consumer need, is generally more persuasive than providing facts. You find many examples of this strategy in current business practices: public utilities include energy-saving tips in their monthly bills; grocery chains launch unit pricing information campaigns; oil companies explain how they are preparing for future energy needs. Such approaches have credibility in image building *to the extent that they are consistent with the company's other actions.* Oil compa-

7. Donald L. Baeder, "Chemical Waste: Fact versus Perception," *Vital Speeches* 46 (June 1, 1980): 496.

nies, for example, have been caught in the unenviable position of promoting conservation of gasoline while trying to sell as much of it as possible. Electric power companies have had much the same problem.

IDENTIFYING WITH SOMETHING THE PUBLIC CONSIDERS POSITIVE

Corporations can create an image, or improve their existing one, by relating the organization to some thing or concept that the public considers positive. This positive thing or concept may have no relationship whatever to the company or its products or service. Sperry Corporation, for example, has built its public visibility around the concept of listening; the company's *products* are computers, farm equipment, fluid power systems, and guidance and control equipment. Texaco's role in promoting the Metropolitan Opera, Philip Morris's commitment to the arts, and Arco's public parks program send messages that the companies involved are ethically responsible. By identifying themselves with opera, arts, or public parks, these companies have tried to build a positive image through *association*. Further, they have sidestepped defending themselves against attacks on their policies.

Communication Strategies for Advocacy

How a company responds to attacks and what it does to head off negative publicity will have an important impact on advocacy responsibilities in the organization. Advocates may choose to ignore or withdraw from attacks or they may answer them. Some prefer to anticipate public relations or policy problems and prevent or minimize them *before* they come to public attention. Here are some of the communication strategies advocates may use.

WITHDRAWAL FROM CONFRONTATION

The withdrawal strategy reflects management's preference that the company not debate those charges made against it. The typical "No comment" response is characteristic of the withdrawal strategy. Another response—though rarely stated so bluntly—is "It's none of your (their) business."

Advantages of the withdrawal strategy are that you do not escalate the debate or put your organization "on the record" on a controversial issue. Disadvantages must also be carefully weighed. Not only does "No comment" suggest that you may be guilty, but "It's none of your business" is likely to be interpreted as arrogance. The withdrawal strategy, therefore, can seriously damage the corporation's image—sometimes even more than the specific charges leveled against you. Finally, the withdrawal strategy allows the attacker (special-interest groups, the media, unions) to draw the issues and present its own case unchallenged.

SLEIGHT OF HAND

Just as sleight-of-hand magic tricks depend on focusing audience attention away from the scarf up the sleeve or the false bottom in the box, a sleight-of-hand communication strategy allows company spokespersons to obscure the controversial issue or fact by shifting attention to something else.

Typically, the corporate advocate who uses sleight of hand focuses discussion on a secondary (perhaps even minor) issue or fact. Because it allows the advocate to sidestep indefensible issues, many corporations view the strategy as an advantageous way to deal with hostile publics. The strategy is ethically questionable, however, and fails to justify corporate practices. After the magic tricks are over, the major objections raised about your company will still stand.

CHALLENGING OPPOSING FACTS AND ARGUMENTS

When your organization is attacked, you may choose to challenge or disprove the facts or claims used against you. If you are successful in doing that, the strategy can reinforce the company position. You will probably weaken your attackers' credibility by proving their facts wrong and their arguments unsound. Your own case, moreover, will remain intact.

A critical question is whether you can successfully refute *all* the negative facts or arguments raised about your company. Unless you can, your position may be weakened. Even if you are able to disprove the opponent's entire case, you may not be able to remove the damage to the organization's image caused by the original charges. Finally, you will have difficulty getting your message to all the audiences your critics initially reached.

REDEFINING THE ISSUES

Often the facts your opponents present against your corporation are true and the arguments they raise are sound. If this is the case, you will have difficulty successfully challenging either. You may need to take a closer look at the central issues of the conflict and redefine them from the corporate position. Sometimes that involves exposing questionable assumptions and hidden agendas. It always involves shifting perspective—from that of the challenger to that of the corporation. The following steps are useful for moving the debate from a defensive battle to an offensive, advocacy campaign:

1. Analyze the questions/attacks for the "real" meaning. In other words, what are the real questions being raised by those who are attacking you?

2. Precede your answer by
   a. restating the issue as a content issue. (See Chapter 5, "Listening," for differences between content and feeling messages.)

b. restating the issue to expose underlying assumptions or messages. Most questions have an underlying statement that shows the opinions or position of the questioner. Restate to clarify these.

c. asking questions to clarify issues. Sometimes those questions will need to be very open-ended. Sometimes they will need to be very closed and specific.

3. Expose inconsistencies and false assumptions.

4. Separate multiple questions or issues and respond to them individually.

5. Respond on the content level. Do not allow yourself the luxury of getting angry or attacking the challenger. You will most likely damage your case.

Probably the most important advantage of reframing issues is that it leads to a clearer understanding of the major points at issue. The major disadvantage is that it may serve to polarize the corporation and its publics.

PRESENTING THE COMPANY POSITION

When answering opponents, corporate advocates usually need to present the company case. Not a substitute for challenging facts and arguments or redefining the issues for debate, this strategy adds an important positive dimension to those approaches.

When presenting the company case, follow these steps:

1. Lay out the corporate position point by point.
2. Explain the reasons for the position.
3. Present materials that support your position.
4. Explore the relative advantages and disadvantages of the corporate approach.

Presenting the company case can be an advantageous communication strategy if critics are willing to listen and if you can demonstrate that public benefits of the company's policies outweigh public costs. Be aware that by giving open, honest information, you may be providing your opponents with ammunition for future attacks. Also, as company spokesperson, your credibility may be questioned.

ADOPT A PROACTIVE APPROACH

The communication strategies used in advocacy discussed so far are reactive. That is, they are strategies useful in *responding* (or failing to respond) to attacks made on your corporation. An alternate approach is to *anticipate* public relations or policy questions and try to resolve them before they come under public scrutiny. Here is a five-step approach that takes a more long-range view of public relations and advocacy issues:

1. Anticipate questions raised about your corporation and its policies.
2. Research facts/precedents/implications of policy or position.
3. Develop public relations or advocacy plan:
    a. Determine issues to address.
    b. Determine "audience" to be targeted.
    c. Determine strategy for adapting to audience.
    d. Determine media (budget/time/access constraints).
    e. Develop timetable.
4. Implement plan.
5. Evaluate results (work with professionals to set up useful evaluation plan).

Advantages of the proactive approach are obvious. The image problems you prevent and the arguments you answer before they become points of contention will most likely result in fewer public relations problems for your organization.

SUMMARY

In considering a career in business or the professions, you may not have been aware of the public relations and advocacy responsibilities you would have. Even if your organization has a professional public relations staff and designated speakers to defend its viewpoint, you, as a member of that organization, have an impact on its image.

This chapter has explored the generally negative image the American public has of business and has suggested two ways of improving that image. When the company is attacked by its critics, you may need to go beyond image making to defend or make a case for your organization's policies. In some instances, your organization will actively work to influence public policy. These tasks may call upon your skill as an advocate.

To be effective in public relations or advocacy, you need to know who your "publics" are and how you can adapt to them. You also need to know the internal media available for communicating with employees and the external media for communicating with your other publics.

When your organization or profession is trying to change or develop its image, you can use any of the three public relations communication strategies discussed in the chapter. These are: providing facts about the industry, service, or product; filling consumer need; and identifying with something the public considers positive.

Finally, when your corporation is attacked, you need to choose a communication strategy that will help you accomplish your advocacy goals. This chapter discussed five: withdrawal from confrontation, sleight of hand, challenging opposing facts and arguments, redefining the issues, and presenting the company position. It also suggested a proactive strategy that will help you anticipate and head off attacks before they occur.

Public Relations and
Corporate Advocacy

EXERCISES

1. Find three annual reports in the library. Compare these reports in three areas:
   a. What audiences are they written for?
   b. What kind of public relations material is included?
   c. What advocacy materials do you find?

2. Find a corporation that is or has recently been under attack for some policy. (See *Business Week, New York Times,* etc.) Assume that you are the advocate for the corporation. Design a strategy for meeting the attack. What specific arguments will you need to use? Write a short paper setting out your strategy and your reasons for choosing it.

3. Prepare a five-minute speech defending the corporation you studied in the preceding exercise.

4. Interview a member of a special-interest group about specific policy concerns. How would you as an advocate respond to that interest group?

5. Find three public policy advertisements paid for by corporations or industries. Bring these to class for discussion.

6. Analyze a speech made by a corporate advocate defending the company position.

7. Visit or write to a large corporation to obtain samples of brochures, flyers, newsletters, etc. What audiences are the materials designed for? How do the formats differ? What public relations and advocacy strategies are used?

Suggested Readings

Burger, Chester. "How to Meet the Press." *Harvard Business Review,* July–August 1975, pp. 62–70.
This article includes ten practical guidelines to use when being interviewed by the press.

Cutlip, Scott M., and Allen H. Center. *Effective Public Relations,* 5th rev. ed. Englewood Cliffs, N.J.: Prentice-Hall, 1982.
A standard treatment of public relations, this book treats public relations as a four-step process: fact finding and feedback, planning and programming, action and communication, and evaluation. Chapter 17, "Working with the Media," will be particularly valuable to the advocate. Separate chapters discuss public relations for business; trade associations, professional societies, and labor unions; voluntary agencies; governments and citizens; public schools and higher education.

Douglas, George A. *Writing for Public Relations.* Boston: Charles E. Merrill Publishing Co., 1980.
This book offers good suggestions on preparing news releases, brochures, annual reports, newsletters, and specialized letters, and gives a clear treatment of public relations and institutional advertising.

Hilton, Jack, and Mary Knoblauch. *On Television: A Survival Guide for Media Interviews.* New York: AMACOM, 1980.
This book grew out of the authors' experiences in training executives for television interviews. A practical guide with much "how-to" advice, it examines the impact of

television on the public perception of business.

Lamb, Robert; William G. Armstrong, Jr.; and Karolyn Morigi. *Business, Media, and the Law: The Troubled Confluence.* New York: New York University Press, 1980.
This work has excellent chapters on the interview, the news business, and advertising, and a comprehensive treatment of legal rights and responsibilities.

MacCarthy, Mark. "Ethics and Occupational Safety and Health." *National Forum,* Spring 1982, pp. 10–12.

This article presents a case for workers to be involved in a free discussion of controversial issues. The author raises questions concerning the moral rights and the ethics involved in deciding questions of public safety.

Sherwood, Hugh C. *The Journalistic Interview.* New York: Harper & Row, 1969.
This book contains practical information on getting, preparing for, and conducting journalistic interviews. Material on the group interview is included.

Successful Speeches for Corporate Advocacy

10

Most corporations are quite conscious of the image they present to the public. Their executives spend millions of dollars to improve the corporate image. They advertise, they publicize grants to worthy causes, and they speak out as corporate advocates on important issues.

An articulate corporate advocate will have many occasions to present the company message. Speeches may be presented to such service organizations as the Lions or the Rotary Club, at conventions of such professional groups as the American Medical Association, or to various citizens' groups concerned about corporate policy.

Professionals such as politicians, physicians, and attorneys know the value of membership in various organizations. They join professional associations, clubs, and service organizations. They attend meetings where they are asked to give public support on issues on which their professional organizations have taken a stand.

As you begin to join professional groups, you will be called upon to explain, to advocate, and to support their principles and actions. As a member of any corporation, you must be able to represent that business and defend its structure, plans, concepts, and actions.

The successful, effective corporate advocate will have a thorough understanding of all the information needed for a speech and for answering any questions afterward. The first step in speaking out as a corporate advocate is to make sure you have the information you need to present the principles in the most effective manner. In addition to your own experience and knowledge, you will want to use information available from various departments within the organization. This information must be accurate and current. Speakers who use incorrect data will lose credibility for themselves and for their corporations.

After you develop a thorough understanding of the organization's principles, needs, values, history, and problems, you must determine what information to use and how to use it to achieve the desired effect. In order to do this, you must analyze the audience and the occasion for the speech. Begin by considering the needs, values, and expectations of the audience. For a guide, you may want to use the Audience Analysis Guide in Chapter 2 (Fig.

2.5) as a reminder of factors that influence the audience's acceptance of your message.

Audiences

The central purpose of corporate advocacy is to get your audiences to respond in the way you want. You want them to understand something or to believe something or to take some action. In order to accomplish any of these goals, *you must understand the people who will be your listeners.* You must know what information they already have, what they already believe, and what action they are likely to take if they do not hear you speak. Your analysis may be based on characteristics of people in general or on characteristics of those persons likely to be present when you speak. For example, you know that the members of a Rotary Club luncheon will be professional people, and you can assume they will have some similar interests and needs. A group of citizens that is meeting to oppose the building of a nuclear plant may have only one common topic of interest, and this topic needs to be considered.

If you fail to adapt to the needs, values, and expectations of your audience, you cannot expect to achieve the response you want. Only by understanding your listeners can you appeal to needs and values common to the group. If you know your audiences well, you can show them how your message can help them fulfill their needs. You can also demonstrate how your message reinforces their values.

Occasions

The occasion for which you were invited to speak will influence the audience expectations. Always ask yourself why your listeners have assembled to hear you. Is there a special occasion such as an awards dinner or a political rally, or is the group gathered for a regularly scheduled business meeting? Decide if you should build the entire speech to fit the occasion, or if a simple reference in the introduction would be sufficient.

Find out whether you will be the only speaker or one of several speakers on this occasion. Plan to adapt your speech to the atmosphere and time limits created by the occasion. Serious occasions demand serious topics. Informal and entertaining occasions need lighter and less significant subjects.

Now that you have analyzed the audience and occasion for your speech, you are ready to organize your ideas into a logical arrangement that will aid your listeners' comprehension.

Strategies for Organizing the Speech

At the simplest level, a speech is organized into three divisions: (1) the introduction, (2) the body, and (3) the conclusion. (See Fig. 10.1 for a speech outline form.) Each of these three parts of the speech has its own purposes. The remaining part of this chapter

Figure 10.1 Speech Outline Form

INTRODUCTION

   I. (Gain attention.)
  II. (Give preview.)

BODY OR CONTENT

   I. (Give main point or write main division.)
      A. (Give subpoint, or material that supports Point I.)
      B. (Give subpoint, or material that supports Point I.)
         1. (Cite example or other supporting material for B.)
         2. (Give additional supporting material for B.)
  II. (Give second main point or write second main division.)
      A. (Give subpoint or supporting materials for Point II.)
         1. (Cite example, analogy, or quotation for A.)
         2. (Give additional supporting material for A.)
            a. (Give supporting material for Point 2.)
            b. (Give additional supporting material for 2.)
      B. (Give second subpoint of Point II.)
         1. (Cite example or other form of supporting material for
            Point B.)
         2. (Give additional supporting material for B.)
      C. (Give third subpoint of II.)
         1. (Give supporting materials for C.)
         2. (Add other supporting materials for C.)

CONCLUSION

   I. (Summarize.)
  II. (Reinforce or clinch.)

will discuss how to achieve those purposes. *The first step in orga-nization is to establish your purposes or goals for giving the speech.*

DETERMINE THE PURPOSES AND GOALS

The foundation of a well-organized speech is a clear statement of purpose or goals. You must be able to list every goal you want to accomplish with your speech and every purpose you have for making the talk. The following are some hypothetical examples of speakers' goals:

- To have an audience understand the nature of a company's expansion problems
- To persuade an audience to support a company's proposal for disposing of nuclear waste
- To motivate people to work for a reorganization plan
- To inspire employees to improve their productivity
- To entertain an audience with the pitfalls of being an office manager

Frequently a speaker has multiple purposes for making a speech. Suppose that, as a public relations officer for your company, you have been asked to address the Lions club about your company's interpretation of the United States's economic policy. Your specific goal might be "to inform the audience about the president's economic policy and what it will mean to them." An additional purpose, however, might be "to improve the company's relationship with this organization so its members will support our plan to buy the city park next year." In other words, you may have an unstated or unrecognized long-range goal as well as an immediate purpose for speaking. Sometimes these unstated or unrecognized goals are referred to as *hidden agendas*. That is, the person hopes to accomplish goals other than the one that is readily apparent. Almost every corporate speaker has several goals to accomplish with a speech: the immediate or specific purpose for the speech, and one or more long-range goals for the corporation.

ORGANIZE THE INTRODUCTION

Design the introduction of your speech to accomplish three purposes: (1) to gain the attention of the audience, (2) to establish your credibility, and (3) to preview the content of the speech. The following strategies will help you accomplish these goals at the beginning of your speech.

Gain attention. Gaining the attention of the audience is an absolutely essential step *before* giving any significant information. Although you think the audience is ready to listen, you still should give them time to adjust to your voice, your mannerisms, and your appearance before you develop the content of your speech. The person who introduced you has focused the audience's attention on you; it is now your responsibility to focus that attention on the information you will be presenting. You must intrigue or motivate the audience to want to hear what you have to say. *The strategy you use to gain attention must be relevant to the material you will be presenting*. The following ideas are possible ways you can gain attention for yourself and your speech.

1. Refer to the occasion or place.
2. Refer to the audience as a group or to individual members of the group.
3. Tell a relevant anecdote.
4. Use a quotation that is familiar or aptly phrased.
5. Quote a person who is held in high esteem by this audience.
6. Startle the audience with a shocking statement or by an unexpected action (be wary, however, of startling to the degree that attention is lost for what follows!).

As you review the above list of strategies, you might observe how some speakers used them to gain attention in the following speech introductions.

It is always good to see so many familiar faces at these conferences. They show the stability of the secondary market in the housing finance field. But I must say that I am extremely pleased this year to see so many new faces. They demonstrate growing awareness of how vital the secondary market has become to American home ownership.

Reference to audience

I'm proud to have the privilege of addressing this 25th annual secondary mortgage market conference. These conferences span a quarter century in which Americans have developed the most sophisticated and responsive system of home financing in world history.

Reference to occasion

This is also the first conference of the 1980's looking forward to a decade of great opportunities, and, as we all know, some large dangers.[1]

***

A major port city such as Los Angeles provides the appropriate forum for a discussion of transportation regulation. It is at the port that we see the interface of the various transportation modes. It is at the port that we can compare the unique characteristics of each transportation mode. And it is at the port that we can gain a full appreciation of the total fragmentation of this nation's transportation system and the parallel fragmentation of its transport regulation.[2]

Reference to place

***

Thank you very much, Herman. (You can be sure I will see to it that you will be paid through the end of the month!) Herman's introduction reminded me of the story of the customer in the barbershop who sat patiently while his chosen barber talked his way through three haircutting jobs. When the customer took the chair, the barber asked: "And how would you like your hair cut?" The customer answered: "In silence."

Anecdote

I am happy, though, that Herman Butler and others of our company presidents are not committed to complete silence. It would be an embarrassment at the end of the month when Corporate Headquarters calls and asks: "How much profit did you make last month?"

Reference to members of audience

Incidentally, Herman does real well.[3]

***

1. From "The Secondary Mortgage Market," a speech by Philip R. Brinkerhoff, president of the Federal Home Loan Mortgage Corporation, *Vital Speeches,* March 1, 1980, pp. 297–98.
2. From "The Role of Regulatory Agencies in the Eighties," by Leslie Kanuk, member of the Federal Maritime Commission, *Vital Speeches,* March 1, 1980, p. 315.
3. From "Prospects and Promises—The Century's Last Decades," by Robert J. Buckley, chairman and president of Allegheny Ludlum Industries, Inc., *Vital Speeches,* March 1, 1980, p. 300.

Aptly phrased
quotation   It is flattering to me, a newspaper man, to be invited to talk about the arts and letters, and especially under the sponsorship of a group dedicated to excellence. Newspapers are not generally held in high esteem today. Norman Mailer wrote some time ago that half the stories in the newspaper are 50 percent incorrect. The rest are 75 percent incorrect. "If a person is not talented enough to be a novelist," he said, "not smart enough to be a lawyer and his hands are too shaky to perform operations, he becomes a journalist."[4]

***

Quotation of highly
esteemed person   Hugh Hammond, the first Administrator of the United States Department of Agriculture's Soil Conservation Service, made the following comment, "Acres are Aces. A richer prize by far than the oil lands of the Caucasus, the iron deposits of the Urals, and gold veins of South Africa, they are the most important of man's earthly possessions."[5]

***

Startling statement   I think it prudent to assume that, for the first time in our national existence, the issue before us is that of survival.[6]

Establish credibility.   Establishing credibility means persuading the audience that it should believe you, that it should accept the information you give because *you* are the one presenting it. Your credibility may be partly established prior to your speech by your reputation or by the way you were introduced. But even if your credentials, qualifications, or experience have been explained, you can further establish your credibility with the following strategies:

1. *Establish common ground*—common interests, goals, or background (the I-am-just-like-you strategy).
2. *Establish goodwill* (the I-like-you-and-I-have-your-best-interests-at-heart strategy).
3. *Establish your expertise* (the Do-you-realize-who-I-am? strategy).
4. *Establish a relationship with those in authority or experts* (the I-know-someone-whom-you-will-believe strategy).

The following excerpts illustrate how two speakers established credibility.

Goodwill   It is always a treat to have a chance to exchange ideas with the press. I believe that our two professions, journalism and intelli-

4. From "No Arts, No Letters—No Society," by Harvey C. Jacobs, editor of the *Indianapolis News, Vital Speeches,* July 1, 1980, p. 562.
5. From "America's Changing Farm Structure," by Lindsay Thomas, farmer, *Vital Speeches,* March 1, 1980, p. 304.
6. From "Ascendency and Decline," by Charles W. Bray III, deputy director of the International Communication Agency, *Vital Speeches,* June 1, 1980, p. 493.

gence, have a great deal in common. We have in common the task of finding the facts about what is going on in the world; you, primarily for the American public; we, primarily for the American government.

Common ground

Beyond that, we both recognize the great importance to each of us of protecting our sources of information. I admire those newsmen who have been willing to go to jail rather than to disclose their sources. I assure you that we too will go to considerable lengths to protect ours.

Goodwill

The appreciation of the value of an exclusive is another common professional characteristic. For you, it can provide an important edge over your competitors. For us, it can give the President of the United States an important edge of advantage when competing or negotiating with others.

Common ground
Relationship with authority

There is also another interest we have in common. We both must possess some fundamental protections under the law if we are to continue to be effective for our country. For you, the most fundamental protection is the freedom of speech which is guaranteed by the First Amendment of the Constitution. For us, it is the guarantee of a reasonable degree of secrecy, without which we simply cannot function. And, it is here that our interests sometimes appear to collide. It may seem to you that we are ready and eager to dispense with the privileges of the First Amendment in the pursuit of secrecy. Nothing could be further from the truth.[7]

Common ground

***

A composite picture of the American business leader of the 1980's is being formed as I speak. Within the next 25 minutes member firms of the Association of Executive Recruiting Consultants—of which I am Executive Director—will locate a dozen or more talented executives qualified to deal head on with the problems of the 1980's.[8]

Expertise

Preview the content. The audience members are giving you their attention: they are ready to believe or accept what you have to say; now they want to know what you will be talking about. The final portion of the introduction should be a preview, a capsule, or the thesis of the body of the speech. In essence, the preview prepares the audience to listen to your main points or ideas. From reading the following introduction, you may determine the nature of the speech and how the speaker plans to develop his main ideas.

> Good morning. It's a pleasure to be with you today. First Union National Bank is a product of some 28 mergers completed during the late 50s and early 70s. . . .

7. From "American Intelligence in the 1980's," by Stansfield Turner, director of Central Intelligence, *Vital Speeches,* October 1, 1980, pp. 753–54.
8. From "The 1980's," by John F. Schlueter, executive director of the Association of Executive Recruiting Consultants, *Vital Speeches,* June 15, 1980, p. 537.

I really believe that the days of easy profits are coming to an end. If bankers are to prosper in the 80s, we have got to realize we are no longer in the commercial banking business, but in the financial services business. We must become more imaginative in the areas of marketing and data processing, or we may find the road to 1990 full of landmines.

That's a term you've heard a lot recently.

Preview   During the next few minutes I want to make 3 points. First, identify for you several key trends affecting bank profits in the 80s. Second, evaluate the impact of these trends on the banking industry. And third, share some of my own views about how bankers can profitably cope with the environment of the 80s.[9]

ORGANIZE THE CONTENT OF THE SPEECH

You are now ready to organize the body of the speech. This portion is, of course, where your major ideas appear. You must develop this section in a well-defined, clear, and logical manner. Your preview already has hinted at the major points (or divisions) in the body of the speech. In arranging those main ideas, you might use one of several patterns. This discussion focuses on five patterns of organization. (See Fig. 10.2.)

Chronological pattern. This arrangement of main ideas is based on a *time* order. Your major divisions are presented as they appeared in time—either from first to last, or last (current) to first (beginning), or any segment in time. For example, if you discuss the history of your organization, you might follow its development from its earliest days, through time, to its current status. The following outline illustrates how a vice-president of Honeywell Information Systems used a chronological pattern to develop one of his major points.

I. As a computer supplier, Honeywell must be concerned and *is* concerned with these issues concerning computer security.
  A. . . . our early work with the Multics Computer system dates to 1964.
  B. . . . last October we announced four DPS 8 models and the GCOS 8 operating system, which was designed to allow full access of all use and system procedures to all hardware resources while at the same time isolating procedures from each other.
  C. Data encryption is another current security project. . . .[10]

Topical pattern. In this arrangement of ideas, you subdivide the main topic into its subtopics. For example, if your main subject is the desirability of your company's *products,* then each subdivision would be *one* of those products.

9. From "Profitable Banking in the 1980's—The Weak Will Merge or Fade Away," by Edward E. Crutchfield, Jr., president and chief executive officer of the First Union National Bank, Charlotte, N. C., *Vital Speeches,* October 1, 1980, pp. 735–37.

Figure 10.2 Patterns of Organization

Organize your main ideas into a logical pattern for easier comprehension. Use one of these patterns:

1. Chronological
2. Topical
3. Causal
4. Problem-solution
5. Reflective

E. F. Loveland, vice-president of Shell Oil Company, spoke to the Corps of Cadets at West Point on "Energy in the Eighties." He used a topical pattern to develop a major idea, as illustrated in the following outline.

So what does this confusing world energy scene mean for us in the United States?

A. *First, it means higher prices.* The cost of petroleum products in this country has not peaked.
    1. cost of crude oil is $42 a barrel
    2. cost has doubled in price in the past 15 months

B. *The second thing the international scene means*—we are even more vulnerable to the decisions of OPEC today than ever before.
    1. in terms of price
    2. in terms of supply

C. *The third thing the international petroleum scene means to Americans*—the decade of the Eighties will be a tough time as far as energy is concerned.[11]

Causal pattern.   The causal pattern is an arrangement in which you first talk about the causes of an event and then discuss its effects. If you wish to change the emphasis, you may discuss the effects first and then its causes. The first aspect you present usually is that with which the audience is already concerned; and the second usually is your explanation or interpretation, which will be "new" to them. For example, you might discuss the *effects* of the energy shortage (something of concern to the audience) and then tell them the *causes* (some causes that are unique or unfamiliar to them).

Problem-solution pattern.   In this pattern of arrangement, the first step or division is to discuss the *problems*—you might analyze those problems; you might even talk about the causes and effects of those problems. The second step is to discuss the *solutions* to

---

10. From a speech by Michael J. Keliher, *Vital Speeches,* August 15, 1980, pp. 662–66.
11. *Vital Speeches,* August 15, 1980, pp. 653–56. Italics added.

those problems—how the solution would work, what its benefits would be, how it would solve the problems, its cost, and its advantages.

The following outline is based on a speech given by Thomas D. Barrow of the Kennecott Corporation, called "International Business Strategies for the Eighties."

A. *Food problems* naturally follow population growth
  1. location of farming centers and the distribution methods mean food shortages in some areas and surpluses in others
    a. of the estimated 4.5 billion people now in the world, fully 1.3 billion may be chronically undernourished
    b. because of population increases, the food supply may have to increase 45 percent by 1985

B. The most obvious *solution* appears to be in technology—technology which can make deserts arable, restore the fertility of eroded land, develop new livestock breeds, increase crop production, guard against pests and disease, develop new food processess and products.[12]

Reflective pattern. The reflective pattern of organization is based on John Dewey's philosophy of "how we think." In Chapter 7, you used those steps as a type of agenda for groups to follow in problem solving. These six steps also may be used as major divisions in the body of your persuasive speech.

1. *Define and limit the problem.*
  a. Tell what it is.
  b. Tell areas of the problem you will cover in this speech.

2. *Analyze the problem.*
  a. Discuss its history if applicable.
  b. Discuss its causes and effects.
  c. Discuss its significance.

3. *Establish acceptable criteria for solving the problem.*
  a. Will it need to be cost-efficient?
  b. Will it have to solve the entire problem?
  c. Should it be an immediate or long-range solution?

4. *Discuss possible solutions.*
  a. Talk about solutions that have already been attempted.
  b. Give your unique solutions.

5. *Arrive at the best solution*—evaluate the possible solutions according to the established criteria.

6. *Demonstrate how to implement the best solution.*
  a. Tell how it will work.
  b. Give its advantages.

As you can see, the reflective pattern of organization is a variation of a problem-solution pattern. Many of the patterns overlap with others. In this case, however, we offer the reflective pattern

12. *Vital Speeches,* August 15, 1980, pp. 656–59. Italics added.

as a special strategy for the speaker who is confronted with a hostile audience. If your audience analysis leads you to believe that the audience is concerned about the problems but is not ready to accept your solutions, then you can develop your information along the lines of the reflective pattern. This strategy allows you to emphasize the lines of agreement:

"We all know that we have a problem, and that is . . ."
"This problem started when . . ."
"We must agree that any solution would have to be economical."
"You are all aware when Company X tried . . . , but have you thought of . . . ?"
"It seems obvious, then, that this solution would be the most economical."
"Let me show you how it would work."

ORGANIZE THE CONCLUSION OF THE SPEECH

The conclusion of the speech should summarize the content and leave the audience something to remember. That is, the conclusion is organized as a reverse of the introduction. In the introduction, you gained attention and then gave an initial summary (preview); in the conclusion, you should give a final summary and end with an attention device. The conclusion, thus, may be divided into two major portions: (1) the summary, which may range from one sentence to a brief paraphrasing of all the major points, and (2) the clincher, closure, or reinforcer for your thesis.

The *summary* acts as a reminder and as a form of closure. The longer the speech, the more important it is that you summarize the salient points. Strategies for the *reinforcer* are similar to those you used in your introduction to gain attention. You might end with a particularly apt quotation. If you opened with a quotation, you might want to quote the same person at the end of the speech. On the other hand, you might need to close with a motivating statement of action. The following excerpt is taken from the conclusion of a speech given by a corporate executive.

The press conference is a great tool . . . an effective technique. Don't be afraid to use it. Through it a company can effectively paint and depict a truly honest mural of public understanding—worthy enough to capture valid and valuable editorial space in newspapers, magazines and on the airwaves. *Summary*

A press conference is a two way method of communications: the reporter seeks information; the corporation wants to get the word out. Thus, two way communications is not merely a perfunctory function of management but is *vitally* essential for the conduct of business.

So, again . . . where there is good news . . . or even bad . . . and the press conference is the way to do it . . . do it and do it well and always, *with style*. The press conference is a truly valuable *Reinforcer or clincher* medium in today's complex and highly competitive world, and as John Milton once said:

> "Good . . . the more communicated . . . the more abundant grows . . ."

Thank you.[13]

Your last step in organizing your ideas is to add transitions to help your listeners realize when you are moving to another idea.

USE TRANSITIONAL DEVICES

Transitional devices are words, phrases, or sentences that allow the listener to follow your movement from one point to the next. Words such as *first, second, next, now,* and *finally* serve as transitional devices that indicate your position in the speech. Such words also act as reinforcers for major assertions.

The following phrases serve as indicators that you have completed the development of one idea and are now ready to develop your next idea:

> "Now that we have seen . . . let's look at . . ."
> "We have now completed X. What should our next problem . . . ?"
> "This analysis leads us to our next problem."

Review some of the speech excerpts given earlier in this chapter to discover how the speakers used transitional devices.

Strategies for Winning Approval

At this point in your preparation for being a successful corporate advocate, you have learned to organize your thoughts into logical patterns of arrangement. In essence, that organizational pattern serves as a skeleton of the body of your message. You are now ready to develop each one of those major divisions or assertions by giving analogies, examples, quotations, definitions, statistical data, and reasons for those points. We call these types of development strategies *supporting materials.* (See Fig. 10.3.) That is, you make your assertion, and you support it with information that will cause your listeners to accept those ideas. *Use supporting material each time you need to clarify, prove, or reinforce your assertions.* Such information must be current, accurate, and acceptable to your listeners. This type of accuracy will aid your credibility and win acceptance for your corporation.

USE EXAMPLES

Examples should be relevant to your assertions. They should also be representative or typical. If examples are used to *prove*

13. From "The Press Conference," by Joseph J. Duome, *Vital Speeches,* May 15, 1980, pp. 473–77.

your point, then they must be actual, *factual* examples. On the other hand, if they are used only to clarify or to provide interest, then you may use a *hypothetical* example. In the following excerpt, the speaker uses several brief examples to illustrate, or clarify, his assertion.

> Sociological changes of the 1970's may have included a declining birth rate, but there have never been more contenders for jobs in the marketplace.
>
>   For example, where once women played an auxiliary, minority role in business, in the last decade they increasingly have postponed children and prepared for careers. . . .
>
>   Further job competition comes from minority groups— Blacks, Hispanics, the handicapped, the elderly. . . .[14]

Assertion

Example

Examples

USE ANALOGIES

Analogies are comparisons; they are useful in helping the listener to understand one occurrence or concept by comparing it with another. Literal analogies are comparisons between things of the same class: one form of government with another form of government. Figurative analogies compare things of different classes: investing in the stock market with gambling in a casino.

In the following excerpt, the speaker used a figurative analogy to compare the oil industry to a supertanker.

>   I'd like to tell you a fable about a supertanker. In accordance with a basic law of physics, a supertanker tends to keep going in a given direction long after the rudder has been turned to a different course. Its captain and crew are happiest when the weather is good, the seas are calm, and they are let alone to run their ship.
>
>   Well, once there was a supertanker known as "U.S. Pete." It had been plying the high seas for many years, under generally

---

14. From "The 1980's: Leadership on Trial," by John F. Schlueter, *Vital Speeches,* June 15, 1980, pp. 537–41.

pleasant conditions, delivering large quantities of inexpensive oil to its customers. And over the years its customers had built a whole society based on this cheap and plentiful energy.

It came to pass that suddenly, seven years ago, supply sources were destabilized and prices skyrocketed. The customers got very upset, and government agents swarmed all over the ship. The seas turned turbulent and the weather whipped up into hurricane force.

Now, the family that ran the supertanker had seven brothers and a lot of cousins. They had such names as Double X (it was formerly Stan but he wanted twice the anonymity), Tex, Moe, Skelley, Phil, Arky and the like. They were very skilled captains, and their whole lives were devoted to running their supertanker.

When conditions suddenly turned ugly, they were faced with a dilemma. They wanted to keep on navigating in the way they knew best. But they realized that this stormy condition was probably going to last a long time and they had better learn some new navigational methods.

They decided to change direction, but they weren't sure which way to go. They asked around and found that nobody had had much experience navigating such a large supertanker in such adverse conditions. And they had this problem of their supertanker's propensity for going straight on, even though the rudder was changed. It was very hard to counter, in the short span of seven years, the momentum built up over 100 years.

But they suddenly perceived terrible shoals just ahead. They saw that they needed to find a way to more quickly turn the ship and learn to cope with a hostile and unfamiliar world.

The moral: Even with supertankers, navigational methods that were adequate in calm seas in good weather must be drastically changed when the weather and seas turn violently hostile.

I think this is an apt description of what's been happening to the oil industry.[15]

USE QUOTATIONS

Another way to reinforce or to prove your assertions is to cite an authority on the issue. *An authority becomes an expert through training, experience, or education in the subject.* This authority may be in the form of a written source such as a reputable book, journal, or magazine. Your audience must accept that source's credibility if such a quotation is to gain approval for your assertion. If the name may not be recognized, then you should "qualify" your source by including the credentials of that person: "Colette Southerland, *the president of the largest industrial firm in the state,* said that. . . ." Citing an authority gives additional credence to your own credibility.

15. From a speech by Kalman B. Druck, vice-chairman, Harshe-Rotman & Druck, *Vital Speeches,* June 15, 1980, pp. 514–17.

USE DEFINITIONS

If there is any possibility that your audience may not share with you the same understanding of your concepts, define those concepts. Definitions are excellent ways of achieving the necessary clarification to effect successful corporate advocacy. The more complex the concept, the more types of definitions you may need.

An *operational definition* is one in which you explain the concept by showing how it operates or functions: "Punctuality is being on time for appointments."

A definition by *negation* tells what is not part of the concept: "The assistants are *not* members of management."

A definition by *classification and differentiation* is one in which you tell the concept's *class* and then how it *differs* from others in that class: "Maslow's hierarchy of needs is a theory [class] which categorizes human needs in an order such that one must be fulfilled before the next one can be met [how it differs from other theories]."

Obviously these types of definitions overlap. The preceding example could be considered an operational definition also. You also might use examples, analogies, and quotations to define concepts.

USE STATISTICAL DATA

Numerical data can add impressive support to a claim. Numbers, however, must be made relevant for the listener. Consider using charts, graphs, and other visual aids that will allow the listener to see numbers as well as hear them. Use an analogy to express a percentage in order to increase understanding. Another method to aid listener comprehension and retention is to round off numbers rather than give specific figures. For example, your listeners will find "almost a thousand" easier to remember than "nine hundred eighty-nine and seven-tenths."

The president of American Motors Corporation made a speech to the Detroit Automobile Dealers Association on trade relations between the United States and Japan in which he used an impressive array of statistical data. In the following excerpt, he used round figures (10,000 and 2,000) and compared the production rate to the current sales rate ("about one-third").

> Just a few days ago, Honda announced it will build a new plant at Marysville, Ohio, to produce 10,000 cars a month. While this production rate represents only about one-third of their current sales rate in the U.S., it is at least a step in the right direction, especially the news that the plant, hopefully to be completed in 1982, will employ 2,000 people.[16]

16. "United States and Japan Trade Relations," by W. Paul Tippett, Jr., *Vital Speeches,* April 1, 1980, p. 373.

SUMMARY

As a corporate advocate, it is essential that you win approval for yourself and for your issues. The following steps summarize the guidelines suggested in this chapter.

1. Analyze the audience from whom you will be seeking approval.
2. Write all the purposes and goals you want to accomplish with this speech.
3. Discover all possible information about your subject.
4. Write one statement that previews the entire speech.
5. List all the major points that develop that preview.
6. Write all the examples, analogies, quotations, definitions, and statistical data that will support *each* point.
7. Review and select only supporting material you need to clarify, reinforce, or prove each point *to this audience*.
8. Return to the introduction and write an opening statement that will gain attention (and establish credibility, if necessary).
9. Return to the conclusion and write a summary and reinforcing statement.

EXERCISES

1. Read a speech published in *Vital Speeches*. Outline the speech, following the outline form found in this chapter (Fig. 10.1).
2. Write an analysis of your class as an audience. Use the form given in Chapter 2 (Fig. 2.5).
3. Present a five-to-seven-minute speech to your class in which you explain or clarify an economic concept, a professional theory, or a managerial philosophy.
4. Select a professional, political, or service organization. Write an analysis of a typical audience found at one of its meetings.
5. Prepare a ten-minute speech to be given to the audience you analyzed in Exercise 4. Select a business, profession, or corporation to represent. You may either (a) defend a controversial action recently taken by your selected profession/corporation, or (b) present a proposal you wish to have adopted by your targeted audience.
6. Find an occasion to hear a business or professional speaker. Write an analysis of the speech in which you describe
   a. the purposes of the speech
   b. the organizational patterns of the speech
   c. the types of supporting materials used in the speech
   d. how the speaker adapted to the audience

Suggested Readings

Heun, Richard, and Linda Heun. *Public Speaking*. St. Paul, Minn.: West Publishing Co., 1979.

The text is a thoughtful combination of theory with skills. The reader should easily be able to apply all the skills of public speaking with the use of this book.

Logue, Cal; Dwight L. Freshley; Charles R. Gruner; and Richard C. Huseman. *Speaking: Back to Fundamentals*. Boston: Allyn and Bacon, 1979.

The authors use a traditional treatment of the basic concepts of public speaking.

Osborn, Michael. *Speaking in Public*. Boston: Houghton Mifflin Co., 1982.

The author provides a thorough public speaking textbook that covers such topics as the art of evaluating speeches, the design and development of informative and persuasive speeches, and conflict management through communication.

Making a Presentation

11

The word *speech,* which was used to describe corporate advocacy talks in the previous chapter, may be properly applied to a large number of types of communication. A sermon may be considered a speech. So may a coach's pep talk to the team at half time or a senator's argument in a congressional debate. The sermon, the pep talk, and the debate, along with a variety of other forms of oral communication, belong to the general category of "speeches." Although these examples of communication have common features, they have their distinctive characteristics as well. A speaker's success depends on knowing the requirements of the particular type of speech being given.

You may have heard of a type of business speech called a "presentation." Some people who give presentations insist they are not speeches at all. As you examine this form of communication, however, you will see that a presentation is a speech in the same sense that the word *speech* can be applied to a sermon or a pep talk or an argument in a debate.

Speakers who make presentations have not arrived at a universal agreement on the proper definition of the term. Many books on business and professional speaking do not recognize the presentation as a special type of speech, and others offer a variety of definitions. Howell and Bormann, for example, state that presentational speaking is a "unique" form of business communication that has been growing in importance since the early 1950s.[1] George Vardaman, on the other hand, considers any "purposive" communication, oral or written, to be under the broad heading of the presentation.[2] For our purposes, *a presentation is a specialized, job-related talk designed to provide information or to persuade.* After looking at some examples that show how presentations are used on the job, you will see how presentations share characteristics of public speaking, and then you can identify the characteristics that distinguish them from what we typically call public speaking.

---

1. William S. Howell and Ernest G. Bormann, *Presentational Speaking for Business and the Professions* (New York: Harper & Row, 1971), pp. 3–21.
2. George T. Vardaman, *Making Successful Presentations* (New York: AMA-COM, 1981), pp. 9–37.

179

Examples of Presentations

Suppose you are the editor of a company magazine and you decide the magazine should have a new format. You find a graphic artist to design a new masthead. You discuss with your printer the cost of adding color, increasing the number of pictures, and using a higher-quality paper. Now you have a clear idea of what you want to do. But the changes will result in an increase in costs. You will need a bigger budget. So you schedule a thirty-minute meeting with your boss, and you go in with all your arguments and your samples to make your pitch for more money. You would not exactly give a talk of the sort required when speaking as a corporate advocate, but you would use at least some of the same techniques. Your appeal to your boss for a budget hike could properly be called a presentation.

To take another case, suppose you are a real estate broker. You have the capital to develop a new office building, but the site you have decided on is not zoned for the type of construction you have in mind. You must appear before the zoning board. You ask your architect to go with you and to bring the sketches or perhaps even a model of the structure you want to build. You also have your lawyer with you. You decide on the topics each of you will cover, and you settle on a time limit for each person. You coach the architect carefully on the personal prejudices of each member of the board. The combined speaking efforts of your team would be called a presentation.

Finally, imagine you are an agent for a health insurance company. You make a presentation to the personnel officer of a small business firm. The personnel officer likes your idea and wants to pursue it further. Then you are invited to make another presentation to a committee of company officers. They decide to buy your policy. You are next asked to appear before a group of company employees to make sure they understand and approve the benefits your policy offers. The first two presentations described are clearly persuasive in nature—the one before the committee is actually a sales presentation. The third presentation might also be persuasive, but it would in many cases serve only to inform.

Common Features of Presentations and the Public Speech

DELIVERY

Like the corporate advocate speaking to a civic club, the person giving a presentation uses the spoken word as the primary means of getting a message over. Anyone giving a presentation must be aware of the added dimension a message acquires as a result of eye contact, gesture, posture, and conversational tone of voice. All the delivery skills useful in any speaking situation apply to the presentation.

RESEARCH AND EVIDENCE

Research and evidence to support ideas have the same significance in a presentation that they have in making a speech. You must both know what you are talking about and know where facts fit best in your presentation. The examples, illustrations, comparisons, statistics, and testimony used in a public speech will have their place in a presentation.

LANGUAGE

Language must be selected with care in all types of speeches. Although a presentation before an audience of experts may make it possible to employ a great deal of technical language, speakers who make presentations must follow the basic principle of all successful speakers who know the value of choosing words their listeners can easily understand. Like a good public speaker, anyone who gives a presentation cannot afford to stumble through a speech filled with vague phrases and excessive repetition.

ORGANIZATION

Presentations must be well organized. The standard organizational pattern explained in the discussion of corporate advocacy (see Chapter 10) will work with a little adaptation for many presentations, especially those intended to inform. A pattern of ideas designed specifically for the persuasive presentation will be examined later as an alternative method of organization.

Now look at some of the characteristics that make a presentation a special kind of speech. Examine features of a presentation that are *usually* present. Not all of these special features will be found in every presentation, but even if only a few of them are present, the presentation will be markedly different from the typical speech.

Special Features of a Presentation

AUDIENCE

Any speaker must carefully size up the listeners who will hear a talk, and in preparing for a presentation, particular attention should be paid to special listener-related features often present.

Decision makers. Presentations are generally given to listeners with the power to decide and act upon the recommendations made by the speaker.[3] A boss, a zoning board, or a personnel officer can approve or disapprove an idea. A presentation in such a situation will almost always be directed toward an action the presenter wants listeners to take.

In a sense the audience for a persuasive presentation may be compared to a jury at a trial. At the end of the presentation—and usually within a rather short period of time—the group will come to a decision. It will decide to buy, to approve, to accept, to rec-

3. Howell and Bormann, pp. 10–11.

ommend, or to take some other action that will determine the practical effect of a presentation.

The decision-making power held by those who hear a presentation means that the customary role of speaker and audience in the public speaking situation will be reversed. It is common (although not universal) for the public speaker to be the authority or the expert who is looked up to by the audience. Though a person who makes a presentation may know more than anyone else present, the presentation will frequently be aimed at listeners who have the power to act on the speaker's ideas.

In the case of a presentation to inform, the audience will not be made up of what we would usually call decision makers, but such an audience will commonly have quite a bit of authority over the speaker. Listeners to an informative presentation are often supervisors, customers, or others to whom the speaker must "report." For example, a press officer giving a presentation to reporters may find that the audience believes that it has certain rights and privileges regarding the information being presented.

Size. Though a presentation may be given to a large audience, many presentations will be heard by a group far too small to constitute an audience in the traditional sense of the word. There may be but a single listener, as illustrated by two of the examples cited earlier. Even though you find yourself sitting at a table with a committee, your presentation should be just as carefully organized and prepared as it would be in speaking to a larger group.

LENGTH

The standard time allowed for a business *speech* today tends to be around fifteen or twenty minutes. Even though the standard *presentation* may not cover as broad a topic as a speech, it will probably take longer to deliver. You would hope to have at least thirty minutes to tell your publisher why you needed more money for your company magazine, and a hearing on a zoning variance could last for a couple of hours. A presentation will usually go into far greater detail than would be possible with a speech.

VISUAL AIDS

"Visual aids," as W. G. Ryckman points out, "are used extensively in presentations and competence in their development and use is essential to a successful performance."[4]

In the examples of presentations mentioned earlier, it would be hard to imagine a request for funds to improve a company magazine without showing what the new format would look like. A

4. W. G. Ryckman, *What Do You Mean by That? The Art of Speaking and Writing Clearly* (Homewood, Ill.: Dow Jones–Irwin, 1980), p. 55.

breakdown of the costs by category will be more clear if depicted in a handout to be left behind after the presentation. In the zoning board hearing, a graphic showing how the proposed building would blend into its surroundings could be essential in gaining the board's approval. A chart or slide showing comparisons of costs and benefits would aid the insurance broker trying to get a firm to buy a new policy. Special consideration to be kept in mind when using visual aids for a presentation will be discussed later in this chapter. The basic principles of using visual aids set forth in Chapter 12 should also be reviewed before making a presentation.

TEAM PRESENTATIONS

For a number of reasons it may be wise to use more than one speaker in a presentation. First of all, if several topics are covered, an expert may be required for each topic. Someone with a legal background may be needed in the zoning case, for example, as well as an additional expert in architecture. Even if other members of the team do not take an extensive part in the formal presentation, they may be badly needed in handling questions from the persons to whom the presentation is directed.

Second, because a presentation may be rather long, a team approach will give it variety. Switching from one person to another gives the audience more than one voice to listen to, and it offers changes in visual focus that may help keep listeners' attention.

Third, the team approach gets more people involved in the preparation of the presentation. Two heads are better than one, and two or more people working together on the task will usually do a more complete and accurate job of getting their message over.

HANDLING QUESTIONS

Public speeches frequently conclude with a question-and-answer session, but speakers are seldom questioned *during* a talk. A presentation, however, because the audience is usually small and because the listeners are in positions of power, may be interrupted by questions at any time. This will not always happen, but speakers must be prepared to answer questions in the middle of a presentation, and they may even stop at several points to encourage listeners to ask questions. A public speaker would almost never find such a practice desirable.

Presentations, then, are likely to differ from speeches because of the audience's smaller size and, in the case of presentations to persuade, because of listeners' decision-making power. Presentations typically will be longer than speeches and will almost always be accompanied by visual aids. Audiences generally feel free to ask questions in the middle of a presentation, and it is not uncommon for presentations to be given by a team of two or more speakers.

ESTABLISHING OBJECTIVES

Early in the process of preparing a presentation, a speaker should write down the specific results to be accomplished. In the case of a presentation to inform, where the aim is to transfer information, the major topics and crucial facts to be understood and remembered should be specified.

For example, a stockbroker speaking to a sales force might prepare, in addition to an outline or manuscript for the talk, a set of objectives, including: "I want every sales representative to know and be able to explain (1) six reasons why a client should invest in Limited Partners Growth Company, (2) the details of the performance of Limited Partners for the past six years, and (3) recent IRS rulings affecting investments in this company."

In the case of presentations to persuade, results should be specified, where possible, as *actions* the speaker wants the audience to take. All possible reactions that a presentation may create should be considered, and the speaker should decide which ones are acceptable and which are not.

To return to an earlier example, your boss may respond to a request for a budget increase by saying, "This was a terrific presentation. You've got a great idea here. I am impressed by your work, and I agree that we need a change. Thanks for coming in." As complimentary as these words sound, they may mean you directed your presentation toward impressing your boss with your idea instead of aiming for the more important objective of having the money for your idea included in the budget. You should have established exactly what your boss *could* do about the budget, and then you should have specified the action you wanted taken. From the start you would need to know whether your boss had the power to include your project in the department's budget. If your boss did not have that power, then the action you wanted might have been a formal agreement to recommend your idea to the next higher level of management.

In establishing objectives, you want to be realistic. The most desirable result from your point of view may be absolutely impossible to achieve, and you may have to aim for a goal you can reasonably hope to achieve. But you should determine what your options are, and you should write down the specific results you want your presentation to bring about.

To set forth objectives, the form below can be used for a presentation to persuade. In the first column all the *desirable* and *realistic* outcomes of the presentation should be listed. These should then be ranked in order by assigning an A to the *most* desirable and realistic result, a B to the next most desirable and realistic, and lower grades in order to the rest of the list. Objective A should then become the focal point of the preparation, with other high-ranking objectives possibly considered as fallback positions.

Next a speaker should list the *likely* and *undesirable* outcomes of the presentation. These should be ranked A, B, C, and so on, with highest rankings given to the results the speaker wants to work hardest to avoid. These negative possibilities should be kept in mind during the preparation of the presentation.

POSITIVE OUTCOMES	RANK	NEGATIVE OUTCOMES	RANK
1. _____	_____	1. _____	_____
2. _____	_____	2. _____	_____
3. _____	_____	3. _____	_____

AUDIENCE ANALYSIS

Just as would be the case in preparing a public speech, a speaker working on a presentation must gather basic demographic data on the audience. The speaker will want to find out how many people will attend. If the speaker does not already know the listeners, then their age, sex, and educational background must be determined. The positions they hold should be ascertained as well as the titles to be used in addressing individuals (Madam Chairman, Mr. President, Father Adrian, Congressman Snort, etc.). We have already seen that an audience for a presentation is likely to be a small group of decision makers, which makes it possible in many cases to evaluate the audience for a presentation on a person-by-person basis.

You must attempt to determine whether there are leaders within the group to whom you are making your presentation. A committee of six may have but two members who will determine the group's response. In some groups only one person can tip the scales for or against the speaker. Of course, in some cases all members will have an equal voice in a decision, but whatever the case may be, it is important to know where the power lies.

Even in the presentation before a large group, there may be subgroups that carry more weight than others. Perhaps the engineers or the department heads or the vice-presidents will be the subgroup toward whom the speaker needs to aim.

Knowing about personal prejudices or other personality traits might be important. Perhaps one of the vice-presidents in a company objects violently to 35-mm slides or to presentations that last longer than half an hour. Maybe the company treasurer likes charts that show details of costs, or the personnel officer is reluctant to support any proposal that fails to give consideration to the work hours involved in implementing it.

A speaker who knows listeners well from previous experience may be able to quickly conjure up a mental image of the audience. When the people who will hear a presentation are not known, it may be necessary to ask several people for facts rather than rely on the response of a single individual. Facts can best be gathered by asking specific questions, although it is always a good idea to include a general catch-all query such as "Is there anything else you think I need to know before making my proposal to this group?"

Here is a summary of the kinds of questions a speaker needs to ask:

- What are the age, sex, education, and other demographic facts about the listener(s) or subgroups who will hear the presentation?
- Who exercises the greatest influence in this audience?
- What personal attitudes and individual traits do I need to keep in mind?
- Are there any special facts I need to know?

If you were to make an analysis of the zoning board for the example of a presentation cited earlier in this chapter, you might find the following facts:

1. The board is chaired by a 47-year-old male lawyer. Its members are, in order of years of service on the board, a 62-year-old woman who runs her own accounting firm, a 52-year-old male druggist, a 45-year-old male building contractor, and a 36-year-old female lawyer.
2. The accountant and the contractor are the most powerful members of the board, and in the past, when they have voted on the same side of an issue, that side has always won.
3. The lawyer who chairs the board is fair in conducting meetings, but he strongly objects to nonattorneys citing legal precedents or arguing legal matters. The female lawyer will vote against any change in the zoning on Elm Street or in any other residential area, but she is frequently in the minority. The druggist will go along with whichever side seems to be winning.
4. Only two zoning variances have been granted by this board in the Elm Street section of the city since the current membership was appointed. Also, the druggist often appears to doze off during long presentations.

Visual Aids for a Presentation

MODELS AND OBJECTS

A public speaker addressing a large audience from a lectern in front of an auditorium will find it difficult to display a model or hold up an object for the audience to see. But in a presentation, where the listeners may be seated around a table, three-dimensional visual materials can be used more easily.

Models or objects can add a dramatic touch to a presentation. An audience that may not be impressed by slide pictures of a building might find a scale model quite impressive. Photographs of a new item of equipment might be regarded by an audience as commonplace, whereas the opportunity to see the actual object could heighten attention considerably. Anyone who has ever watched a carnival vendor demonstrate the "hundred and one uses of this dynamic new kitchen gadget" knows the appeal of seeing an object in action.

PROJECTING IMAGES

Speakers usually rely on slides or film to show pictures to their audiences. Both of these media can be somewhat distracting in a presentation. Think how awkward it would be for someone giving a presentation to set up a screen and show a ten-minute film to one person. A slide projector, which might be relatively unobtrusive in a room with fifty people, can become a major distraction in the middle of a table where five people are sitting to hear a presentation.

A presentation, however, may be much more likely to succeed if a short film or a series of slides could be shown. An insurance agent may need to demonstrate to a client the size and efficiency of the home office by showing computers at work processing claims. If the film is to be shown to an audience of only one or two people—or perhaps to as many as a dozen—the solution to the problem would be to use either rear screen projection or video.

When speakers give presentations in their own company headquarters, they often have available conference rooms with rear screen capacity. In such a case, regular 35-mm slides and 16-mm film can be used because the projection equipment will be out of sight.

When traveling with slides or film, a speaker obviously needs to make other arrangements. One solution is to use a portable self-contained rear screen projection unit. About the size of a briefcase and weighing a little over ten pounds, such a unit will easily handle short films. The screen will usually be less than a foot square, but if the film needs to be shown to a larger audience, an enlarged image can be projected on a wall or a regular movie screen. To use this equipment to show slides, the slides must be transferred to film.

Although the equipment would be much harder to transport, video has the same advantages as rear screen projection. With either video or rear screen the small size of the screen becomes an advantage rather than a disadvantage. Whereas slides or a film may seem intrusive in a speech, images projected on a small screen can add a feeling of intimacy to a presentation.

Another way of presenting images is to use an overhead projector. Transparencies may be prepared in advance or created as the presentation develops. The overhead projector is generally associated with teaching or training. Though it may not be suitable for most public speeches, it can be useful in making presentations.

HANDOUTS

It may be possible in a presentation not merely to let the audience see the aid but to let them hold it, touch it, move it, or operate it. In such a case, the listeners learn not just from the senses of sight and hearing but also from touch. Many modern museums have applied this in learning through a "hands-on" experience. While a public speaker can almost never afford to relinquish control of the situation by allowing material to circulate among listeners, the smaller size of the typical presentation makes the handout a viable possibility.

When you want your employer to appreciate the value of printing the company magazine on a higher-quality paper, you can have samples on hand to give the feel of the paper and to show its quality. The idea will come across much better if your listener can hold a printed page of the actual material, and both see and handle a piece of the new publication just as a reader would.

Some handouts can be left with listeners. This has the advantage of making it easier for the members of the audience to keep material that will help them remember what you said.

Of course, in distributing handouts, a speaker must be prepared to cope with the temporary shift of attention while listeners have something before them. A speaker may have to make a special effort to help a listener relate what is being said to what is being shown. And when the speaker gets ready to move on to a new idea, it may be necessary to increase the force of the delivery slightly to direct the audience's attention back to the speaker.

Delivery of the Presentation

A speaker accustomed to speaking from a lectern may find that some presentations require a considerable amount of adaptation. For example, it will often be advisable to speak while sitting rather than standing. Or, when using a variety of visual aids such as an overhead projector, a chalkboard, and a scale model, a speaker will have to move from place to place. In such instances it might not be possible to use notes or a manuscript on a lectern in the way most public speakers do. Presentations may be given in a number of unusual locations: in an office, in a laboratory, or on a factory tour. Presentational speaking requires adaptation of the delivery skills used in normal public speaking.

Organizing the Ideas in a Presentation

Many times the parts of a presentation may be organized in the same way as the speeches discussed in Chapter 10. This is especially true of presentations to inform. They can easily take the form of ordinary informative speeches. However, for presentations designed to get action, the six-step pattern described below may be more effective. Each of the six steps will be described and then illustrated by referring to the three hypothetical presentations mentioned earlier: the company editor, the insurance agent, and the real estate broker.

THE OPENING

The opening of a presentation usually does not require as much "softening up" of an audience as is needed in making public speeches. Depending on the circumstances, the opening of a presentation can be highly formal or quite informal, but typically it will be short.

A formal opening might be found in the case of the real estate broker appearing at a zoning hearing: "Mr. Chairman, my name is Larry Jones. I am president of Jones and Company Land Development, and I am here with Ms. Betty Rogers of the law firm Rogers and Rogers and Mr. Tom Scribner, an architect with Casey Associates." An informal opening would be found in the case of the company editor who might say to his boss, "Morning, Bob, I'm glad you were able to fit me into your schedule so soon."

THE BACKGROUND

People who attend presentations are often being asked to shift their attention quickly from some other aspect of their work to the presentation. They may have just left another conference or stopped work on some demanding project. They usually need to be reoriented, and this can be accomplished by supplying needed background information.

If you were the company editor, you might remind your boss that the two of you talked two months ago about improving the company magazine. You could quickly sketch your activities on the project during that time. As the real estate broker, you might find it necessary to give a lengthy account of your company's past work as well as the development of the Elm Street area where you plan to build.

THE CRITERIA

This step will not always be required, but it may be advisable after explaining the background to identify the criteria listeners will use in judging your idea. As company editor, you might say, "Following your instructions, Bob, I've had these guidelines in mind: (A) a higher-quality publication, one that has a thoroughly professional look and feel, (B) a more dynamic, colorful, exciting format, one that will attract and hold attention, and (C) reasonable cost, a budget that will increase only moderately." As the insurance agent making a sales presentation, you could review the chief concerns of your client. These might include faster and more efficient processing of claims, expanded coverage to include dental and psychological care, or more coverage for major costs, with employees picking up more of the bill for smaller problems.

THE PROPOSAL

At this stage of the presentation the speaker should set forth in concrete terms exactly what is being offered. You would tell in detail the kind of magazine you want to publish, the kind of policy you have for sale, the kind of building you want to construct, or the specific insurance policy you are offering. At this stage of the presentation, speakers do *not* usually state what action they want taken.

THE JUSTIFICATION

The justification step contains the "arguments" for the proposal. Here the speaker explains how the proposal meets the criteria set forth in the third step. Advantages of the plan are offered in such areas as cost, efficiency, practicality, and desirability. The speaker should stress the benefits the proposal or product will bring the listener. It may be wise to deal with arguments against the proposal by showing they are not significant or they are not legitimate or they are balanced by the positive features of the proposal.

If you were the real estate broker, you would want to develop arguments showing how your development would be compatible with the surroundings on Elm Street, you might want to demonstrate community support for your plan, and you could emphasize the advantages that would be gained by the city in such areas as taxes or stabilizing property values.

The justification step can be the longest section of a presentation. It provides the basis on which listeners will accept or reject a speaker's ideas.

THE ACTION

Finally, the action to be taken must be specified. If a speaker has properly planned a presentation, then the most desirable and realistic outcomes have been decided upon and the speaker should know exactly what the audience is expected to do. As a rule it is a good idea to spell the action out precisely. If your boss has the power to approve your request for a new magazine format and a higher budget, you should appeal for this approval directly at the end of the presentation. Do not leave the initiative for action in the hands of your listeners.

In the sales presentation, this step in the organizational pattern is called "the close." It is the step where the sales representative attempts to get the buyer's signature on the dotted line. Although it is true that some salespeople use reprehensible pressure tactics to drive a sale to a close, there is nothing wrong with recognizing the importance of the need to ask for the desired action. Many speakers stop short of this critical step.

At the end of some presentations it will be impossible for a decision to be made immediately. A zoning board, for instance, may have to have further hearings or deliberations before it can act. The decision could be a week or more away. Where possible, however, a speaker should try for an immediate decision. The longer the delay, the weaker the force of the arguments may become.

When a presentation is given by more than one person, a careful division of responsibilities must be made. The presentation should be a team effort. Rather than have a series of disjointed speeches, the organizational pattern described above might be used by having segments within the pattern presented by the person with the best qualifications for that segment.

In the zoning hearing you could give the opening and part of the background. Your attorney could give additional background material, and you could handle the criteria step. Then your architect could make the formal proposal, and all three of you share in developing the justification step. You would close the presentation with an appeal for action.

In some more loosely constructed patterns, the appropriate member of the team might speak spontaneously as the need arises. This same flexibility would also be required in answering questions; each member of the team must be alert to contribute part or all of an answer.

COORDINATION AND REHEARSAL

Even when you are making a presentation alone, many people will be involved. A speaker may depend on others for ideas and may even have to get approval of a higher authority for some of the material to be offered.

Anyone planning a presentation should prepare a schedule of events covering all phases of preparation. In case of a team presentation, this task should be assigned to one specific individual who should have the responsibility for coordinating the activities of the team.

The schedule should give the exact timetable for the development of the presentation. It should be distributed to all who are involved. A sample schedule can be seen in Figure 11.1. Several features shown in the example are of particular importance in almost any effort to coordinate a presentation.

You should bring together all of the people involved for a conference about the presentation. Include all the names on the distribution list except perhaps for the supervisor of audiovisuals, who might be contacted separately to make sure the demands for slides or film can be met. At the initial conference the general direction and tone of the presentation should be established and duties in research and writing assigned. Only one conference may be necessary, but several may be required in special situations.

In some cases presenters will be responsible for doing their own research and outlining; in other cases help may be available. But

Figure 11.1

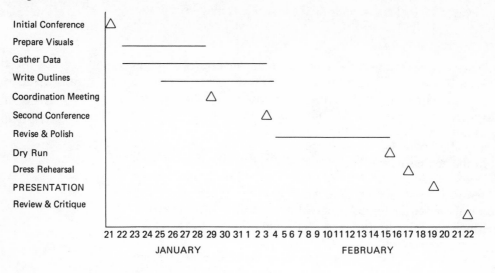

presenters are always responsible for learning and rehearsing their own material. Even so, formal practice sessions are advisable.

Both a dry-run session and a dress rehearsal should be part of the formal schedule. In the dry run the participants talk through their material. Their remarks do not have to be in final form, and the visual aids may not yet have been completely integrated into the presentations. In the dress rehearsal, the presentation should be given as closely as possible to the way it will actually be presented. The dry run and the dress rehearsal should be video-taped to make performance evaluation easier and more exact.

PRESENTATION REVIEW AND CRITIQUE

The process of evaluation should continue through the actual presentation. When it can be done unobtrusively, a video tape should be made. This tape can be valuable in reviewing the strengths and weaknesses of the delivery and the structure and content of the presentation. Audience reaction can be studied in an effort to discover the most successful parts of the presentation.

When a video tape cannot be made, a simple audio recording will provide many useful clues. If the presentation is witnessed by someone from the presenters' organization, that person can give useful feedback. In a team presentation, the presenters should critique each other.

The information collected in a presentation review and critique will often be used to alter a presentation for future use. But even when a presentation will never be repeated, the review serves a useful function in improving the skills of the participants.

SUMMARY

As a specialized, job-related talk intended either to inform or persuade, the presentation has several special features that are *usually* present. The audience for a presentation tends to be small and generally has authority to act. Listeners may feel free to interrupt presentations with questions. Visual aids are commonly used in presentations, and presentations are sometimes given by teams of two or more speakers. In planning presentations, speakers should set their objectives, analyze their audience, adjust their delivery, and plan their visual aids in accord with the particular demands of presentational speaking.

EXERCISES

1. Work with a fellow student to prepare a presentation to your class on some volunteer project that class members should participate in (such as giving blood, helping in a specific project for the underprivileged, buying tickets for a benefit performance). Be practical. Judge your success on the basis of action taken by the class.

2. Design a presentation you can give by yourself to get a college administrator or administrative body to approve some needed improvement in campus life.

3. Visit your school's recruiting office or fund-raising division and find out how many presentations they give. Observe one of their presentations in action and write a report on it, or write a report evaluating the presentation as it is described to you.

4. Find someone to play the role of your potential customer or customers and then deliver a sales presentation to that person. Video-tape the presentation and turn in the tape to your instructor. You might consider such sales situations as (a) selling a set of encyclopedias to a husband and wife with children in school, (b) selling life insurance to newlyweds, or (c) selling a used car to a fellow student. As part of your preparation, interview a professional salesperson who sells the product or service you select.

5. Give an informational presentation to your class on a school topic.

Suggested Readings

Linkugel, W. A.; R. R. Allen; and Richard L. Johannesen. *Contemporary American Speeches: A Sourcebook of Speech Forms and Principles,* 5th ed. Dubuque, Iowa: Kendall/Hunt Publishing Co., 1982.
The speeches in this book illustrate many of the principles of effective public speaking. The speakers were students, corporate executives, and a variety of professionals.

Morris, John O. *Make Yourself Clear!* New York: McGraw-Hill, 1980.
The author advocates a simple step procedure to improve business communication and provides interesting case studies for application. An easy-to-read-and-follow procedure to help the communicator be succinct and clear.

Smith, Mary John. *Persuasion and Human Action: A Review and Critique of Social Influence Theories.* Belmont, Calif.: Wadsworth Publishing Co., 1982.
The author provides a thorough examination of theories relating to persuasion and information processing. The serious student will be interested in applying these theories to presentations, especially when the presentation is to convince the decision makers.

The 3M Company offers a number of pamphlets on presentations, available from Visual Products Division, 3M Center, St. Paul, MN 55101. There is some redundancy among the publications, but they illustrate how business speakers give presentations as part of their work. The titles are *How to Make a Better Financial Presentation; How to Make a Better Technical Presentation; How to Present More Effectively—and Win More Favorable Responses from More People in Less Time; Is There a Sure Way to Be More Persuasive in Meetings and Presentations?* (includes the results of a Wharton School study on use of visuals in presentations).

Visual Aids

12

Business speakers frequently use visual aids out of habit without considering whether or not the aid makes a useful contribution to a speech. Visual aids should *not* be used simply because "everyone else at the meeting will have one." A decision based on such a premise may produce a speech with dull charts or meaningless slides that do little to help the speaker get a message across to an audience.

Visual aids may create certain difficulties even when they are used well and for a valid reason. First of all, an aid gives a listener something other than the speaker on which to focus attention. The listener can become more interested in the aid than in the idea, and as a result the visual material actually works against the speaker. A speaker showing pictures of homes to illustrate various ways of using solar energy will necessarily offer viewers an incidental opportunity to see (1) color schemes in the decor of the home, (2) shrubbery and landscaping, (3) a glimpse of furniture, and (4) a great variety of other things that do not relate to the speaker's point. A good visual aid will keep distractions to a minimum, but they cannot be eliminated altogether.

Second, a speaker cannot assume visual material will always be easier to understand than a verbal explanation. The old saying "A picture is worth a thousand words" is true of *some* pictures and *some* words, but it does not express a universally valid claim. Speakers must remember that all communication takes place through a process of interpretation of symbols before communication occurs.

Speakers should recall that most listeners have not had a great deal of experience interpreting many of the types of visuals shown during speeches. Graphs, for example, can be quite confusing to members of an audience who have not had many opportunities to interpret data distributed along the X axis and the Y axis. Charts with diagrams showing complex relationships do not make the relationships less complex simply because they are two-dimensional and drawn on a piece of heavy paper. You might discover in your own reading of books and magazines that you skip over any but the most attention-getting visual materials.

Before using a visual aid, you should make sure that the aid safely passes at least one of the following tests.

1. Does the visual aid clarify? If you had to describe a Rubik's Cube to someone who had never seen or heard of the device, you could probably do it with words alone. But if possible, you would almost certainly bring one out to aid in your explanation. If you were speaking to a large group, you might decide that a series of charts would be required. Or you might under special circumstances find it necessary to have a huge model of the cube constructed. While the object by itself would not automatically make its nature clear to a listener, a proper combination of words and visuals would be more useful than either words or the object used alone. You can use a visual aid, then, if it helps make your idea clear.

2. Does the visual aid cause the listener to remember? If you have ever seen a professor write key concepts on a chalkboard during a lecture, you probably were watching an effort to help you remember. Key words are not usually more clear in the written form than they are when merely spoken. But when they appear in print at the same time they are spoken and elaborated upon, the speaker is enlisting two of your senses to fix the material in your mind. Both the eye and the ear pick up the information and, one hopes, send it off to be stored in the brain.

A TV commercial asks the question "How do you spell relief?" and the answer written out for the viewer at the same time it is spoken is "R O L A I D S." Whatever you may think of the technique, it does cause listeners to remember the product. A business speaker may want a listener to remember six ways to save energy or three types of investments or four steps in making a workplace safer. A visual with key words and phrases on it may be shown to increase the possibility that listeners will later be able to recall the points.

Displaying nothing more than words as an aid to memory is not always advisable. Many audiences are annoyed to find they are watching an elaborate slide show that does nothing but provide them with a copy of the speaker's outline. Key words should not be displayed merely to prove that the speaker can operate the company's fancy projection equipment. The words must be important enough to justify their presence on the screen. Often key words or phrases are accompanied by diagrams or pictures. The words "Stop, look, and listen" on a safety poster may be illustrated by a stop sign, an eye, and an ear. Much more sophisticated word-picture relationships can be devised by a good art department. But always the speaker's purpose in showing words should be to make concepts easy to remember.

3. Does the visual aid impress? Some visual aids function primarily to impress the audience with the speaker's firsthand knowledge and experience with the subject. A speaker who holds up a tiny solar battery in front of an audience does not expect the object to be seen. But simply having the battery available may impress the audience with the speaker's familiarity with the object. A popular oil company speaker often displays a piece of oil shale when talking on energy exploration. The explanation of the difficulty of removing the oil is made somewhat clearer by seeing the shale, but the chief effect of the aid is to demonstrate the speaker's experience. A speaker might carry a copy of a report being quoted in a speech just to prove that the original document is available. One speaker brought in a two-foot-high stack of forms and reports to point out the work required to meet government regulations on a company project.

The examples given of visual aids to impress the audience fall into a category of aids commonly called "props." They can add variety to a speech in situations where audiences are pleased to see something fresher and more interesting than the routine charts and slides they expected.

Since visual aids may compete with speakers for an audience's attention, it is useful to categorize visuals according to the degree of *audience focus* on the visual material. The highest level may be called full focus, the next level primary focus, and lowest level variable focus. (See Fig. 12.1.)

The Degree of Audience Focus on Visual Aids

FULL FOCUS

Movies, multimedia shows, and filmstrips are full-focus visual aids. The audience will concentrate exclusively on the screen. The speaker will function only to introduce the visual material or to follow it up with comments and responses to questions. In a presentation, as discussed in Chapter 11, a visual aid of the full-focus type may be integrated into a speaker's total presentation. In the normal public speech, however, a movie or a multimedia show will tend to stand out as an independent piece of communication.

The "independent" nature of a full-focus visual aid makes it possible for a film or multimedia show to stand on its own with no help from a speaker. Some films can be mailed to an organization that needs a program so that it can show the material with no outside comment. Schools and senior citizens' groups are typical audiences for these films, which cover such diverse topics as the

Figure 12.1

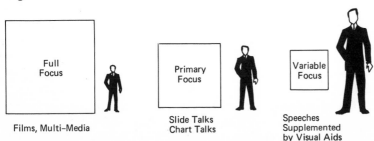

Full Focus — Films, Multi-Media

Primary Focus — Slide Talks, Chart Talks

Variable Focus — Speeches Supplemented by Visual Aids

history of steelmaking and the growing of peanuts. In another independent deployment of films or multimedia shows, they may be set up to run at several scheduled times during a convention or trade show. A person strolling past may decide to watch part or all of the showing and may come back to see it repeated. The rest of our discussion of full-focus visuals, however, assumes that a speaker usually will accompany the aid.

The decision to use a full-focus visual aid should take into account the major weakness of this medium. First, *these visual aids are not readily adaptable.* This problem is especially acute with a film. Once the film is produced, the message is set and cannot be expected to meet the varying needs of different audiences. A college recruiter may use a film in going from one high school to another on the assumption that most high schools are alike. If the recruiter is wrong about the similarities of the different audiences, the film will not be a valuable medium of communication.

Multimedia shows can be altered more easily than films. A change in 35-mm slides can update material or shift emphasis slightly without a revision of the whole show. But the basic message cannot be changed without considerable effort.

A second weakness of full-focus visual aids is that *they can be expensive.* While a company movie does not require the multimillion-dollar investment of a Hollywood film, its cost can quickly escalate into the tens of thousands of dollars. A multimedia show may require a dozen or more projectors and an elaborate sound system, all coordinated by computer. Although the heart of the show is the 35-mm slide, the cost can be as great as film.

A third problem of full-focus aids is that *they demand a more elaborate setting in order to be shown to an audience.* Both multimedia and film appear to best advantage if offered in a room especially designed for them. Anyone who has seen a movie while sitting in a folding chair in a gym knows that such surroundings do not compare favorably with the technical advantages and comfort of a theater. To demonstrate a giant fan for electric power plants, Westinghouse Corporation once designed a fifty-minute multimedia presentation that it took to thirteen cities. The show required a thirty-by-ninety-foot room, in which Westinghouse technicians set up swivel chairs surrounded by ten rear projection screens. The company used quadrophonic sound in this theater-in-the-round facility to give an audience the illusion of being inside the huge piece of equipment. Operation of the show required four technicians, thirty projectors, and two computers. Most full-focus visual aids do not require such a complicated setting, but physical facilities will always be a matter of concern.

PRIMARY FOCUS

Unlike a movie, where the full attention of the audience is riveted on the screen, a slide talk or a chart talk divides the focus between the visual aid and the speaker. The speech may be said to have primary focus on visual aids when the aid stays in view of the audience during the entire speech and the speaker's role is limited to reading a script or reciting an explanation of the material shown on the visuals. The most common example of primary-focus visual aids is the slide talk. Another example is the speech accompanied by a constant display of material on charts rather than 35-mm slides.

The slide talk has sometimes been derisively called a "talking head" speech. This description, of course, refers to the typical situation in a darkened room where the speaker's face is illuminated by the reading light on the lectern. As the slides change, the "talking head" reads from the text. Much of the criticism of the slide talk can be blamed on the poor quality of many such talks rather than on the slide talk as a medium of communication. A well-planned slide talk can be an effective way to present a message.

The cost of slide talks will be less than movies or multimedia shows. Although a professionally prepared single slide might easily cost fifty dollars or more, slides can be made from pictures taken by anyone and developed at the same price charged for home photography.

Slide talks are more flexible than full-focus visual aids because slides and script can be rather easily changed. Even elaborate diagrams and graphs on slides can be modified in a short time as new data become available. Many companies purchase their slides from such firms as Genigraphics, where the slides are made by computers and are kept in computer memory for ready access and rapid alteration to depict updated figures on profits, growth, or whatever data may be required to make the speech current.

Another advantage of slide talks over full-focus visual aids can be seen in the relative ease with which slides may be set up and shown. Almost any darkened room with a blank wall will do. A simple slide projector and a folding screen can be carried from place to place by one person. By adding a second projector and a dissolve unit, a speaker may achieve a high degree of sophistication as one slide from projector A smoothly replaces one from projector B.

Almost everyone has seen a good slide talk. An excellent one was prepared by the C & P Telephone Company on the one hundredth anniversary of Alexander Graham Bell's invention of the telephone. With 140 slides in a twenty-minute script, the talk enlivened the telephone story with quaint photographs of early equipment as well as slides showing the latest technological advances. The script was delivered dozens of times by the company's speakers bureau speakers and was made available to other companies as well.

Preparing a Slide Show

A good slide talk should be more than a speech with slides thrown up on the screen as the talk progresses. The words and pictures must be integrated with an understanding from the outset that the pictures will attract the primary focus of the audience and carry a major portion of the speaker's message.

Since no picture should be on the screen for longer than about ten seconds, it is apparent that not every subject will be suitable for a slide talk. For subjects that are suitable, a large number of slides will be needed and careful planning will be essential.

Outline. Start by preparing an outline of the material you intend to cover. The outline should have sufficient detail so that you will be able to prepare enough slides to cover every concept mentioned in the talk.

Planning cards. After you have a detailed outline, you should prepare a series of index cards, each representing one slide you intend to use. By using a 3 × 5 or 5 × 8 card for each slide, you can easily "shuffle ideas, add new ideas, or discard some ideas."[1] The cards will be easier to work with than pictures, and they make it possible for you to know precisely what you want when you get to the picture-taking stage. The cards also allow you to get suggestions from any advisers before you reach the point where changes would be time-consuming and expensive.

A useful format for each card consists of the following items. (1) In the upper left-hand corner of the card, sketch the *picture* you plan to use. A rough pencil outline will be enough, although if you already have a photograph or a diagram, you can attach it to the card. (2) In the upper right-hand corner, indicate the *slide number*. Use pencil to make changes easier. (3) Beneath the slide number and to the right of the sketch, put your *production notes*. These notes should include any information you will later need when you take your pictures. You might want to consider the camera angle if the slide shows a building, or the background color you want if the slide is to show a graph. (4) At the bottom of the card briefly summarize the *text* that will be used for the slide you are planning. (See Fig. 12.2.)

The planning board. After all the cards are prepared, spread them out on a planning board to see the scope of the show and to consider possible adjustments in the sequence of slides. A planning board is simply a large piece of heavy cardboard with slots for the cards. (See Fig. 12.3.) Attaching the cards to a wall with masking tape or spreading them out on a big table may be satisfactory alternatives to a specially designed planning board.

The script. Before you actually begin to take pictures, you should complete the text of your talk and coordinate it with your

1. *So You Want to Make a Tape-Slide Program ... Here's Why and How* (Richmond, Va.: University of Richmond Learning Resources Center), p. 4. The suggestions presented in this booklet form the basis of the above discussion on making your own slide show.

Figure 12.2

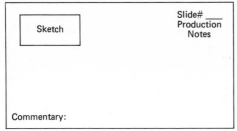

Planning Card

Figure 12.3

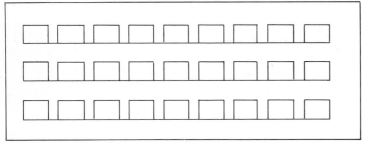

Planning Board

planning cards. At this stage you may also indicate any sound effects you might want to record. To study the relationship between the visual and the spoken parts of your talk, you can use the following form for your script.

SLIDE #	SUBJECT	NARRATION	MUSIC & EFFECTS
24	View of computer and operator	Our home office*† has the latest and	Hum of computer
25	Close-up of computer	best in equipment.*	
26	Close-up of operator	We also have highly* skilled personnel to ensure that our service	
27	Picture of printout	will be as fast and*† as efficient as possible	Sound of printer

The narration column of the script should indicate where slides are to be changed and where sound cues appear. In the sample shown above, an asterisk (*) is used for a slide change and a dag-

Visual Aids

ger (†) for a sound cue. In the language of a script, you should not mention the slides. Do not say, "This slide shows our sales rose twelve percent in Kansas City"; instead say, "Our sales rose twelve percent in Kansas City" as the slide comes on the screen. Do not let the speech become cluttered with references to "the red bar on the graph" or "the green line on the diagram." If the audience needs to have its attention directed to a place on the slide, use a pointer instead of references to the picture. Of course, a particular slide should be simple enough to be readily understood. The principles underlying the effective use of visuals, which will be discussed later in this chapter, apply to the slide show as well as to any other visual aid.

Final steps.   Once you have written your script and made last-minute adjustments in your plans, you are ready to provide the pictures for your slides. Any good 35-mm camera with a close-up lens should be adequate for most of the pictures you will need. You may require professional help if you need to photograph pictures or drawings taken from printed material. After your slides are developed, they should be checked carefully to see that they carry the message you intended. Then they should be numbered and filed. After you prepare any sound effects you need, your slide show will be ready.

Preparing the room and your equipment.   Any speaker should check out in advance the room where the speech is to be held, but that requirement takes on special urgency when you are giving a slide talk. You must determine the location of electrical outlets so that you can provide enough cord to put the equipment where it ought to be. Avoid being forced to put it in a poor location simply because that is where the power source happens to be. Make sure the room can be darkened adequately, and find out where the light switches are located. If coordination with someone to turn off the lights or operate the projector proves necessary, this also should be taken care of in advance.

Tape is necessary to secure electrical cords to the floor to prevent the danger of tripping. You may need an extra bulb for the projector if you are not using one of the newer models that automatically replaces a bad bulb. Never assume you can operate a projector unless you have worked with the particular model you are using. Make sure immediately before the speech that your equipment is in good working order.

VARIABLE FOCUS

When the speaker rather than the visual aid attracts the major share of an audience's attention, then that person is using a variable-focus visual aid. The room will not be darkened, or it will be darkened for only a short time during the speech, and the visuals appear only when they help the speaker make a point. A speaker may choose from a variety of types of visual aids using this approach. Each type is described in the following paragraphs, and then some guidelines for handling visual material are discussed.

The instant writing-surface visual. In spite of all the equipment available to the modern business speaker, at times nothing more elaborate than a writing surface will be needed. There can be an element of drama as a sales representative for a land developer calculates costs and profits on a proposed deal by working them out on a chalkboard during a speech. A speaker for an electric utility company may effectively use a felt-tip pen and a large pad to quickly sketch a graph showing the way in which consumer demand for power rises to a "peak load" on a summer day. An accountant may display a transparency of a 1040 tax form on an overhead projector and then fill in the blanks with a water-soluble marking pen. The chalkboard, the writing pad, and the overhead projector are the most common forms of instant writing-surface visuals.

The instant writing surface has significant advantages in cost, flexibility, and ease of operation. At a very low cost, colored pens or chalk can add a vivid touch to an otherwise drab diagram. Writing out a visual must not be allowed to interrupt a speech, so material used on an instant writing surface must be kept simple. Speakers who write on boards or pads or transparencies should *not* stop talking while writing. Ideally they should continue their explanation of their material, but if the writing requires their full concentration, some "patter" will be needed. A speaker adding up numbers written on a transparency can at least say something like "Let's see what we have here now" or "We will need to total the figures in this column."

The prepared chart. Use a prepared chart for material that would require too much time to write on a pad or chalkboard during a speech. Also, some simple visuals such as certain graphs or diagrams may demand greater precision than you can manage while giving a talk and should be put on charts ahead of time. Charts may also be used for some material ordinarily shown on slides. A blowup of a photograph of a computer or a greatly enlarged picture of the IRS 1040 tax form, which were cited earlier as examples of slides, might be used as charts.

Like the writing surface, the prepared chart can be used almost anywhere. You need only make sure that an easel or some other means of displaying the chart is available. Speakers quickly learn not to carry their charts rolled into cylinders and bound with rubber bands; after a few hours in this condition, charts are extremely difficult to unroll and keep flat.

The cost of charts varies considerably. If artwork must be purchased, the price can be quite high. Professional help may be advisable in some cases, however, because audiences expect a somewhat higher quality of drawing on a chart than they do when a speaker sketches a diagram on a chalkboard. Color can be an inexpensive but helpful feature of charts, just as it is in the case of a writing surface.

Slides.   Although the slide show has been considered a primary-focus visual aid, slides may be employed in a subordinate role during a speech. For example, if six slides were to be shown during a four-minute segment in the middle of a talk, the technique would be quite different from that used in a slide show. The ten-second rule would not apply, so a slide might be exposed for a minute or longer. Also, the speaker would still be the more dominant presence. Rather than become a "talking head" in a corner of the room, the speaker would be wise to choose a position in the front and center while relegating the screen to a less commanding position in front but to one side. See Figure 12.4 for possible room and screen arrangements when using variable-focus visual aids.[2]

Props.   A prop may be defined as any three-dimensional object a speaker displays before an audience. As was noted earlier, props may build a speaker's credibility without significantly adding to the clarity of the speaker's explanation. In a speech urging listeners to invest in a real estate venture, for example, a speaker cited information from both the *Wall Street Journal* and a report of a local certified public accountant. In both cases the speaker held up copies of the documents being quoted.

Props also may be used to clarify. They frequently appear in demonstrations of new products, for example. In one typical case, representatives of the telephone industry often give speeches on the technology of fiber optics, the system in which tiny, clear fibers replace copper wire in carrying telephone messages. Holding a piece of the fiber, which is about the thickness of a human hair, and actually showing light beams carrying sound through it can both impress an audience and make the concept clear.

The range of props is as wide as the speaker's imagination. A dollar bill may help make an economic point, a block of insulating material may help make an energy point, or comparing an old textbook with a new one may help make an educational point.

Props are flexible and can be replaced, updated, or discarded as necessary, although size can be a problem. If the object you want to display is too big, a scaled-down model of it may be constructed.

Handouts.   Handouts should be held to the end of a speech, except when making a presentation to a small group. If distributed during a talk, handouts may be a major distraction. Listeners have the habit of not looking at the part of the handout the speaker wishes to discuss.

Handouts can serve the function of providing a written record of the speaker's main ideas or supplying data too complicated to remember. They can also furnish information that listeners need

2. *Leaders Digest,* Visual Products Division/3M, St. Paul, Minn., 1979.

Figure 12.4

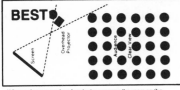

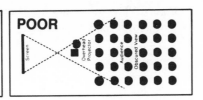

When using an overhead projector, arrange the room so the audience's view of the screen is not obstructed.

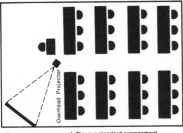

Classroom arrangement. This is a standard arrangement suitable for any size group.

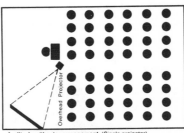

Auditorium/theater arrangement. (Single projector). Suitable for any size audience, but most efficient for large groups.

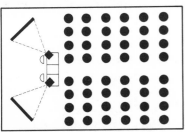

Auditorium/theater arrangement. (Dual projectors). As above, this arrangement works well with large groups. Two projectors and screens give the presenter more latitude in his presentation.

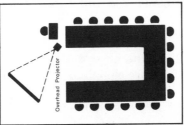

U-table arrangement. Suitable for 30 people or fewer. This arrangement is ideal for group discussion and interaction.

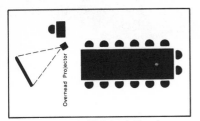

Center table arrangement. Suitable for under 20 people. This set-up promotes discussion and is best for long meetings.

in order to take further action. This information might include anything from order forms to instructions on how to contact the company complaint department. Some companies give their speakers ball-point pens, reusable bottle caps, rulers, or other "favors" to be distributed largely as an incidental effort to get goodwill. Some of these items, however, have telephone numbers or addresses that companies hope audiences will use.

Handouts are flexible, they are usually easy to handle, and their cost is generally modest.

Visual Aids

Guidelines for Using Visual Aids

Ineffective use of variable-focus visual aids can almost always be traced to a violation of one or more of six guidelines (see Fig. 12.5). These guidelines offer a simple, commonsense approach to combining visual and spoken communication.

1. Subordinate the visual aid to the speaker's ideas. As has been noted, a visual aid should not be an end in itself. No direct reference to the aid need be made; the speaker should talk about ideas, not pictures.

2. Maintain eye contact when displaying visuals. Few sights are more ludicrous than that of a speaker standing in front of an audience while speaking earnestly to a visual aid. The speaker should not need to look at a visual except quickly to make sure the correct aid has been exposed and perhaps to find a particular feature of the aid on which to focus audience attention. A glance will serve that purpose, and the speaker should resist the urge to gaze at the visual. While the audience looks at the visual, the speaker looks at the audience.

3. Expose the visual aid only when needed. A speaker should not display visuals before the speech begins. When this is done, the audience tends to look at the aids instead of listening to the speaker, and by the time the speaker refers to the aid, the audience will have lost interest in it. Speakers should also be concerned about getting visuals out of sight after they have served their purpose. Leaving a visual exposed after use is not so big a distraction as exposing one too soon, but it will generally be helpful to erase, remove, or cover aids no longer being used.

Speakers should plan ahead to make sure visuals will be set up before a talk begins and if possible before the audience arrives. A speech will get off to a weak start if a speaker must take two or three minutes to arrange some charts or set up a projector.

Visual aids should be in place, but concealed, before the speaker is introduced. Props may be placed under the lectern or covered with an unobtrusive cloth to keep them hidden. The first chart on an easel should be a blank, and other blanks should be inserted between charts. If charts are affixed to a wall, they may be covered with strips of paper that can easily be pulled away when the chart is needed.

Separate parts of a visual should be exposed one at a time when all parts do not immediately relate to the speaker's point. For example, suppose a speaker wanted to show an audience a diagram of a planning card used in preparing a slide talk. The four parts of the card should come into view one at a time. If the card were shown as a blowup on a chart, each part could be covered with a separate piece of paper that could be removed as the idea was explained. Or the chart could be exposed with only the outline of the card shown, and the words indicating the four parts could be added as "stick-ons" made of small pieces of cardboard backed by masking tape. If slides or transparencies were used to show the planning card, five visuals could be made. The first would show a blank card, the next would be a card with a sketch added to it, the third would include the slide number, the fourth would show the production notes, and the last would display the commentary, so that the complete planning card was exposed.

The "overlay" approach just described has many variations. By placing a blank transparency over the 1040 tax form, for example, you may work out a tax case, and then, by replacing the top transparency with another one, you may work out another sample case. The principle involved is a simple one: expose any visual only when it will be relevant to the point you are making at the time.

4. Make sure the visual aid is big and bold enough to be seen clearly. Except for certain aids used only to make an impression, visual material should be big enough to be seen without strain. A speaker usually will not get a warm response from an audience by apologizing with the remark "I know you can't see this clearly, but. . . ." In preparing visuals, a surprising number of speakers forget the simple fact that although they may prepare a chart at arm's length, it will be viewed by people sitting at a much greater distance. The only sure test for proper size requires the speaker to try out the aid by walking as far away from it as the farthest seat in the room where the speech will be delivered.

The lines on a diagram or graph should be heavy and dark. Beware of thin spider-web lines that disappear from view only a few feet away from the drawing. Colors should be bold. Red or black carries better than a pale yellow. Letters should be big. A visual aid may have a clear diagram, but it will be ineffective if the important words used to label the parts are far too small to be seen.

5. Keep the visual aid simple. Ideally a visual aid should support a single idea. It should not be cluttered with so much detail that the audience has a wide choice of places to look. If a visual begins to become cluttered with too much material, some of it must be discarded. You may discover that several aids are needed instead of just the one with which you began. Following the rule of simplicity will make it easier for you to follow the guideline that calls for you to expose visuals only when they are actually needed in your speech. A supply and demand curve represents a complex idea captured in a simple diagram.

6. Establish an open line of sight. Perhaps you have had a professor who put important material on the chalkboard and then stood directly between you and the information you needed to copy. Unfortunately, some business speakers also fail to provide an open line of sight between visual aids and the audience. They stand in front of their charts or place objects too low to be seen beyond the first row. Often this problem results from a failure to go to the room where the speech will be given in order to determine the best location for visuals. Last-minute efforts to adapt to a poorly equipped room do not often prove successful.

If possible, your planning should extend to determining the arrangement of chairs in the room. You must give particular attention to the placement of screens and projection equipment. Figure 12.4 illustrates the right and wrong approaches.

Working with the Audiovisual Department

Although much of our discussion of visual aids has assumed that you as a business speaker will be responsible for preparing your own visuals, you may discover that this task is largely in the hands of a professional audiovisual department in your company. One corporation, Standard Oil of Indiana, has an Audiovisual Services Division which occupies most of the twenty-fifth floor of corporate headquarters in Chicago. The division has four sections: production, television, photographic, and art. An operation of this scope can handle everything from a simple slide to an animated film.

Most audiovisual departments are much smaller, but you can expect a high degree of technical expertise either in a company you might work for or in an outside firm called in to help you on a project. A sample contract for the preparation of a slide talk, shown in Figure 12.6, illustrates the kinds of services an audiovisual company can provide and indicates the cost involved in a fairly typical case. It will be important to cooperate with technical experts and to coordinate your efforts with theirs. These experts keep up with developments in the audiovisual field, and you should respect their judgment, at the same time making sure the material they supply does in fact accomplish the task you have in mind. You will want to take great care to make sure you allow enough time for the technicians to do their work. Last-minute requests or changes on your part will hamper their efforts to give you the best possible service.

Figure 12.6

Video Services of Virginia

Terry Goldman   804 353-4431
P.O. Box 312
Richmond, VA.
23173

SEALED BID   3/1/82

Bid to: ACME Floor and Tile Corporation
         123 Granite Ave.
         Richmond, VA 23222

         Attention: Mr. R. Wheeler, Vice Pres. Corporate Public Relations

Production Specifications: 1 dissolve or single projector multi-image
                       sound/slide program. Stereo.

Description: VSV will produce for ACME Floor and Tile, a sound/slide
            program for utilization by their sales organization to
            acquaint marketing representatives with their new 1982
            spring line of products. Show length: 15 minutes/250 slides.

Costs: A. Scripting: Program will be co-produced/scripted with
            assistance from R. Wheeler, ACME Floor and Tile.

         $200.

      B. Sound studio production: 1/2 day @ $400 per day........

         $200.

      C. Talent. 1 male voice....2 female voices 1/2 day.....

         $600.

      D. Art work/phototype/layout for slide production

         $500.

      E. On site-field location production (2 days) 300.

         $600.

      F. Slide film costs:Duplication/internegatives/custom slides/graphics

         $250.

      G. Editing/Mixing/Synchronization Studio Time (1/2 day)

         $200.
Total Cost:
         $2550.   ****This includes two separate playback screenings for
                 corporate personnel.
                ****Additional screenings charged at the rate $150 per day
                ****Price above includes one original program and one du-
                plicate program. Additional duplicates $150. each.
* Representative bid sample. Prices subject to alteration by program
   requirements.

SUMMARY

Visual aids should be used with discretion. They should be employed only if they clarify ideas, help the listener remember, or impress the audience. Speakers have available a wide range of visual aids including (1) full-focus aids, such as movies or multimedia shows, where the visual aids constitute almost the total communication effort; (2) primary-focus aids, such as slide talks or chart talks, where the speaker plays the "talking head" role; and (3) variable-focus aids, such as writing surfaces, prepared charts, limited slides, props, and/or handouts—aids that play a less important role than the speaker. Business speakers may prepare their own visual material but should be able to work with the skilled audio-visual technicians available both privately and in many companies.

EXERCISES

1. Watch the evening network or cable news for a week. Observe the role of visual aids. Keep a log in which you describe the visuals. Write a critique evaluating their usefulness.

2. Bring a three-dimensional model or an actual mechanism to class to show how it works. Choose something not well understood by the class and complete your explanation in five minutes or less.

3. Find a magazine article with an interesting segment that would take you three to five minutes to read. Prepare a set of planning cards to show how you would make the segment into part of a slide talk. Make sure you have a card for at least every ten seconds of your talk.

Suggested Readings

Conference Room Planning Guide. St. Paul, Minn.: 3M Company, 1979.
An excellent brief guide to setting up a room so that audiovisuals can be used to best advantage. It includes some suggestions concerning planning meetings.

Materials for Visual Presentations: Planning and Preparation. Pamphlet No. S-13. New York: Kodak.
This pamphlet includes an excellent guide on preparing a slide talk.

Public Relations Journal. Public Relations Society of America, New York.
One issue a year has an emphasis on audiovisuals. The September 1978 issue offers an especially good survey of applications.

Speechmaking: More than Words Alone. New York: Kodak.
This short booklet shows equipment and methods used in business communication.

Delivering a Message

13

In an ideal world, people would listen to your ideas without paying any attention to the *manner* in which you spoke. In our real world, however, when you stand up to speak as a representative of your business, you will be judged on how you conduct yourself as well as on what you have to say. Poor delivery skills can all but destroy your message; good delivery can help you express your thoughts successfully.

During the fifteen or twenty minutes of a typical business speech, you are at "center stage." Every eye is on you, and every aspect of your behavior will be a part of your message. You should work to ensure that nothing your audience sees or hears distracts from your ideas. Have you ever had a teacher who paced aimlessly during a lecture? Have you ever had a date who conversed in a listless tone? Have you ever found yourself counting the number of times a speaker's eyeglasses had to be readjusted? If so, you know that such behavior leaves a distinctly negative impression.

Good delivery is the effective use of your voice and your body when speaking. If used properly, the spoken word has many advantages over cold print. Your tone of voice can add an extra dimension of meaning to a word or phrase. Your sincerity and conviction will come across not just because of the language you choose, but also because of the stress you put on your words. The way you stand and move can help make your ideas both interesting and clear. This chapter considers the specific patterns of behavior you will want to follow in speaking.

Modes of Delivery

You have four basic delivery modes from which to choose: you can read your material from a manuscript, you can memorize it, you can speak "off the cuff," or you can speak from notes.

READING A SPEECH

On rare occasions you may be required to read a speech from a prepared text. A highly important talk, one in which the implications of each phrase you utter will be studied, might be read from a manuscript. Such speeches can range from brief statements on a sensitive legal matter to the carefully worded text of a keynote speech before a major business or professional convention. As you will see in Chapter 14, "Speech Writing," a manuscript speech is usually studied carefully by a number of people in an effort to see that every word is exactly right.

This method of speaking has many disadvantages and is used for only a small minority of business and professional speeches. Most speakers find it difficult to use a conversational tone of voice in reading a speech. Also, the speaker reading from a text will not be able to make major adjustments in the message when, for example, the audience fails to understand an idea in the speech.

MEMORIZATION

Memorizing a speech may be the most dangerous of all the choices a speaker has. Even more than the speaker who reads a talk, the person who memorizes will find it hard to sound conversational. And, of course, if a speaker's memory fails at some point in the speech, the result will be highly embarrassing.

OFF-THE-CUFF DELIVERY

Speakers who depend on last-minute inspiration may discover that it does not always come to them. Going before an audience to speak off the cuff should be reserved for rather informal situations in which the speaker has an absolute mastery of the subject. Two major problems must be kept in mind. First of all, slips of the tongue may occur. An innocent remark may have a double meaning that may confuse or amuse the audience. Second, speakers may have trouble keeping within time limitations. If no thought has been given to precisely how the speech is to be presented, a speaker may talk at great length without being able to express an idea adequately.

The question-and-answer session at the end of a talk will force a speaker to give at least some off-the-cuff responses, since not every question can be anticipated. Techniques for handling questions are considered later in this chapter.

SPEAKING FROM NOTES

The best method of delivery for most situations is the speech from notes. Such a speech should be well prepared, although the preparation will be represented not by a text but by a written outline. The outline contains the points and subpoints you plan to develop and also briefly indicates the material you will use to explain the points.

Your notes may be quite unintelligible to anyone else. For example, if a speaker's first main point is "The first step toward regaining our share of the market must be to continue to improve productivity," the outline may contain only "1st step market share prod." A cryptic comment such as "Ex of Sp Parts" may mean to the speaker "Give the example of the way we improved productivity by speeding up the shipment of spare parts." Be careful not to make your notes *too* cryptic, though, or you might forget what they mean.

Quotations and statistics may be written out in detail in notes, but notes are not generally intended to be read. Notes *remind* you of an idea. Once the idea has come to your attention, you do not need the notes until you refer to them for the next idea. This approach means you will be thinking about the ideas when talking about them to an audience rather than merely reciting what is written on a piece of paper.

As you consider the attributes of good delivery, it will be clear that speaking from notes maximizes a speaker's capacity to give a speech in a conversational manner.

Conversational Delivery

Although many untrained speakers do a poor job when standing before an audience, the fact is that almost all of them use delivery skills in a highly effective manner when they are engaged in normal conversation. When two friends meet after not seeing each other for a long time, their eyes "light up," they smile, and their voices reflect their feelings. Or when a parent scolds a child, the parent's face shows concern, the gestures add emphasis, and the voice acquires a stern edge to it.

In giving a speech, you should talk "to" and "with" an audience instead of "at" them. Never regard a speech as a performance in which you are putting on a show. Your best speech delivery will result from learning how to apply the skills you already use in everyday communication.

EYE CONTACT

Anyone engaged in earnest conversation almost always looks directly into the eyes of the listener. Experience has taught you that looking at someone provides you with valuable clues to how your communication is being received. The public speaker, then, must both look at *and* see the members of an audience gathered to hear a speech.

Recognizing lack of interest. Listeners send clear signals to show when a speech fails to hold their interest. They yawn, they look out the window, they check their watches, or they talk to one another. You must have eye contact to be alert to such behavior. While a small amount of boredom can be expected in almost any speech, too many negative reactions tell you that something must be done.

A good public speaker responds to demonstrated lack of interest with the same devices used in a conversation in the home or office. The speaker changes behavior to keep the listener interested. Speaking louder may help. Or the speaker may add variety to the voice by altering rate or intonation. The speaker may increase the action in the speech by making more forceful gestures or moving from behind the speaker's stand.

Spotting signs of confusion or disbelief.   Some signals picked up by good eye contact give you information about problems in the speech that cannot be corrected by changing behavior. A listener may have a puzzled look or a frown, suggesting that information in the speech has not been understood. A speaker talking from notes can adjust to this response by adding additional evidence or merely by repeating a point in clearer language.

The planned content of the speech must also be changed when you see signs of disbelief. Listeners may shake their heads negatively or exhibit facial expressions indicating that they do not accept the speaker's point. Again, supplementary material or explanation may be required. If you have analyzed the audience well before preparing the speech, only minor adjustments should be required.

Getting positive audience feedback.   Naturally, all signs seen in an audience will not be negative. At times listeners will smile or nod. Their eyes will reflect understanding and appreciation of your ideas. This information, too, is valuable because it permits you to continue with some assurance that the message of the speech is being understood and accepted.

Mechanics of eye contact.   Eye contact during a speech can be quite systematic. Talking from notes will enable you to look at everyone in a small audience. Take care not to leave out those seated in the back or on the edges of the group. You should not focus too much eye contact on a few listeners; they may feel they are being "stared at." In large audiences of several hundred listeners, you will be unable to look at every single person and must select a few listeners from various parts of the room. The responses from the sample can be treated as representative of the audience as a whole.

POSTURE

Posture plays a key role in projecting an image of a speaker. A speaker who stands off-balance while shifting about will telegraph a note of uncertainty and insecurity to the audience. A speaker who has a relaxed but alert posture and who stands straight will project an image of being solid, sound, and dependable.

Problems with the speaker's stand.   The lectern can easily become an embarrassing security blanket for a speaker. Do not cling to the stand or lean on it for support; if you do, you may look like a human pretzel, so that posture will not be a positive force in your speech. The speaker's stand exists to hold speaking notes, if required, and not to provide a resting place for the person giving the speech.

Standing squarely.   When speaking, you should keep some weight on each foot. When the weight shifts to only one foot, your shoulders slant at an awkward angle. Movement becomes clumsy in this position, and the audience might be distracted from what you have to say.

Avoiding stiffness. Good posture does not mean standing at rigid attention, with knees locked and hands stiffly at your side. Unnatural stiffness in posture will make both you and the audience feel uncomfortable. Remain "relaxed but alert."

GESTURES

For some reason, many people are embarrassed by the fact that they use gestures when speaking. There is no reason to feel apologetic for using movements of the hands and body to help convey meaning. Gesture is a fundamental medium of communication; it can help convey an idea even when people do not speak the same language. In speeches, gestures help reinforce a message. Gestures describe by showing action, direction, shape, speed, or size. They emphasize by demonstrating the intensity of a speaker's feeling about an idea. They help to hold the audience's attention, because movement attracts the eye. Some gestures even convey ideas as well as words: a clinched fist, a shrug, or a cautioning gesture may express meaning as well as or better than the spoken language. No speaker should regard gesture as an unnatural part of communication.

Speakers sometimes feel that gestures are unusual because they become aware of gesturing only when engaged in formal speaking. The problem is compounded by the need to find something to do with hands when they are not being used. An audience can easily be distracted by a speaker whose hands move about aimlessly or are positioned in awkward resting places when not in use. This distraction can be removed by letting hands hang naturally at the sides or by resting them lightly on the lectern.

Timing. A gesture usually comes at the same time you utter the thought that the gesture reinforces. Occasionally a gesture may precede the thought slightly. Rarely does a good speaker gesture *after* the thought. A delay in timing may result if an effort is made to plan gestures by writing "stage directions" into the notes for a speech. When such a delay occurs, an audience may find the gesture ludicrous rather than helpful.

Size. Beginning public speakers sometimes make their gestures too small to be effective. A motion intended to emphasize your thought will be of little help if it is hidden at your side or concealed by the lectern. Gestures big enough to be seen by an audience may at first seem excessively large to you, but with experience you can soon become comfortable with the larger gestures.

Rhythm and force. Gestures should not appear mechanical. They should be smooth and relaxed. If a gesture is a natural physical response to your thought, it will usually have the right amount of vitality to aid in the expression of your message.

VOICE

Without thinking about it, most listeners pay a great deal of attention to the sound of a speaker's voice as well as to the words being spoken. Subconsciously, many decisions about a speaker's confidence and sincerity are made on the basis of voice. Four major features of the voice—rate, volume, pitch, and quality—may be a problem to the public speaker, but each can be controlled.

Rate. Speaking in public causes many people to increase the rate at which they speak. This often gives an impression of uncertainty and may seem to indicate that the speaker does not know the subject well. As a rule, most beginning speakers find it advisable to make a deliberate effort to slow down. Remember that you are not obligated to fill every second of a talk with sound. Silence will be far better than meaningless vocalizations or nonfluencies such as *ah, er,* and the often-heard *y'know.* The rate of a speech can be varied so that some parts are slow and deliberate while others are at a brisk pace.

Volume. A speaker who does not talk loudly enough will obviously not be heard, but in addition to that, the speaker may appear to an audience to be insecure. When speaking to a large audience, do not resort to blasting a listener's eardrums. The best advice calls for projecting or "aiming" the voice at the most distant person in the room. This will usually result in an adequate volume without making you sound unnatural. If you have to yell to be heard, a microphone should be used.

Pitch. While most speakers think a low pitch sounds impressive, no effort should be made to force the pitch of the voice down to an uncomfortable level. Excessively high pitch can be avoided by slowing down, staying calm, and concentrating on the ideas in the speech. More important than pitch level is the variety of pitch in your voice. Most speakers who read their talks word for word use a monotonous tone without the normal rise and fall of everyday vocal pitch. Again, the solution to this problem is to think of the idea while it is being spoken.

Quality. No effort should be made to speak in an artificially dignified or "stage" voice. Many speakers do not like the sound of their own voice as they hear it on audio or video tape. They should not, however, attempt to alter vocal quality while speaking, for two reasons. First, most audiences soon adjust to the sound of a speaker's voice. All speakers are not expected to have the voices of professional announcers. Second, an effort to make a radical change in vocal quality may result in a voice that sounds "fake." The voice may even crack from the strain of attempting an unnatural sound or of holding an unusually low pitch. Speakers should focus on their ideas and not on their voices. Any speaker with a voice problem that seriously interferes with communication will need to consult a professional voice expert.

The one rule that should determine the way you dress for a speech is this: wear nothing that will distract from the speech. Dressing extravagantly will be just as bad as dressing shabbily. From hair style to jewelry, a speaker should try to avoid any aspect of personal appearance that will call attention to itself. In those situations where acceptable dress for a particular audience has a range of formality, you will usually be safer dressing at the upper end of that range.

Since most business speeches are given before a group where normal office dress will be acceptable, students might want to give classroom speeches in somewhat more formal attire than usually worn to class. Although some businesses are conducted in a blue-jeans environment, most are characterized by the business suit. Frequently, wearing standard business clothing will have a positive effect on the way a student presents a talk. The classroom is a good place to practice speaking in dress appropriate for the business and professsional world.

As a speaker, you begin to communicate with an audience *before* the first word of a speech. In fact, a speech can be said to begin as early as the moment you rise to approach the lectern. A good speaker will move purposefully and deliberately. Without rushing immediately into the speech, you should arrange your notes on the lectern and establish eye contact with the audience. It will make a weak impression on the audience if you begin to speak with head bowed and eyes fixed on notes.

At the end of a speech, do not rush away. The last line of the speech should be given directly to the audience before any move is made away from the lectern. After a moment of eye contact following the last word of the speech, you can then walk away.

Most business and professional speakers are expected to remain for a question-and-answer session after a speech. As was noted earlier, this session cannot be fully planned and must be delivered off the cuff. Some preparation can be made, however, and there are a few fundamentals a speaker should understand before attempting to face the questions.

To avoid a potentially clumsy transition from the speech to the start of the questions, you should work closely in advance with the presiding officer of a meeting. One good approach calls for two important steps. First, make sure the audience clearly understands that questions will follow the speech. This helps ensure that listeners will be ready with inquiries. Second, have the presiding officer start the question-and-answer session by calling for the first question. This procedure permits the speaker to leave the stand at the end of the talk. Remaining at the lectern can be embarrassing if no questions are asked or if, as is often the case, the questions start slowly. Once the first questioner has been recognized by the presiding officer, the speaker can return to the stand to answer the question and to take control of the rest of the session.

Since the session typically starts slowly but ends with a flurry of questions, you should plan to end the questions on time without hurting anyone's feelings. One way to do this is to announce the approaching end of the session when there are still two or three minutes to go. This warns the audience that only a few more questions can be answered and reduces the risk of offending people who have their hands in the air when the questions are abruptly terminated.

TYPES OF QUESTIONS

Not all questions are sincere efforts to get information. Knowledge of this fact can help a speaker cope with the pressure of answering a variety of queries in the off-the-cuff mode of delivery.

Some questions are intended to state the questioner's position on an issue. A question that begins with "Isn't it true that ..." may be of this type. In almost every instance, it is bad form to respond with "What is your question?" Many people will regard such a response as clumsy or arrogant behavior on the part of a speaker. Usually a better response takes the form of recognizing the questioner's point of view. If you agree with it, your response may indicate agreement. If you do not agree, your response can be a simple "I see. Thank you for that observation," or "That's an interesting point of view. I appreciate your concern."

Some questions have a hostile tone and are primarily intended to attack the speaker. If you respond with equal hostility or "put down" the questioner, you run the risk of actually helping the questioner win audience sympathy. A more effective approach is to respond calmly and factually to the question. If the question permits it, you can indicate concern for the *feelings* of the person who asked the question. For example, if someone asks a utility company speaker an unfriendly question about rising rates, the speaker could both state the facts about rate increases and acknowledge the questioner's legitimate concern. It is seldom a good idea to try to minimize the problem stated in a question if that problem directly affects the questioner.

The delivery of answers to hostile questions should be to the audience rather than directly to the person who asked the question. Continued eye contact with the questioner might encourage the questioner to break in and thus allow the question-and-answer session to degenerate into an argument.

In answering any question, hostile or not, do not be afraid to say, "I don't know," when necessary. In such a case, it is a good idea to offer to get the name and address of the questioner after the meeting and then to supply the requested information.

Speakers should also make an effort to keep answers short. Those speakers who use questions as an opportunity to give another speech will not be good representatives of their organizations. Answers can be kept short by "front-loading" them. With this approach, you give the essence of the answer immediately and then briefly explain it. If the answer starts with the explanation, you may find it hard to get to the answer briefly.

Be aware of the need in some cases to repeat a question. If members of the audience in the back of the room failed to hear a question, then obviously your answer will not make much sense. In repeating a question, you may shorten it or even remove some offensive language, but avoid distorting or twisting the question.

The last question you answer may not always provide the most graceful or appropriate ending to an appearance before a group. To solve this problem, many speakers follow their last answer with half a minute of concluding remarks. These can often be prepared ahead of time, or they can grow out of the situation surrounding the speech.

Using the Microphone

A microphone should not be used simply because one is available. A speaker whose voice can comfortably carry to everyone in an audience will generally be better off if the mike is turned off. Microphones pose many problems for the speaker. In the first place, they often malfunction. They go dead at odd moments or they make unpleasant noises. Even the highest-quality equipment can betray a speaker.

Also, microphones usually require adjustment. This can be difficult, as a number of speakers use the same mike and each one is required to move it up or down. The adjustment process is distracting enough, but it is made worse when the sound of the adjustment is amplified through the system. If a microphone must be adjusted, it should be done in one smooth, decisive movement. If the adjustment must be tested after it has been completed and with an audience present, the speaker should never blow into a mike or tap it. Nor should a speaker ask the rather inane question "Can anybody hear me?" It will usually be possible to tell from audience response to the first few words whether the equipment is working properly. If not, someone in the back of the room should be called on specifically to ask if the sound is reaching the rear.

Most microphones have the additional disadvantage of limiting a speaker's movements. Leaning toward or away from the mike sends the volume of the sound sharply up or down. Moving away from the stand to work with a chart or other visual aid eliminates the amplification altogether. An exception is the lavaliere mike, which can be worn around a speaker's neck. This arrangement permits the speaker to walk as far as the length of the cord while keeping the mike at a constant distance from the speaker's mouth.

Stage Fright

Most speakers feel some degree of stage fright. Although this anxiety is seldom apparent to the casual observer, most speakers think everyone is keenly aware of what they are feeling. Since the symptoms are not obvious, there is little point in mentioning the problem during the speech. Of course, stage fright or speech anxiety is important to the speaker. The perspiration or trembling or vocal tension or upset stomach or temporary loss of memory is real and cannot be ignored by the speaker.

These symptoms can be controlled, but they cannot be eliminated in most cases. Speakers, then, should recognize that stage fright is natural, and they should expect to live with some discomfort, especially in the early minutes of speaking. With experience, the signs of stage fright decrease and become more bearable. Even highly experienced speakers will find that the anxiety can return in full force, but they also know that stage fright does not keep a speech from being successful.

Some speakers believe a touch of anxiety is necessary for a good speech. They feel that if the symptoms of stage fright are not present, the speaker does not care enough about the speech and may do poorly.

Although the uncomfortable signs of stage fright cannot be totally eliminated, they can be kept within reasonable bounds. To keep speech anxiety under control, have a positive attitude and practice your speech adequately.

Anyone speaking as a company representative will ordinarily have been selected for the job. This is a compliment to any speaker and should give confidence. Almost always a speaker is called upon because he or she has special knowledge about the subject of the speech. One who is not an expert in the field will at least have had experience with the topic. This knowledge, plus an appreciation of the audience's need to hear the speech, should inspire a speaker with a positive attitude.

Practicing a Speech

The best way to practice a speech is to deliver a dress rehearsal in the room where the actual talk is to be delivered. Except for the absence of the audience, everything should be just like the real thing. Unfortunately, this method of practice is not always feasible.

Not having an audience for a practice run makes many speakers uncomfortable in rehearsal. Partly for this reason, speeches are often practiced silently. By going over a speech several times mentally, you can become familiar with the material. Saying at least part of the speech out loud often proves to be the only way to be confident that you will handle strange words, names, or phrases well in the speech.

The goal of practice ordinarily is not to get every word and gesture and tone exactly as they will appear in the speech. The delivery of a speech will, as was noted earlier, often be adapted to the responses of the audience. But rehearsal should give you the opportunity to learn the ideas of a speech well enough to be confident and also to be free to observe how the speech is being delivered so that adjustments can be made as necessary.

SUMMARY

Voice and body play an important role in communication during a speech. A business speaker should use a conversational tone and should not hurry the rate of speaking. Speakers can learn to monitor their own behavior by checking their use of eye contact, gestures, and posture. In most cases, a business talk should be delivered from notes rather than off the cuff or from memory or a manuscript. Speakers should, however, be able to read a speech text when required and should be able to give off-the-cuff responses to questions after a speech. When a microphone is not absolutely necessary, it should be turned off. When a speaker does need amplification, the mike should be adjusted properly.

EXERCISES

1. Write an evaluation of the use of eye contact by three of your professors. Include a statement for each professor indicating the effect you think eye contact or the lack of it has on that professor's ability to communicate.

2. Read the summary paragraph at the end of this chapter aloud and tape-record your reading. Then make notes on the points covered in the summary and use your own words to say the ideas into the tape recorder. Listen to the two versions, and carefully note the vocal differences.

3. Watch any one of the popular TV evangelists deliver a sermon. Write a detailed account of the speaker's delivery. For at least five minutes of the sermon, turn the sound off to devote full attention to the speaker's actions.

4. Watch a TV program such as "Meet the Press" or "Face the Nation," and write an evaluation of how well the guest answered questions. Make a tape recording of the broadcast to play back in assisting your memory. As part of your evaluation, indicate the percentage of questions to which the speaker gave a direct answer.

Suggested Readings

Anderson, Virgil A. *Training the Speaking Voice,* 3rd ed. New York: Oxford University Press, 1977.
Brief concepts are followed by exercises designed to improve or correct vocal problems. The book would be used best with a tutor trained in the principles.

Ehninger, Douglas; Bruce E. Gronbeck; and Alan H. Monroe. *Principles of Speech Communication,* 8th brief ed. Glenview, Ill.: Scott, Foresman and Co., 1980.
Chapter 4 on the use of the body and Chapter 5 on the use of the voice give a detailed look at speech delivery.

Rodman, George. *Public Speaking: An Introduction to Message Preparation,* 2nd ed. New York: Holt, Rinehart and Winston, 1981.
Chapter 7 includes a brief passage on controlling stage fright.

Verderber, Rudolph F. *The Challenge of Effective Speaking,* 5th ed. Belmont, Calif.: Wadsworth Publishing Co., 1982.
This standard public speaking text offers a chapter on delivery that includes how to deal with fear, the vocal mechanism, and a program to improve delivery.

Speech Writing

14

Speaking from notes after careful preparation usually is the best way to give a speech. Some occasions, however, call for a speech to be written out in full prior to delivery. It would be hard to imagine the president of the United States giving an inaugural address from an outline, or the head of a corporation speaking without a manuscript as a keynote speaker for an important business conference. Executives at various levels in the business and professional world sometimes decide that a speech should be committed to paper before it is presented.

Speaking from a prepared text offers a speaker several significant advantages. The language of the speech can be carefully controlled without the risk of making an unfortunate slip of the tongue or using a clumsy expression. The content of the speech can be checked in advance with informed advisers to ensure that the material used and the policy expressed are suitable.

Some speakers are simply too busy to write their own speeches. Writing a speech can consume an enormous amount of time. Even professional writers may require twenty hours or more of writing time to complete a fifteen-to-twenty-minute speech. The demands on an executive's time may simply make it impossible for him or her to do the physical preparation for a speech.

Some critics of speech writing regard the practice as unethical. Having a speech written by someone other than the speaker has been compared to cheating on a test. This criticism overlooks an important distinction between speakers and students in the classroom. Speakers in the business and professional world are not being evaluated to see what they have learned about communication. The speaker's prime responsibility is to make certain the ideas in a speech are accurate and responsible. Business executives constantly call on the help of experts in such areas as advertising, accounting, and engineering. An executive with final responsibility for producing a product would be foolish, for example, to attempt to write the ads, keep the financial records, and design the product.

As long as the speaker and the speech writer believe in the ideas expressed in a speech and have confidence in the accuracy of the material used, their collaboration does not differ significantly from the many other examples of cooperation found in a large company. Some speech writers argue that it is not even necessary for a writer to believe in the position espoused in a speech. These writers compare their role to that of a lawyer, who advocates a client's cause without always believing in that cause personally.

The History and Status of Professional Speech Writers

This age has seen the rise of many types of jobs that were unknown only a generation or two in the past. The writing of speeches for someone else to deliver, however, is not a new profession. Demosthenes, the famous Greek orator, was a speech writer early in his career. George Washington had considerable help from Alexander Hamilton in the writing of "The Farewell Address."

Under Franklin Roosevelt, speech writing became a specialized staff function in the White House and began to attract increasing public attention to the role of speech writers. As presidential writers such as Ted Sorensen for John F. Kennedy and William Safire for Richard Nixon became well known for their contributions to presidential speeches, corporate speakers and government speakers from mayors to governors increased their demands for speech-writing help. The growing openness of speech writing in higher levels of government also coincided with rising pressure on business leaders to address both public and employee audiences. As a result of all these factors, the ancient profession of speech writing has grown rapidly in the last twenty years.

Speech Writing in Business and the Professions

In spite of the increasing amount of speech writing in business and the professions, most organizations do not have full-time speech writers. The overwhelming majority of those who write business speeches spend most of their time on other assignments. Speech writers are commonly located in the communications or public relations departments of a company, where their other duties might include writing annual reports, editing employee publications, or managing the company's speakers bureau.

A typical speech writer may have a background in speech, journalism, or English, while others come from such varied fields as economics or computer science. Since almost no one prepares for a career in speech writing while in college and few people entering the business world find speech writing a part of their first job, the task becomes a part of someone's job largely by chance. A person far removed from the communications office could be asked to become involved in speech writing. Someone in marketing, for example, might contribute to a speech by supplying information to the speech writer, submitting a few pages to be included as part of a speech, or serving as an evaluator of a speech written on a marketing subject.

Since anyone entering the business world may become involved in speech writing, some knowledge of the process could be useful. A full appreciation of the speech-writing task must include an understanding of the complex interrelationships involved when a writer prepares a speech for someone to read.

Unfortunately, some writers are forced to prepare a speech without any direct contact with their speakers. This lack of contact between speaker and writer almost always means the speech will not be so good as it could have been. To do the best possible job, a writer needs direct access to the speaker. No administrative assistant or other executive "gatekeeper" can do an adequate job of telling the writer what is on the speaker's mind.

CONFERENCES

In an ideal situation, the writer should meet with the speaker at four points during the preparation of a speech. First, the speaker and the writer should hold an initial conference when the speech-writing assignment is made. The speaker should tell the writer what impact the speech should have on the audience and should work with the writer in preparing a list of major ideas to be covered in the speech. The speaker should pass on any information about the audience that he or she may have and may even suggest people in the company to whom the writer should turn for further information.

Second, the writer and the speaker should confer after each draft of the speech has been prepared and read. The speaker should use these face-to-face conversations to explain any changes desired in the manuscript.

Third, the speaker should rehearse the final draft of the manuscript with the writer present. This practice gives the writer a chance to correct any minor problems and also increases the odds that the speech will be delivered well. In the case of an especially important speech, the rehearsal could be recorded on video tape and played back for a critique.

Fourth, the writer should hear the speech and hold a conference with the speaker to assess the success of the talk. This meeting can be as informal as a conversation while riding back from the speech, or it can be a regular office meeting.

These four types of meetings between speaker and writer are, of course, possible only in ideal circumstances. For some minor speeches one or more of the meetings may not be useful. The level of interaction described in the four meetings, however, will improve the quality of speeches in most cases.

THE APPROVAL PROCESS

From speeches to press releases, almost any official company pronouncement has to be seen and approved by a number of people before being made public. As was mentioned earlier, a speech writer may have to call on expert help from a number of departments in a company. Many speeches must be read by the company lawyers to protect the organization from legal complications. If the speech writer does not report directly to the speaker in the company organizational chart, then the writer's supervisor may wish to read the speech and suggest changes in it.

Anyone involved in the approval process ought to recognize that a speech cannot be easily written by a committee. A good speech needs the guiding hand of one writer if it is to have a consistent style and a clear theme. This is not to say that speech writers do not benefit from advice. The advice, however, should be made to the writer, and those involved in the approval process should follow an important rule: *no one should make a change in the speech without sending it back to the writer.*

The Language of the Speech

ORAL STYLE

The language of a speech differs considerably from the language of a written report even if the speech and the report cover the same material. If a speech writer uses "language for the eye" instead of "language for the ear," the speech will sound artificial. Although all of the characteristics of conversational language do not appear in a formal speech, some of them are of special importance.

Informal words. Most people understand many words they seldom say out loud. If you encountered the word *agog* in print, you would know it described a state of great interest or surprise. The word, however, seldom appears in casual speech. The speech writer who wrote, "This invention has the scientific world agog," probably left the audience agog at the speaker's unusual word choice.

Not all "eye" words are long or complicated. *That* usually sounds more natural than *which,* for example, although neither word is complex. There are two simple words that, while correct, would seem out of place if the following sentence were spoken: "I left the book upon the desk, for I wanted you to see it." In normal speech you probably would say, "I left the book *on* the desk, *because* I wanted you to see it."

Here are a few words from a short newspaper editorial: *voracious, presage,* and *salubrious.* A speech writer might be able to use one of these terms occasionally, but such formal language appears far more frequently in good writing than in good speaking. Members of an audience, even if they are quite well educated, simply are not accustomed to hearing such words and may begin to focus attention more on a speaker's language than on the ideas in the speech.

Ease of pronunciation. President Gerald Ford had trouble with the word *judgment,* which he pronounced with an extra syllable, and President Jimmy Carter could not manage to give the word *nuclear* its standard pronunciation. If a speaker cannot say *statistics* or has the habit of reading *adapt* as if it were *adopt,* the writer must respect the individual speaker's problem and avoid the troublesome words.

In any speech, a writer should avoid letting tongue twisters find their way into a text. The *sts* and *sks* combinations can be especially difficult for many speakers, so expressions such as "the trusts' tasks" or "insists on risks" should be replaced.

Distracting phrases and clauses. Normal speech seldom employs a phrase or clause to qualify an idea. For instance, you would be less likely to say "Joe Smith, the governor, reported . . ." than "Governor Joe Smith reported. . . ." You probably would not say, "Virginia, a state that grows a lot of tobacco, needs this law." A more natural expression, without the clause, would be "Virginia grows a lot of tobacco and needs this law."

When speakers do need to insert a clause, it should be a major interruption and should be set off by dashes rather than by commas in the manuscript. Here is how such a clause might appear:

"Joe Smith—a man I am proud to have as our governor—reported. . . ."
"Virginia—a state with a long history of tobacco production—needs this law."

Sentence length. If you were to capture informal speech on a tape recorder, you would discover some extremely long sentences. Speakers frequently accomplish this by stringing sentences together with conjunctions. As a result, the sentences may be long, but the units of thought within each long sentence are fairly short. Speech writers sometimes achieve this effect by starting many sentences with *and* or *but* or *or.* In this way they capture some of the natural flow of everyday speech without producing sentences that would look strange on the pages of the manuscript.

Not all sentences in a speech should be of the same length; if they were, the delivery would sound monotonous. A few short sentences should be included for variety. Speech writers also get variety by occasionally using a sentence fragment. Here are samples of incomplete sentences from President Reagan's inaugural address delivered on January 20, 1981:

"This breed called Americans."
"A man of humility who came to greatness reluctantly."
"Off to one side, the stately memorial to Thomas Jefferson."

Personal language. A speech writer should not be afraid to use *I* or *me* or *we* or *us.* Except in unusual instances, *one* should be avoided as a substitute for the personal pronoun. Personal references are relatively easy at the beginning and at the end of a speech. The writer should make sure that they are also employed in the body of the speech.

Rhythm. Spoken language has a beat or cadence to it. Speech writers should try to capture the rhythm of speech and should learn to "listen" to the flow of a sentence or phrase while writing it. Good advertisements demonstrate how rhythm can give an idea emphasis without sounding like bad poetry. "Progress is our most important product" sounds better than "General Electric believes in progress." The closing line of Patrick Henry's most famous speech is quite a bit too oratorical for today's tastes, but its rhythm may be examined to make a point. Henry said, "I know not what course others will take; but as for me, give me liberty or give me death!" Try reading the sentence with the last phrase changed to "give me liberty or death." With two words missing, the flow of the passage is destroyed and the impact of the conclusion is weakened.

CLARITY

Language must be clear whether written for the ear or for the eye. Because words convey clear meaning only if they are familiar to a listener, the speech writer must always be aware of the audience when choosing words. Achieving clarity can be particularly difficult in business communication because many companies use technical language and frequently give ordinary words highly specialized meanings. Such words are used so often in a business organization that it may be hard to remember *not* to use them when writing for outsiders.

Technical language, or "jargon" as it is sometimes called, has an important place inside an organization. Members of a college community, for example, find it convenient to talk about "three hours credit" for a course. A worker on an assembly line might well be confused by a college speaker who is rewarded with only three hours of credit for going to class for fifteen weeks. The same kind of confusion can occur when a business speaker refers to the "plant department." How many different meanings might the word *plant* have to an audience not familiar with the speaker's company? A flowering plant? A factory with a smokestack?

Abbreviations should not slip into a public speech without explanation. Many listeners will not know that a speaker uses *R & D* to stand for "research and development" and *R.O.I.* to mean "return on investment."

Some public speakers use jargon out of carelessness, but others seem to be motivated by a desire to sound important by speaking in code. Speech writers should not fall victim to this temptation.

FORCEFUL LANGUAGE

Language has the capacity to evoke all of the human senses. Because listeners associate words with experiences they have had, a reference to "a plump, bright yellow lemon" may cause some who hear the phrase to react as though they had actually tasted or smelled the lemon. A TV commercial about headache pain can use language and pictures that will literally cause a viewer to hurt.

The easiest of the senses to evoke, and the one most useful to speech writers, is the sense of sight. By painting a vivid word picture, a writer can fix an image in the listener's mind. The language does not have to be fancy or high-flown, but it should give details that will cause the listener to "see" the scene. Words that show action and give color and shape will help. Here is an example:

> We have made improvements in the environment. Ten years ago water in the Pine River had the color of weak coffee. Foul-looking foam lined the banks, and about the only fish you ever saw were floating belly up. But now you can watch fish swim over the spillway in water that is sparkling and clear. People are swimming in Pine River again too. And families enjoy picnics at Pony Park and play volleyball on the clean sand below the bridge.

STYLISTIC DEVICES

Rhetorical questions. In an effort to reduce the barrier a manuscript may create between speaker and audience, a writer may decide to use rhetorical questions in a speech text. Rhetorical questions involve the audience and add a touch of drama to the speaker's point. Sometimes rhetorical questions can be clustered in groups of two or three or even more. A question may be used to introduce each main point of a speech. As a rule, the answers to rhetorical questions are left to the audience to supply silently, but occasionally a speaker may both pose and respond to a rhetorical question. Several of the functions of the rhetorical question can be seen in the following illustration.

> First, let us ask if we can continue to bear the cost of a balance of payments deficit. Can we stand by while this enormous sum of money flows out of the country each year? Are we helpless to stop this dreadful drain on our economy? I say the answer is no.

Alliteration. When Spiro Agnew was vice-president of the United States, his speech writers used so much alliteration in his speeches that it almost became a game. One of the better-known examples was Agnew's reference to "nattering nabobs of negativism." Such a deliberate effort to call attention to alliteration would seldom be made by a corporate speech writer, but a touch of alliteration can be useful to emphasize an idea or perk up audience interest. Such phrases as "dreadful drain" or "foul-looking foam" are usually safe and effective.

Balance. Some writers associate balance in the phrases of a speech with the eloquence found only in major speeches such as Lincoln's use of "of the people, by the people, and for the people" or Kennedy's "Ask not what your country can do for you; ask what you can do for your country." But even a routine business speech can benefit from attention to balance: "Improved productivity makes money for the company, it saves money for the consumer, and it pays money to the worker."

INOFFENSIVE LANGUAGE

Words must be chosen to fit the occasion, the audience, and the speaker. A writer must try to think like the speaker while trying to imagine what the occasion will be like and how the audience will react. Almost nothing challenges the skills of a speech writer more than the ability to choose appropriate words for one speaker one week and another one the next.

In adapting speeches to suit the audience, a speech writer should be careful to eliminate sexist language from a speech and to do so in a way that does not distract from the message of the speech. Such instances of sexist language represent bad taste in word choice as, for example, in the use of *girl* to refer to women who are not children. Other instances of sexist language grow out of problems with English grammar, like the use of *he* or *his* in reference to a person whose gender is not specified. Both types of error can be avoided without distraction by choosing among five simple methods.

Use the plural. Perhaps the simplest way to avoid using *he* or *his* is to make the noun to which the pronoun refers into a plural. Instead of writing "When a speaker talks to his audience, he must have eye contact," write "When speakers talk to their audiences. . . ." Many listeners will be annoyed by the use of *man* or *mankind* as a generic term intended to include both sexes, so a better choice would be to use *people* or *human beings,* words that safely and explicitly include both men and women. Use of the plural will not work with a sentence such as "When a worker is named employee of the month, we give him the day off." Another method would solve the problem better.

Repeat the noun. The need for a sexist pronoun may be eliminated by repeating the noun to which the pronoun makes reference. For example, the sentence cited at the end of the previous paragraph could be changed to read, "When a worker is named employee of the month, we give that employee the day off." Or the sentence referring to a speaker could be altered to say "When a speaker talks to an audience, the speaker should have eye contact."

Substitute. Neutral terms can be found to replace most sexist words. *Girl* should obviously be replaced by *woman* in reference to adults. More subtle instances are found in the need to remove such terms as *businessman, paper boy,* and even *salesman* in favor of *business executive, paper carrier,* and *sales representative* or *sales clerk.* It would be hard to imagine someone becoming offended at any of the substitutions, but it is easy to see how female managers could be hurt by a speaker who says "As all you businessmen out there know. . . ."

Particular care should be taken to substitute in cases of "unequal yoking" of terms. Instead of *man and wife,* which defines the female by her relationship to the male, use *man and woman* or *husband and wife.*

The word *chairman* presents special difficulties. Replacements for this term cannot always be made without calling attention to the change. Many people resent hearing *chairperson,* and if the reference in a speech is to the "Chairman of the Board of Exxon," the substitution would be awkward. The substitution of *chair* is acceptable to some people; in other instances a writer must determine the most likely audience reaction and then choose between the lesser of two evils. Where appropriate, as recommended in the suggestion below, the use of the term *chairman* might be avoided altogether.

Cut the sexist word.   Many times the sexist term can simply be crossed out of the text. "A manager must communicate well with his employees" loses nothing by the omission of the *his.* Deleting two words *(to him)* would improve the statement "When I talk to an executive, I always say to him that. . . ."

Give alternatives.   While a writer should be guided by the general rule that nonsexist language does not call attention to itself, some exceptions may be made. In some situations a speaker wishes to make a point of including both sexes in a comment. "When an employee retires," a company officer might say, "he or she will receive substantial benefits." Or a manager might want to be sure not to leave anyone out with the statement "The top sales representative next month will find a five-hundred-dollar bonus in his or her pay envelope." Using *he* in one example and *she* in another may serve the same purpose if the examples are close together in the speech.

In deciding not to use nonsexist terms, a writer should remember that the intention of the speaker does almost nothing to undo the harm of offensive language. Even if the speaker believes that "girls in the office" is a friendly phrase and even if the women in the office actually call one another "girls," the speech writer must keep in mind the fact that many listeners will still be offended. Nor should a writer be deterred from using nonsexist language by those who argue that consistency calls for *manhole cover* to be replaced by *personhole cover* and *woman* by *woperson.* Such examples are absurd because they ignore the basic principle of adaptation to audiences by implying that *woman* and *manhole cover* are offensive when they are not.

In addition to sexist language, writers should avoid terms that offend minorities and other groups who are increasingly taking exception to language discrimination. Anyone who speaks extensively will eventually talk to audiences made up in part of homosexuals, older people, and handicapped persons. Most business speakers need to appeal to such individuals in their roles as citizens and consumers. Nothing is gained by tasteless remarks about sexual preference, stereotyping comments about the elderly, or loose references such as "helpless as a cripple."

Humor in the Speech

Most speakers have difficulty determining when and how to use humor. The difficulty becomes even greater when decisions must be made about humor in writing for someone else.

Humor should not be used in a speech as a matter of routine. Do not believe that "every speech should start with a few jokes." Humor should appear in a speech only if it meets three tests. First, is it relevant to the aims of the speech? Second, is it in good taste? Third, is it fresh?

RELEVANCE

Unfortunately, many writers get their idea of humor from watching professional comedians. The comedians' humor differs significantly from the humor needed by a speaker. Humor in a TV comedy show can be judged simply by the amount of laughter. The more laughs, the better the comedian. But in a speech you need to ask *not* how much the audience laughed but rather how well the humor advanced the speaker's objectives. A humorous comment in a speech may be quite successful if it gets only a smile or a chuckle while making a point clear, or showing the speaker to be a friendly person, or holding the audience's interest in the speaker's subject. The speech writer, then, should use only that humor that advances the speaker's aims.

TASTE

A funny story that gets a big laugh may be a disaster for the speaker if the laugh comes at the expense of good taste. It is possible to laugh at someone's humor while at the same time deciding the person lacks sensitivity or even credibility. The speaker can get a laugh without winning the audience over to the point of view in the speech. Stories that show "the old farmer" or "the Polish immigrant" in an unfavorable light may undercut the audience's respect for the speaker unless it is clear that the speaker belongs to the group that is the butt of the joke.

FRESHNESS

Writers should avoid the temptation to include in a speech the latest joke making the rounds. If the writer has heard it three times, the audience probably has heard it too. Unless the speaker has considerable skill at relating jokes, it may be best to avoid them altogether. Several substitutes can be used if humor is needed. First, humorous anecdotes from the speaker's own experience can be told. Such humor cannot be familiar to the audience, and it has the additional advantage of not setting up the high expectations for quality of humor that are implicit in the telling of a joke. D. C. Staley of New York Telephone once began a banquet speech by telling of the time he identified himself as a telephone company employee when he arrived at a banquet. He was promptly escorted not to the meeting but to an office where he was put to work installing a telephone.

As a second choice, a joke can be replaced by a "one-liner." This form of humor also has the advantage of not building up great expectations, and it can be delivered in much less time than a joke. A business executive speaking of a day when things had gone especially badly on the stock market said, "But I went home and slept like a baby—I woke up every hour and cried awhile."

A third option is to use "integrated humor." Integrated humor consists in taking an idea that stands on its own in the speech but wording it in a light, clever way. For example, John Hanley, president of Monsanto Chemical Company in St. Louis, began a speech in Houston by using the common bond technique. While this approach can be serious, he chose to note that Houston and St. Louis were alike in hot weather and losing baseball teams. While his remarks would strike most local citizens as a friendly, humorous way to begin a speech, the content of his observations could be taken at face value and the failure of the audience to laugh would not have been a major difficulty.

Humor should be used with caution. Excessive or careless use of humor can offend an audience, and humor can easily be misinterpreted.

The Speaker's Manuscript

The text of a speech carried to the lectern by the speaker has certain requirements quite different from the manuscript form needed for the typical essay or report. A larger-than-normal typeface usually is necessary for the speaker to see the text clearly. Most speech writers use Orator or Presentor type, which is about twice as big as regular type. Some writers have access to bold, heavy type used in printed headlines, which can make a manuscript easy to read.

The margins of the reading text of a speech should be quite generous. Extra space, perhaps as much as a third of a page, should be reserved in the left-hand margin for notes the speaker may want to include. The lines should not run to the bottom of the page because this will cause the speaker's head to drop too low while reading. Again, about a third of the bottom should be left blank.

A sentence should never be continued from one page to another.

Breaking sentences at the bottom of the page can cause an interruption in the middle of a thought while the speaker turns the page. Some writers insist that paragraphs not be carried over. This practice can result in a fifteen-to-twenty-minute speech having forty or more pages.

The pages should be numbered but never stapled. Stapling would result in making the turning of pages too obvious. It is better for the speaker to slide a completed page to one side. Numbering permits the speaker to rearrange the pages quickly in case they get out of order.

The texts for major speeches are sometimes put on video prompters, but this practice is rare. With a little practice a speaker can learn to handle a manuscript and to pick up several words at a glance in order to establish brief eye contact with an audience. Many speakers mark a manuscript with highlighting pens or underline for emphasis. The speech writer's hard work can be readily destroyed by a speaker who is not able to handle the manuscript well.

The Manuscript as a Guide to Speaking

Not all speakers read their manuscripts word for word. A speech writer's text may be used by some speakers as the basis for a talking outline. Indeed, some writers provide such an outline in the left margin of the text so the speaker can follow either the exact wording or the key concepts in the margin.

Speech writing practices vary widely. The good speech writer must have both skill in writing and the ability to adjust to a variety of situations. Anyone with the ability to write a good speech might very well find this talent in great demand.

SUMMARY

Speech writing, with a history stretching back to ancient times, is becoming increasingly important in business. In order to write a good speech, a writer must establish a good relationship with the speaker and with others involved in the speech-writing process. Speech writers also need to understand the characteristics of oral style and be able to write clear and forceful speeches. The writers must be able to employ such stylistic devices as the rhetorical question, alliteration, and balance. Speech writers achieve appropriateness in their speeches by matching their words to the needs of the speaker, the occasion, and the audience. They must take particular care to avoid language that offends because of sexist, racist, or ageist connotations. Speech writers should use humor with caution and should be aware that one-liners and integrated humor can be used as well as the more common jokes or anecdotes.

EXERCISES

1. Collect and bring to class newspaper editorials containing at least a dozen words you understand but do not hear in normal conversation.

2. Write a five-minute description of an event you have witnessed, such as an accident, an athletic contest, or a scene from a movie or play. Use language that will cause members of your class to see the event in their own minds.

3. Divide the class into pairs. Each student should write a speech for the other one to deliver in class. The manuscripts should be turned in. The time limit is five minutes for each speech.

4. Interview a speech writer from a local company or government agency. Find out what the writer thinks makes writing speeches different from other forms of writing. Prepare a report on what you learn.

5. Find three jokes in a magazine and rewrite them as they would be said aloud. Identify the characteristics of "oral language" you have used in changing the material.

Suggested Readings

Grayson, Melvin J. "The Last Best Hope: Words." *Vital Speeches of the Day,* July 15, 1981.
The author offers a defense of using the manuscript speech.

Kelly, Joseph J., Jr. *Speechwriting: The Master Touch.* Harrisburg, Pa.: Stackpole Books, 1980.
This book is a description of writing speeches for others by a writer with thirty years of experience.

Ott, John. *How to Write and Deliver a Speech.* New York: Cornerstone Library, 1976.
This brief sketch of some of the problems and techniques involved in speech writing is by an author who worked as a professional writer.

Safire, William. *Before the Fall.* New York: Tower Publications, 1975.
This is an excellent account of the inside workings of the White House by a speech writer for President Nixon.

Stone, Janet, and Jane Bachner. *Speaking Up: A Book for Every Woman Who Wants to Speak Effectively.* New York: McGraw-Hill Book Co., 1977.
This easy-to-read paperback illustrates speech writing, using the microphone, and some pitfalls to avoid. The principles are applicable to men as well as women.

Tarver, Jerry. *Professional Speech Writing.* Richmond, Va.: Effective Speech Writing Institute, 1982.
This is a guide to techniques of speech writing and suggestions for career advancement for speech writers in business and government.

Appendix
Parliamentary Procedure

In business and the professions, you'll find that some of the meetings you attend will use parliamentary procedure; in others you will make decisions more informally. The effective manager has a working knowledge of parliamentary procedure and is able to use it when the situation dictates.

Parliamentary procedure is essentially a set of rules that prescribes how a group will frame issues, debate them, and reach a decision about whether to accept or reject them. Following are some very simplified points of parliamentary procedure that you may use in meetings. For more comprehensive rules, see either *Robert's Rules of Order Newly Revised* (1970) or Alice Sturgis's *Standard Code of Parliamentary Procedure.*

1. *Issues or ideas must be framed into position statements called main motions.* Typically, main motions are stated as follows: "I move that. . . ." A motion must be seconded before it can be debated, and only one motion can be "on the floor" at a given time.

2. *Main motions may be either debated or amended; they may not be ignored.* Debate should always be germane, or relevant, to the motion being considered. Exceptions to that rule are certain procedural motions. Debate should be as open as possible, though a group member may move to limit the debate—either to a given issue or to a time frame.

3. *A main motion may be amended by another motion (first-degree amendment).* Motions to amend qualify or change the original motion. An example of a motion to amend is "I move to amend the motion by adding the words *July 3.*" The motion to amend must be seconded or it "dies."

4. *A motion to amend may be either debated or amended (second-degree amendment).* A second-degree amendment might read: "I move to substitute the date *August 1* for *July 3.*" The second-degree amendment must be seconded, debated, and voted upon *before* the first-degree amendment can be considered. *Only one amendment may be debated at a time.* The second-degree amendment may not be further amended. There is no such thing as a third-degree amendment.

5. *Amendments must be voted on before the main motion.* If a second-degree amendment is on the floor, it must be voted on first. Then the first-degree amendment *as amended by the second-degree*

amendment is debated and voted on. Finally, the main motion *as amended* (by both first- and second-degree amendments) is debated and voted on.

6. *Groups may set their own rules for voting.* They may choose among several options: a majority (more than half); plurality (more than any other person/option/suggestion gets); part-of-the-whole (percentage of those voting); or consensus (all those voting).

Procedural motions are motions made in the course of the debate. They allow participants to limit the debate, put the motion being debated aside, clarify procedure, ask a question, make a personal observation, or revote on an issue. The most common of these procedural motions are outlined as follows.

Procedural Motions

If you wish to curtail debate, then move to

1. *limit debate* to x number of minutes
   (requires a second; amendable but not debatable; two-thirds vote)
2. *call for the question* or ask for a vote
   (requires a second; not debatable or amendable; two-thirds vote)
3. *adjourn*
   (requires a second; not debatable or amendable; majority vote)

If you wish to put the motion aside, then move to

1. *table,* which puts aside until recalled—maybe forever
   (requires a second; neither debatable nor amendable; majority vote)
2. *postpone definitely*—that is, specify the time you want the motion recalled
   (requires a second; debatable and amendable; majority vote)
3. *refer to a committee*
   (requires a second; debatable and amendable; majority vote)
4. *withdraw*—in order only if you made the original motion
   (no second required; not debatable or amendable; no vote)

If you wish to clarify procedure, then move a

1. *point of order*—question whether correct procedure is being followed
   (no second required; not debatable or amendable; no vote)
2. *point of parliamentary inquiry*—ask for correct procedure
   (no second required; not debatable or amendable; no vote)

If you wish to ask a question or make a personal observation, move a

1. *point of personal privilege*—not germane to motion
   (no second required; not amendable or debatable; no vote)
2. *point of information*—ask a question
   (no second required; not amendable or debatable; no vote)

If you wish to revote on a motion that was earlier passed or defeated, move to

1. *reconsider*—applies only to motion voted on in *same* meeting (requires a second; not amendable but debatable; majority vote)
2. *rescind*—applies to motions voted on in earlier meetings (requires a second; amendable and debatable; majority vote)

Index

Index

Active listening, 60
Advertising, 151–152
Advocacy strategies, 154–157
Affect display, 39
Agenda, 126–127
    personal, 113–114
Aggressive behavior, 54
Alliteration, 229
Amendments to motions, 237–238
Analogies, use in corporate advocacy, 173–174
Annual reports, 148
Appearance
    in nonverbal
        communication, 7, 36
    physical, 36, 217
Appraisal interviews, 86–88
Aristotle, 10, 14
Arrangement of office furniture, 33–35
Audience Analysis Guide, 27, 161
Audiences, 26–27
    analysis, 27, 161
    of corporations, 141–146
    expectations, 162
    hostile, 171
    for presentations, 181–182, 185–186
Audiovisual department
    working with, 208–209
Authoritarianism, 49
Authoritarian leadership style, 121

Balance
    in language, 229

Borman, Ernest G.
    quoted, 179
Breakout/buzz sessions, 104
Brochures and flyers, 147–148
Bryan, William J., 7
Bulletin boards, 8, 146–147
Bureaucratic leadership style, 121–122
Buzz sessions, 104

Charts
    as visual aids, 203–204
Clarity
    in language, 228
Cohesiveness, 101, 111–112, 122, 124, 127
Committees, 103
    ad hoc committees, 103
    meetings, 103
    standing committees, 103
Communication, 21–29
    in business, 4–9
    codes, 26
    definition, 21
    feedback, 22–26
    gaps, 24–27
    interpersonal, 45–56
    messages, 26
    model, 24, 25
    nonverbal, 31–41
    process, 28
Conferences, 103
    rooms, 33
Conflict resolution, 9, 132
Consensus, 130
Conventions, 103
Conversational delivery, 213–217

Coordination
    of presentations, 191–192
Corporate advocacy
    public relations, 139–157
    public speeches, 7–8, 161–
        176
Corporate image, 139–141
Corporation's audiences, 141–
    146
Counseling interviews, 83–86
Credibility
    and corporate speeches, 12–
        18
Customers, 141

Definitions
    use in corporate advocacy,
        175
Delivery, 211–220
    off-the-cuff, 212
    of presentations, 180, 188
Democratic leadership style, 122
Dewey, John, 107, 170
Dogmatism, 49–50
Dyad, 46, 47, 75

Educational materials, 151
Employees
    as the audience, 143
Ethical concerns
    about speech writing, 223–
        224
Examples
    use in corporate advocacy,
        172–173
Exit interviews, 89–90
Extemporaneous speaking
    see: Notes, speaking from
Eye contact, 63–64, 213–214

Facial expressions, 39
Fairness Doctrine, 146
Federal Equal Employment
    Opportunity guidelines, 80
Feedback, 22–26

Forcefulness in language, 228–
    229
Forum, 103

Gestures, 36–37, 215
Gordon, Thomas, 58
Grievance interviews, 88–89
Group process, 106

Handouts, 187–188, 204–205
Haney, William, 66
Hanley, John, 233
Howell, William S.
    quoted, 179
Humor, 232–233

Impromptu speaking
    see: Off-the-cuff delivery
Influence of leadership, 117–118
Information
    -giving interview strategies,
        91
    -seeking interview
        strategies, 91–92
    -sharing model (meetings),
        104–106
Instant writing surface
    as a visual aid, 203
International Association of
    Business Communicators, 4,
    12
Interpersonal communication,
    5–6, 45–56
    aggressive behavior, 54
    atmosphere, 52–54
    authoritarianism, 49
    barriers, 50–52
    definition, 46
    dogmatism, 49
    open-mindedness, 48
    self-behavior, 51–52
    self-disclosure, 48, 52–53
    trust, 47–48

Interview plans, 79, 84, 87, 89, 90
Interviews, 75–94
  characteristics, 75–76
  functions, 76–78, 91
  job, 6
  kinds, 78–90, 91
  strategies, 90–93

Japan
  communication in, 3

Koehler, Jerry, 151

Language
  avoiding sexism, 230–232
  clarity, 54, 228
  forcefulness, 228–229
  oral style, 226–228
  for presentations, 181
  stylistic devices, 229–230
Leadership
  formal and informal, 118
  leader functions and responsibilities, 125–133
  leadership styles, 121–122
  nature of leadership, 117
  personal leadership characteristics, 118–120
  situational leadership, 123–124
Lecture, 104
Letters, 148–149
Lincoln, Abraham, 8
Listening, 57–73
  active versus passive listening, 60
  false assumptions, 57–58
  listening checklist, 72
  listening models, 70–71
  listening skills, 62–70
  listening steps, 61–70
  reflecting, 61
Loden, Marilyn, 6

Manuscript
  for reading speeches, 233–234
Mass media, 143–144
Media for corporate messages, 146–152
  external, 148–152
  internal, 146–148
Meetings, 99–115
  conducting, 129–133
  evaluating, 128
  functions, 104–111
  guidelines for having, 99–102
  interaction factors, 111–114
  planning, 125–129
  types, 102–104
Memorizing speeches, 212
Messages, 21–23, 26
  channels for, 23
  codes, 22, 23, 26
  effectiveness, 54–55
  unintentional, 22
Microphones, 219
Mirroring, 68
Models and objects
  as visual aids, 186–187
Motions, 237–239
  amending, 237–238
  main, 237
  procedural, 238–239

Networking, 6
Newsletters, 146
Nominal group, 106, 109–111, 129, 130
Nondirective leadership style, 122
Nonverbal communication, 31–41
  appearance of communicator, 7, 36
  definition, 31
  facial expressions, 39
  gestures, 36, 37
  objects, 38

Nonverbal communication
  (*continued*)
    paralanguage, 38
    space, 32–35, 53
    strategies, 32–39
    time, 35–36
    touch, 37–38
    voice, 38
Norms, 112
Notes
    speaking from, 212–213

Observation
    inference confusion, 65–66
Occasions
    for corporate advocacy, 162
Office arrangements
    furniture, 33–35
Off-the-cuff delivery, 212
Open-ended questions, 131
Open-mindedness, 48–49
Oral style, 226–228
Organization of speeches and
  presentations
    attention, 164
      strategies, 164–166
    conclusion, 171
    credibility, 166
      strategies, 166–167
    introduction, 164
      purposes, 164
    patterns, 168–171
    purposes and goals, 163
    speech outline form, 163
    strategies, 162

Panel discussion, 104
Paralanguage, 38
Paraphrasing, 54, 68
Parliamentary procedure, 130,
  237–239
Participant responsibilities
  (groups), 133–134
Personal agendas, 113–114
Persuasive interview strategies,
  93
Physical setting, 64

Plato, 10, 16
Posture, 214–215
Practicing
    a presentation, 191–192
    a speech, 220–221
Presentations, 6–7, 179–193
    audience for, 181–182,
      185–186
    coordination, 191–192
    defined, 179
    delivery of, 180, 188
    examples of, 180
    language in, 181
    length of, 182
    objectives for, 184–185
    organization of, 181, 188–
      191
    questions and answers in,
      183
    rehearsal of, 191–192
    research and evidence for,
      180
    review and critique of,
      192–193
    special features of, 181–183
    team approach, 183
    visual aids for, 182–183,
      186–188
Press conferences, 150–151
Press releases, 144, 149–150
Problem solving
    interview strategies, 92–93
    model, 107–109
Projection of images
    in presentations, 187
Proof, 172
    analogies, 173–174
    definitions, 175
    examples, 172–173
    quotations (authorities),
      174
    statistical data, 175
    supporting materials, 172–
      175
Props, 204
Public relations and corporate
    advocacy, 21, 139–158
Public Relations Society of
    America, 4

Public relations strategies, 153–
154

Quality circles, 4
Questions, 67, 104
    and answers for
        presentations, 183
    and answers sessions, 217–
        219
    direct and indirect, 67
    follow-up (probe), 67, 92
    open and closed, 67, 92,
        132
Questions and answers, 183,
    217–219
    for presentations, 183
    sessions, 217–219
Quotations
    use in corporate advocacy,
        174

Rationalizing, 52
Reading speeches, 211–212
Reflecting, 61, 67–68
Reflective thinking, 106, 129
    model, 107–109, 170–171
Rehearsal
    of presentations, 191–192
    of speeches, 220–221
Research
    for presentations, 180
Restating, 68
Résumé, 80–82
Review and critique
    of presentations, 192–193
Rhetorical questions, 229
Rockefeller, David, 8
Rogers, Carl, 61, 68, 71
Roles, 65, 75, 112–113, 125
    social role, 113
    task role, 113
Room size, 127

Selection interviews, 79–83
Self-concept, 65
Self-disclosure, 48, 52–53

Sexist language, avoiding, 230–
    232
Sisco, John, 151
Situational leadership, 123–124
Size (of group), 111
Slides
    slide talks, 199–202
    as visual aids, 204
Speakers Bureau, 7, 148
Speaker's stand
    approaching and leaving,
        217
Special-interest groups, 144–145
Speech writing
    in business and the
        professions, 224–225
    ethical concerns, 223–224
    history and status, 224
    relationship with speaker,
        225–226
Staff meetings, 102–103
Stage fright, 220
Staley, D. C., 233
Statistical data
    use in corporate advocacy,
        175
Status, 53, 65, 76, 114, 119
Stereotyping, 50
Stockholders, 141–143
Stogdill, Ralph, 118–119
Stress interview strategy, 83
Stylistic devices
    in language use, 229–230
Summarizing, 54–55, 68
Supporting materials
    for corporate advocacy
        speeches, 172–176
Symposium, 104

Tarver, Jerry
    quoted, 12–18
Team meetings, 102–103
Team presentations, 183
Telephone "hotlines," 148
Territoriality
    or space, 32–34
Time, 35–36
Toastmasters, 11

Touch, 37–38
Transitional devices, 172
Trust, 47–48, 65, 124

Unions, 144

Vardaman, George
    quoted, 179
Visual aids
    charts as, 203–204
    degree of audience focus,
      197–199
    difficulty in using, 195–197
    full focus, 197–198

    guidelines for using, 206
    handouts, 187–188, 204–
      205
    instant writing surface, 203
    models and objects as, 186–
      187
    for presentations, 182–183,
      186–188
    primary focus, 198–199
    projections of images, 187
    props as, 204
    slides as, 204
    variable focus, 202–205
Vocalizations or nonfluencies, 64
Voice, 38, 216–217